SOME THINGS YOU SHOULD KNOW

SOME THINGS YOU SHOULD KNOW

Truman Locke

BLOOMSBURY ACADEMIC
LONDON • NEW YORK • OXFORD • NEW DELHI • SYDNEY

BLOOMSBURY ACADEMIC
Bloomsbury Publishing Plc
50 Bedford Square, London, WC1B 3DP, UK
1385 Broadway, New York, NY 10018, USA

BLOOMSBURY, BLOOMSBURY ACADEMIC and the Diana logo
are trademarks of Bloomsbury Publishing Plc

First published in Great Britain 2020

Cover design: Chris Trotman
Cover illustration © Dex

A catalogue record for this book is available from the British Library.

A catalogue record for this book is available from the Library of Congress.

ISBN: PB: 978-1-3501-1340-4
         ePDF: 978-1-3501-1324-4
         eBook: 978-1-3501-1325-1

Typeset by Integra Software Services Pvt. Ltd.
Printed and bound in Great Britain

To find out more about our authors and books visit www.bloomsbury.com
and sign up for our newsletters.

FOREWORD

The original, intended publisher of this book was disappointed with the manuscript I delivered:

Dear Mr Locke,

Copeland Fischer is one of the oldest and most respected publishing houses in London.

18 months ago we commissioned you to produce a record of your activities as a leading executive producer, during the course of a calendar year, for the edification of students of television and the general reader. You have produced a record of recklessness, dishonesty, criminality, violence and sexual depravity, which will surely edify no one.

It is clear that your standards and ours are completely incompatible.

I trust we will have no further dealings of any kind.

Sincerely,
Dominic Taylor
Publisher

I'll admit that year didn't go the way it was meant to. I'm not proud of all the decisions I made.

What can I say? Some things that are lies can feel true when you say them. Some things that can only spell danger don't look that way at the time. And I never claimed to be flawless.

So fuck you, Dominic Taylor. Real life is full of mess and trouble.

I don't know why I carried on keeping the diary, once things had started to slip. To make sense of what was happening, perhaps. To help me find a way out.

Which makes it a record of what?

Of an adventure, I suppose. Of curiosity indulged and secrets uncovered.

And of doing what it takes. Of the bad things you have to do, sometimes, to do just one thing that's good.

I'm in no position to offer advice. But if you want to work in TV, or just understand how it really works, these are some things you should know.

Truman Locke

CHAPTER ONE: JANUARY

January 1

'I feel like I don't know you', Boo said. 'I'm not sure anyone does.'

I said, 'I'm sorry.'

She said, 'No you're not.'

I'd planned for us to spend the day together.

Boo is a lovely and patient girl. But something came up, as it always does, and I let her down, as I generally do. This time will be the last.

'It's an opening', I said. 'An opportunity.'

She looked away and said nothing.

She quietly collected her things – a half-read book and some underwear – kissed me on the cheek and went outside to wait for a cab, dignified and stiff, like a fallen woman in a film from the '40s.

'I hope it's worth it', she said as we parted, more in sadness than spite. 'I hope you get what you want.'

Which leaves me here, at a train station in a seaside town at dawn on New Year's Day, cold and hungover, in yesterday's clothes; very good at TV, very bad at everything else.

I feel awful, of course, but not bad enough. I wish that I felt worse.

It's 7.45 am. I've been loitering for over an hour, not sure what to expect. Crowds come and go. A policeman is keeping an eye on me, and nods my way to let me know. A train pulls in, and the station fills up again. A tall man in a long coat comes over and catches my arm. He walks me down a sooty alleyway to the back of the station, past a row of overflowing dumpsters, and opens the rear door of a big black Jag. I suddenly think that no one knows where I am. And then that it doesn't really matter, which feels oddly comforting.

We set off and I make a fumble at conversation, about whether winter is colder by the sea. I can't remember the science of it. I think that it isn't, though it tends to feel like it is. The man in the car says nothing.

We go along the coast, and then down a ramp to an underground garage. He parks and we get out and into a 4x4. Then off to another garage and into a big black Merc, driving back the way we came. We get to an abandoned bed factory, and drive in through a pair of cast-iron doors. I want to seem relaxed, like I do this all the time, but I can tell by the light that someone is closing the doors behind us.

The car pulls up next to another, just the same. The driver jerks his head towards it. 'You're welcome. Chop chop.'

Sitting in the back, low and comfortable, is the man I've come to see.

'Get in, then', he says. 'I haven't got all fucking day.'

January 3

I once met a great political figure, a key player in one of the defining struggles of the late twentieth century, an episode that almost brought down the government. He's a northerner, like me, though I moved away when I went to university, and have rarely been back since. He's never spoken of the events that made his name, and I wanted to make the definitive film about him, a sort of authorized biography. I wrote him a long and thoughtful letter, and he agreed to meet me. I was very excited – so much so, I made two basic mistakes. When he asked me if his old nemesis was on board, I said yes, which wasn't true. I think he could tell. And when he asked about my personal politics, I was clumsily evasive, which was far worse than simply saying that I thought he was wrong. The next day, he politely scuppered the project, and I learned an important lesson: if you want to make TV, you need to be straight with people. Or get much, much better at lying.

The man in the car was a gangster called Rankin, an arms dealer who customized guns and then sold them on to the rest of the criminal fraternity. He's just been released from prison; he did a deal, and now he says that 50 people want him dead. He's reputed to have left his mark on every gun he sold – a sort of designer logo. Which is how come the police know his guns were used in most of the murders committed in London over the last ten years – at least according to the guy's own boasts. But he says the murders are nothing to do with him – *people* might be violent, whereas guns are just tools, not inherently better or worse than cars or shovels – and he's smart enough to almost persuade you he's right. He's as sharp as anyone I've met.

We drove along by the sea, listening to some sort of compilation opera tape, turned up loud. We got to an empty restaurant, formally laid out for dinner, and he asked me his only question – what's the angle? I could have said there isn't one, but of course there always is. Or at least there always should be. Access to a person or place is nothing without a take. A perspective, and a sense of purpose. If there's no real reason to make a film, there's no real reason to watch it.

'You say you love guns. That they're things of beauty. That everyone should have one. I want to change your mind.'

Specifically, by taking him on a journey to meet the families of people shot with the guns he sold.

'I'll look like a cunt', he said.

Not necessarily. 'How you come across is down to you. If what you say about guns is true, you've got nothing to worry about. In fact, you'll be in a position to change other people's minds. So the question is, do you really believe the things you say?'

I.e. are you full of shit? Quite a risky line to take.

'I asked some people about you', he said. 'Quite a varied response.'

He stared at me, weighing my balls. Then smiled, awkwardly, like he didn't know how, and his face transformed, all the menace gone.

'You're bold', he says to me. And then to the driver, 'I think we can work with this guy.'

So far so good. All I need now is to persuade a broadcaster to commission it.

But that's not going to be easy. Because as a rule, TV is warm and fuzzy. It's there to comfort and reassure us, and distract us from harsh realities. Hence all the shows about pets, weddings and baking. That's where the money is – in shows that people love. The sensible thing to do is go with the flow. If you have ideas for a living, that's certainly what your boss is going to want. And if you're even slightly interested in money, that's what you should want as well.

Now, I'm definitely interested in making money. It's the money at stake that gives TV its edge. A six-part factual series might attract a budget of 150k an episode – call it a million, all in. And a company's margin on that is around 10%, which you might get half of, if you're a good negotiator, which is 50k, plus the same again if you've got yourself a share of programme sales. All multiplied by however many series your show might run to.

That's how come today I'm sitting in a crowd of 200 restless executives at a dreary venue on the South Bank in London. We're half-listening to commissioners from one of the main broadcasters explain at length what sort of ideas they're after. Which is to say, where the opportunities lie on their channels to win commissions and make some money. The broadcaster's annual programming spend is close to £3 billion, and we all want a piece of the action. So here we are, like seagulls around landfill. We're half-listening because the presentations are sinkingly dull and devoid of meaning or substance. In place of the hoped-for tips and leads, vague requirements for ideas that are soothing 'like a bubble bath' or 'a cuddle from your mum'; propositions that are 'sunny' and 'generous'; shows that 'you can come home to'. It's an ever-evolving lexicon conceived to express (and perhaps also disguise?) those two basic, unchanging requirements: a) warmth and b) fuzziness. Commissioning's not that hard, but commissioners like to pretend that it is.

To meet these requirements, I've been working on an idea about knocking down the backyard fences at a row of terraced houses, to give mollycoddled, cooped-up kids a park of their own, and another about a small, down-to-earth, family-run business that specializes in moving around huge and ludicrous pieces of art for millionaire and billionaire clients.

My problem is that playgrounds and family businesses don't get me very excited. The subjects I love are challenging and chewy: individuals who've lost their way; people struggling with their choices; characters *in extremis*. It's what attracted me to TV in the first place, when the industry was full of outsiders and mavericks, making films about the world as they saw it. It's why I'm mainly thinking about Rankin, the gangster, rather than taking notes. And it's why I've got a Glock in my bag, in a velvet-lined presentation case. It's a gift from my new gangster friend to this broadcaster's Head of Documentaries.

Everyone in the room will be pitching ideas to this guy – some smoothly, wrapped up in a bit of urbane chatter, as though the thought had just occurred; others cringingly, in a lift or in the loo. He's like a French king, grandly in demand, always on the move, outpacing petitioners and hangers-on. A gun in a box should get his attention.

January 4

I've been in the office since 6 am, reading every newspaper and magazine you can think of. I do it every day, but not because I think I'll find ideas. By the time an idea appears in the papers – a feature about an unhappy singleton tracking down all her exes to work out where she's going wrong, for example – it's old; someone has already thought of it, and suggesting it to a commissioner will make you look lazy or lacking in spark (you and all the others who've written the exact same email to the exact same commissioner). Rather, I read the papers because I need to know what's happening – what's fashionable and what's not, what books are being written, what's happening in politics, what people are fantasizing and fretting about. If you want to have ideas, you need to immerse yourself in society, read the patterns of the culture you're part of, and predict what will be on people's minds six months down the line. Your ideas need to connect with the audience they're aimed at. They need to resonate with the wider world.

But once you've filled your head up with memes and blogs and emerging trends, you need to empty it again. Because the best ideas not only connect to the culture but also have a sort of simplicity and innocence about them, a childlike quality that sets them apart. You have to daydream and let your mind wander. You have to remember all the things that amazed and delighted you when you were young. So I'm nursing an idea about playing the San Francisco suspension bridge like a ginormous musical instrument.

For no particular reason a few weeks ago, I remembered when I was a boy, my dad would take me to see the Humber Bridge being built on the Yorkshire coast. I never really felt like I knew my dad, because he never really talked about the things he liked. But he loved the Humber Bridge. We'd stand on the headland, me looking way up at him, so I must have been very small, the wind whipping and strumming the cables, and the bridge zinging so loudly you could shout and not hear yourself. It was awesome. What if we composed a symphony for the Golden Gate Bridge? And filled it with a choir of commuters who've abandoned their cars just to sing? Wouldn't that be joyful? And maybe you could play a tunnel like a flute? Or the lift shafts in a skyscraper like a giant church organ? We could take the humdrum world and make it a little bit magical. It all speaks to a new enthusiasm for creativity and celebration in these straitened and uncertain times, so I think it stands a chance. But I haven't told anyone else about it yet; I'm keeping the idea private for now, taking it out from time to time to polish and admire it.

You can think about such things when the office is empty. It's the best part of the day. But today there's another reason for coming in early; I need time to prepare for my annual appraisal with my boss, Charlie, the chap who owns the company.

It was just Charlie and two friends at the start, more than 20 years ago now. Today the company is established and respected, not huge but not small either – a proper indie, specializing in documentaries and high-end factual television. Charlie's done everything in TV, but he doesn't have ideas any more. Somewhere along the line – maybe after his kids were born, maybe after he'd won his awards – he stopped keeping up with the culture. These days, having ideas is what he pays me for.

We sit in the boardroom, trying to act casual in the whitewashed, formal space. He says, 'I think you can do better', by which he means make more money. 'So no more chasing sordid little stories, for everyone's sake.' He's referring to an incident last year. I had him down as my next of kin. I couldn't think of anyone else.

'I want you to … make me smile', he says. Which is another way of saying the same thing about money.

We gossip a bit about people we know, and then go back to work.

I thought it wise not to mention the gangster we're now very much in bed with. Or the story I'd just devoted my morning to, when I should have been thinking of impressive things to say. It's beyond sordid, but it's singing to my soul.

January 7

I'm sitting in a pub in Paisley, part of Glasgow's urban sprawl, opposite an old enemy.

It's a student place, so we stand out a little, but less than we would in a regular pub; Paisley is a tough sort of town.

The guy's name is Nicolas Sanderson. He's an exec from another company. Same sort of professional (though not social) background, same age, same interests. We've both spent the day trying, and failing, to find an infamous local man. And before today, several years going toe-to-toe over enticing bits of access. We came up, separately, on the first flight from London, together with half a dozen other TV types I vaguely recognized. In other circumstances, we'd be enjoying a (relatively) friendly pint. As things stand, I just want to know what he knows.

'Charming story', he says.

'Bit grubby for you? You're a very long way from Westbourne Grove.'

'Where there's muck there's brass', he says, with a cloddish attempt at a northern accent. It's meant to embarrass me, but it's Sanderson who looks down and away. We both take a mouthful of beer.

There's one important exception to the rule about not pursuing ideas from the papers – real-life stories so extraordinary that everyone wants to know more. The sort of story that generates its own media cyclone: the world's first pregnant man, or the unmasking of Josef Fritzl. If you can reach the people at the eye of the storm, and persuade them to talk only to you, there isn't a channel in the world that wouldn't commission it.

On the morning of my meeting in the boardroom with Charlie, one story dominated the headlines: a 30-year-old man revealed to be the father of 20-odd children, by 20-odd different mums. The tabloids were calling him the world's worst dad; feckless and shameless, a national disgrace. By lunchtime, media around the world had seized on the story as well. It's very possible that when my boss spoke of sordid stories, he was specifically referring to this one. I'm risking a lot on the hunch that there's more to this guy than meets the eye.

When my session with Charlie was over, I went to a run-down cafe I like to hang out in, partly because I feel at home there, but mainly because it's totally private, a great place to make illicit phone calls. The key with sensational stories that lots of other people will also be chasing is to find a way in that no one else will have thought of. From there, you can build up your access, and find your way to the heart of the story and the people who really matter. A nice lady who runs a baby-wear shop said she'd be happy to meet me; she says she knows most of the mums.

Ordinarily I would have booked my tickets on the strength of that, and let the rush of adrenaline carry me all the way up to Scotland, but Charlie's made it clear that times are changing. So I phoned Tourist Information for a cover story, a plausible reason to dash to the airport. Officially, I'm here for a new kind of dog show, in which furry breeds are dyed and groomed to look like pandas, camels, cartoon characters and anything else you can think of. The winner becomes 'Britain's Creative Dog Groomer of the Year', and goes through to an international final in LA. 'Sort of spectacular, but less funny than you'd think', is what my report will be; I don't need to see it to form an opinion.

I buy Sanderson another beer. We both tracked down a fair number of the mums, and wasted £50 paying the same journalist a tip-off fee for the father's last known address, which is boarded up and lifeless. We've hung around in the sort of places we imagine he might frequent, and we've visited his mother, from whom he is estranged. He's gone to ground, and no one knows where he is. I've been told some remarkable things about the story and the people involved in it, but nothing will be commissioned without access to the dad.

Someone thought his oldest daughter might be able to help, but she was entirely blank when I went round; wary or wasted, it's hard to say. A dead end either way. I say as much to Sanderson, and he nods and looks at the floor. He doesn't have the dad, or he wouldn't be wasting his time with me. But I think he knows something I don't. Something about the blank-eyed girl.

We drink up; there's a freezing fog and it's getting late. We shake hands and make noises about heading home to London. I wave him off in his cab, and drive back to the daughter's tenement, parking two streets away this time. Hire cars make you look like police.

January 8

I bought a bottle of off-brand vodka and slipped into the tenement through a fire-escape door, hanging off its hinges. The stairs were bare concrete, and they stank of bins and piss. It felt colder inside than out. The daughter answered the door, her eyes still glazed. She took the vodka and showed me inside. Another girl, just as young, was smoking in the kitchen, staring down at the foggy street. The daughter's best friend. And sitting on the sofa was her boyfriend, making faces at a newborn baby; her first, his 25th.

His name is James Lovell. He prefers Jocky or Jimmy, or Big Jim.

'You're a hard man to find', I told him.

He said, 'Not hard enough.' Then, looking up from the baby at last, 'Is there something you wanted to ask me?'

My theory is that his behaviour is not evidence of misogyny or laziness; it's far too extreme for that. I think he's responding to the bleakness of his environment, falling in love to spin a little magic, starting a family full of hope and excitement, and then moving on as soon as reality starts to bite. I felt the same sort of thing as a boy, desperate for little bits of privacy and perfection as the mining town I grew up in was slowly, catastrophically, shutting down around me.

He told me that he was a TV repairman; that he loved taking things that are broken and bringing them back to life. I filmed him on my phone, watching the little screen as he talked about his kids, twinkly-eyed, and showed me the tattoos he got for each of their birthdays. It's easy to overcomplicate TV; people just want to be understood.

We talked for the rest of the night. Now it's 8 am. I'm on the first flight back to London, on the tarmac waiting for take-off. Sanderson is two rows behind, scheming on his mobile, ignoring a tutting stewardess. I've just emailed the footage I shot to a commissioner who specializes in this sort of thing.

January 10

Back in the office, brainstorming with the rest of the team. We're having another crack at the Holy Grail for TV companies around the world – a returnable series idea for the American market. But today we're pepping things up with a package just in from Mumbai: a shipment of dodgy pills. I've sold an idea to one of the main channels about the fact that there's a pill for everything these days – maybe we could get a celebrity to spend a month popping them, and then see what happens, in a pseudo-scientific sort of way? A kind of medical/consumer/obs doc hybrid. The commissioner liked it a lot, because it would probably rate, but worried that nothing would really happen. I said sure it will – and we'll prove it. So everyone in development is on a daily dose of something: pills to make you thinner, pills to give you bigger tits, pills to make your hair grow, pills to make it stop. And this morning, all of us will be taking a 'smart drug', a pill that's said to make you three times sharper and ten times more productive, developed to treat narcolepsy and 'excessive daytime sleepiness'. We wash them down with a big pot of coffee.

There's an etiquette to brainstorming. It only really works if everyone feels relaxed, so you keep it light and polite. You try to be generous, and never dismiss or ridicule someone else's idea. Usually they're jolly occasions – flirty and funny, meandering, if you're lucky, towards something new and interesting, an idea you can develop and pitch. But it's not like that today. Today we're like a roomful of Wall Street lawyers, shouting each other down, and speaking fast and loud. Someone suggests 'space archaeology' as an avenue to pursue, satellite photography revealing lost cities in the desert. Someone else wants to talk about teenaged Mormons. Another about destroying art that is 'bad', and another still about 'trans-regret', whereby people seek to undo their sex change operations. I want us to discuss a half-thought I've had about using cutting-edge technology to scan the brains and read the minds of animals. What do whales think about all day? How does it feel to be a wolf or lion? We know how animals behave, but what about their thoughts and emotions? If we knew about their inner lives, how would it change the way we treat them? Might it spell an end to pets and meat? Everyone is talking. No one is listening. It's chaos. Fun, but not constructive.

Then the new girl, Aimee, who's half-American, says, 'Where I grew up, everyone rents a storage unit. It's cheap, but if you miss payments, they auction the contents off.' They crack the lock and people can look but not touch, to prevent squabbles and keep things moving; at a big facility, five or ten units might be auctioned every day. The highest bidder for each unit takes the whole lot away, including whatever is hidden away in boxes. It might be treasure, it might be trash. 'I think it would make a very good format', she says.

Everyone goes quiet, because everyone agrees.

January 11

The more ambitious your TV idea, the simpler it needs to be. You chisel and chip till there's nothing left but a single, sparkling thought, so pure it seems perfectly obvious, and you'd swear you've already seen the show.

So is the storage idea a competition? Between who? Is there a presenter? Is it for a daytime or prime-time audience? How long are the episodes? Which parts of the process do we use the format to foreground? Which is the same as saying where exactly is the jeopardy and the drama? Who will the audience be rooting for, and what's the payoff? And in a world of a hundred channels, where shows must sell themselves, what are we going to call it?

Two people hit the phones, and the rest of us spend the day arguing. Then the rest of the office leaves, and we order in pizza and red wine. Then the cleaners come round, and we order in beer. We're in a little island of desk lamps in a pitch-black, open-plan office when the breakthrough arrives, four people squinting and thinking slowly, half-exhausted, half not wanting it to end. It's 7 pm in New Orleans; very late indeed in London.

January 12

Meet Daisy and Joe, a bickering, likeable married couple from Louisiana in their early thirties. They scrape a living at storage auctions up and down the East Coast. Mostly the units contain things people are too lazy or sentimental to take to the tip. But very occasionally they'll strike it rich, with something exquisite or rare. There's natural competition, because around 20 other teams follow the auctions – fathers and sons, brothers and sisters, school-leavers and retirees, and other couples like Daisy and Joe.

In this world, it's a golden rule that you shift whatever you buy as soon as possible, to make money to invest the next time around. So there's natural suspense when the auction is running, natural energy after it's closed, and natural, ongoing jeopardy, with each day ending in profit and loss, and disaster never far away. Best of all, the whole thing unfolds like a road movie, in truck stops, motels and lockups on the edge of town, a portrait of everyday life in small-town America, a peek into places that are usually very private. It doesn't need formatting because it's completely, compellingly real.

We'll pitch it on our next trip to the States, in two weeks' time.

January 13

The first call of the day is from Britain's most popular tabloid: is it true that I've done an interview with the guy with the 25 kids? I assure them it is not. The second call is from a commissioning editor at Channel 4: well done on finding the chap with the 25 kids. So unexpectedly charming and gentle! Such an articulate man! We'd be delighted to commission the film. The third call is from Charlie, my boss: good morning and would you mind telling me exactly what the fuck is going on?

By the time I get to my desk, everyone knows I was less than honest about the purpose of my trip to Scotland, and most people are standing off, unsure whether they'll be helping me celebrate a commission tonight or buying me drinks to say goodbye. The boys are mainly impressed, the girls shy and disapproving.

In the context of TV at least, I believe that friction is progress. That if you're not occasionally in bother, you're probably not doing enough. No doubt you can go too far, though. Charlie seemed incensed on the phone.

So I'm back in the whitewashed boardroom, trying to explain.

I've always been at my best when there's plenty of pressure and lots at stake. My creativity, for what it's worth, is a sort of survival instinct. It just doesn't function if everything gets too comfy. I need to feel up on a wire. And the more things are okayed and agreed, and planned and put into spreadsheets, the safer and duller it all becomes.

Charlie is saying nothing.

I'll get you the series you want, I tell him. But it won't come from mild-mannered pondering and keeping my nose clean. It'll be an adventure. 'A death-or-glory romp.'

Speech over. And possibly my career at the company, too. It's sort of what I meant to say last week, before I got distracted. Following my nose does often lead to single, stand-alone films, which are time-consuming and tough to make, and not very profitable, if at all. And my taste and interests being what they are, those films are often about sordid and difficult subjects. But not always. In any case, taste and instinct are really all I've got to go on.

'Sometimes', Charlie says, 'I think you want me to sack you.'

He was pink with rage when we sat down – not the first time I've induced that response in a boss. Now he's observing me closely, head tilted to one side. He says he felt the same as a younger man, so he's not going to fire me. Do it your way, but you'd better get results; and lie to me again and you're finished.

Which means we're celebrating after all, spending the money Charlie has put behind the bar to show everyone else that we're cool. But a text comes through, from the guy who's just commissioned the film. It's occurred to him that the philandering dad's behaviour might be a sign of mental illness; are we sure that he's right in the head?

I say yes, we talked and he's fine. I already knew he was not.

January 15

Feeling good today, so I take my producer out for lunch. TV is full of posh young women called Tamsin and Tamara, with lots of confidence and education, brought up to follow the rules. My producer isn't like that at all. She's called Mills, and she's from an ordinary, working-class background, a school-leaver at just 16. And she's absolutely *brilliant* at TV. Brilliant at knowing what people want to watch. Brilliant at seeing things from a fresh perspective. And, because she's down-to-earth, determined, tough and utterly ruthless, she's brilliant at finding people.

'There's something I need to tell you', she says.

Most documentaries need to be about something extraordinary to be commissioned. Anything that feels gentle or poetic, a portrait of something or a slice of everyday life, doesn't stand much of a chance; it won't stand out in the schedules, which means that too few people will watch. You can wait for the right sort of thing to come along and then pounce, like we did with the chap in Scotland. Or you can dream things into being – imagine something so strange and remarkable that everyone would want to tune in and watch, and then roll up your sleeves and make it real.

Perhaps there's a support group for compulsive helpers? Can one twin be obese and the other anorexic? Is it possible to hypnotize a whole stadium full of people? What happens to kids who've been expelled over and over, till there are no more schools to take them?

Mills is investigating all of this, and lots of other things besides. She found Rankin, our gangster, after we conjured him up over coffee in the run-down cafe. London is in the grip of a gun crime epidemic, which everyone is talking about. But where do the guns come from, we wondered? Could we trace the life story of a single gun, from military service to criminal use to seizure by the police? How do criminals get their guns? Maybe there's a go-to guy we can find? Someone who can explain how it works? Wouldn't it be amazing to put him on TV, even if it's just an actor speaking his words? Wouldn't that be a great contribution to the debate? Wouldn't that be a coup?

'You're not going to like this', Mills says.

I order us a glass of wine.

She's a bit in love with Rankin. We both are, I suppose, seduced by the sense of danger, the immorality, and the glamour of it all. The gold-plated Uzis and blacked-out German autos. The triumph of getting there first.

Mills says, 'I'm worried it's not really true.'

January 16

I'm on the sixth floor of the offices of Britain's biggest broadcaster, with no bag or files or notebook. It's an important meeting, but I don't want it to look that way. I want it to seem like I've dropped by casually, on my way from one difficult-but-surmountable challenge to another. A doer, not a salesman or intellectual.

I'm seeing the Head of Documentaries, and hoping he liked his gun.

Everyone has their own way of pitching. Whatever you do has got to come naturally, or you'll never hold your audience, like an unfunny man telling a joke. So if you're a serious sort of person, go with it. If you're good at telling stories, it's best to paint them a picture. I just like to chat about things I think are interesting, so that it feels like a conversation. Anything you've rehearsed will only sound stale, and a formal pitch reduces the range of possible responses, perhaps down to just two. And of those two, a busy commissioner put on the spot will always choose the one you don't want to hear – he lives in a blizzard of ideas, and his main goal in life is to escape the heavy weather and sit somewhere warm and dry. With a cosy conversation, if you're lucky, you might not even have to pitch at all; the commissioner will arrive at the idea all by himself, and then he'll love it and fight for it, and make it happen.

If there's one thing I'm good at, it's chatting.

So we chat. About a collective of prostitutes we've found who only go with disabled clients, so they're two parts social workers and one part happy hookers. Many of their clients would never have sex any other way, and isn't sex essential to a happy and fulfilling life? And we talk about my dad, and all the fathers and sons like us who don't get along or understand each other, because the dads were all miners and the sons work in middle management, because the mines all closed and management is what people do now. What if we reopened a mine? And the fathers and sons worked together for a while, just as they would have done if times hadn't changed so suddenly when I was a boy? It would be a way of exploring our changing society, and what it means now to be a man. We chat about the rising number of young women having babies in prison. And we chat about the gangster and his guns.

The head of documentaries didn't open the box I gave him straight away. I told him not to. Here's a present, I said; open it later. And I left it at that, with a note inside suggesting we meet. The first he knew about the gun was when he triggered a major security alert trying to get back to his office. The building was evacuated, and word got around that the cause was a commissioner packing a semi-automatic.

That must have been rather awkward. But now we've both got a story to tell. And he really likes the idea.

January 19

There's 5k on the table to make a sizzle reel about Rankin – a five-minute film to showcase his character and the story we want to tell. If it's as good as I'm claiming, a full commission will follow.

But sizzle reels are tricky. It's easy to paint a pretty picture in words. Now all the grand and airy promises you made in the pitch have to be honed and realized. With not much time or money, and the knowledge that a bad taster can leave a good idea stone dead.

We need to decide what to shoot, and what sort of tone we want to achieve. Too worthy and we'll be wasting an opportunity to make something complex and good. But we can't just give the guy a platform for opinions that no one sane will embrace. You've got to like the guy, despite what he stands for. You've got to believe he can change.

I call Mills to talk it over and tell her what I'm imagining.

'You can imagine whatever you like', she says. 'There are things I think we should *know*.'

Two hours later, she's on a train to the coast; it'll be clear what we should shoot when we find out more about him, she says. And all we really know so far is what he himself has told us.

Her instincts are better than mine, and they're telling her that something's not right.

January 21

Fat, blurry snowflakes are falling slowly, in the gloom at the end of the day. Everything is muffled, the way things sound after a blow to the head. I can see and hear my breath.

The office is way too warm. When my phone rang, I brought it outside to speak. The cold on my face feels good, and some conversations are best held out of earshot.

'This film', says Big Jim Lovell. 'You'll want to dig things up. You'll only cause trouble. And I've got troubles enough.'

Two more mums have been named in the press. 27 kids in total now, with more revelations to come, perhaps.

He's not good on the phone. Not used to conversation. He says all this in a rush. A speech he's been working up to.

'It's not an investigation', I tell him. 'It's all about the present. Who you are and how you live. What you think and feel.'

He says, 'I've done things I'm not proud of.'

'Me too', I tell him. 'None of us are saints.'

'Wrong things', he says. 'Bad things.'

'Me too.'

'I've hurt people', he says.

'Me too.'

He's silent for a moment. He says, 'Physically, I mean.'

That night in the flat in Paisley, after we'd finished filming, just talking and drinking the vodka, he took a call on his mobile. It was very late by then. He listened without saying anything, apart from 'K' at the end. He stood up, wide awake now, and said he'd be back soon. I watched from the window as a car loomed up in the fog. The driver got out. They exchanged words, Lovell towering over him. Then he bounced the guy's head off the bonnet, over and over again.

When he came back to the flat, his eyes were wild and his face was spattered with blood. He went straight to the bedroom and slammed the door. The baby woke up and started to cry. That's when I left.

I passed the guy in the street. His face was a mess. He was groaning and gurgling from the blood in his throat.

I tell him about a time not long ago, at the end of a long day of filming, when some toe-rag stopped me and a producer in the lift of a multi-storey car park. He wanted the equipment. I said sure. It was only rented stuff, covered by insurance. No problem, help yourself. Then he said, 'Your bag as well.' But the bag contained the rushes, and the rushes that day were good. He pulled out an old-fashioned flick knife, eyes wide with excitement. Dangerous, but not very. The producer was outraged, like she'd got bad service at a posh hotel. That's the sort of woman she was. She gave him a piece of her mind. He spat in her face.

I only needed to hit him once, but I did it a few times anyway, because I liked the way it felt. He wasn't expecting an educated type to punch him in the throat, especially in the middle of a sentence. But rage is not the preserve of the ignorant or poor. There's nothing I hate more than a bully.

I put him in the recovery position and helped myself to the money in his pocket, enough for a decent bottle of wine, and drove us back to London. The producer said I was worse than the guy with the switchblade. I don't know. Perhaps she's right. She left the film the following day. I've still got the switchblade. I use it for opening letters.

'We both come from tough places', I tell Lovell. 'You learn to stand your ground. Protect your interests when they're threatened. Not everyone understands that. Especially people with comfortable lives. But I understand. Not all anger can or should be managed. Sometimes it just needs to be vented.'

Lovell's dad was black. He walked out before his son's first birthday. The town is almost totally white. Growing must have been hard.

He says nothing. For a moment I think he might have hung up, but he's considering what I've said. I can hear him breathing, thoughtfully.

'Occasional acts of violence don't make you a violent man.'

He grunts in agreement at this.

'Is there anything the police want you for right now?'

'No', he says. 'Nothing at all.'

'Anything relating to your girlfriends? Or your kids?'

He vents some anger at that. Immediate and volcanic. I tell him to calm the fuck down. It's something I have to ask.

He says he'd never hurt women or children. Says he loves the kids, and all their mums.

I tell him the benefits of being in a film. It's a special thing. A privilege. Not many of us get to see our lives from without. Like an out-of-body experience. It's something you can learn a lot from. It can change the way people see you, and the way you see yourself.

'So trust me, okay? Talk to me. Let me in. And I promise everything'll be fine.'

He says, 'Okay.' And then he's gone.

I think he wants to change.

I think this film could be good.

January 23

Salvatore Donato Valverde, known by his stage name Godín, died at the age of 54 at 1.36 pm on Sunday October 27th, 1929, the day before the Wall Street Crash. An illusionist and escapologist, he had swerved death hundreds if not thousands of times. News of his final demise was greeted with disbelief. Was this, wondered the *New York Times*, one more trick? A final act of vanishment?

By 1900, playbills were already proclaiming Godín the most famous man in the world. He was also one of the richest and most influential, with industrialists, monarchs and presidents amongst his many friends. He is credited with influencing policy on matters of poverty and social mobility in half a dozen countries. For the masses – oppressed, worn and starved of hope – he was living proof that circumstances could be surmounted; that a man could always escape. For that, above all else, Godín was adored.

He was, however, not without enemies. His pioneering movies – abandoned at the peak of his popularity in favour of live performance – were said to be made with mob money, and dangerous men were left exposed when he chose to break his contract. The Church of Science and Light, of which Godín became a leading convert and financial supporter, was all but destroyed when he suddenly denounced it as a cult. He was quick to sue anyone he suspected of copying his illusions, driving several of his rivals into ruin. And by the time he turned 50, he had been named co-respondent in over 200 petitions for divorce. When details of his death began to emerge, many suspected foul play.

His final performance was delivered at the thousand-seater Kendrick Music Hall in Boston on the evening of October 26th. That morning, on the Longfellow Bridge, the brakes had seemingly failed on his automobile, a customized Studebaker Roadster, resulting in a fearsome crash. It was the third such incident involving Godín that same year. In an embryonic gutter press, rumours of drug addiction and syphilis swirled. A doctor no one was later able to trace administered a very large intravenous dose of 'energy serum' to settle Godín's nerves and restore his focus.

In the afternoon, Godín complained to his dresser of a pain in his heart – a legacy perhaps of an incident six months earlier when he was apparently shot mid-performance by an outraged husband. On that occasion his life had been saved by an eminent surgeon who happened to be present, operating there and then, live on the stage, as the audience held its breath, though some suspected the whole thing was merely showmanship. Godín later claimed that the bullet was lodged too close to his heart to be removed; that superhuman strength was all that was keeping him alive. A stage-hand with the Godín Theatre Company reported that for several weeks he had refused all forms of sustenance 'save from sources he knew he could trust'; by the 28th of October, he 'was nothing but skin and gristle'.

In the evening, an hour before his performance began, Godín put himself into a trance. Witnesses spoke of him whispering a strange and urgent incantation, his eyes wide open, oblivious to their presence. He emerged unsteady and wet with sweat.

A little after seven, he took to the stage and announced a change to the advertised programme. Instead, Godín said, something new. An impossible escape, from a sealed glass tank of full water, assisted by 'the angel of death'.

He entered the tank suspended upside down and bound hand and foot in chains and manacles, as local policemen padlocked the roof of the tank in place. As Godín began to struggle, a screen was wheeled into place, blocking his escape from view. The audience heard the clanking of iron, the breaking of glass, the sloshing of water, gasping breaths and heavy, exhausted footsteps. The screen was pushed aside, and there, still suspended in the tank, still bound and immersed, was Godín, completely inert. For a moment there was silence.

The curtain came down, the lights went up, and pandemonium ensued.

Godín's embalmed body lay in state for three days at Grand Central Station in his home town of New York, to accommodate the huge crowds clamouring to see him. A real-life superhero, finally undone. He was buried in an ancient Egyptian sarcophagus, at the Calvary Cemetery in Queens. No postmortem was conducted. His insurance company paid double indemnity.

What, in the end, was the cause of the great man's death, if indeed he died that day at all? We're planning to dig up his body to discover the truth.

So we're on a plane to New York. In 12 hours' time, we'll be taking Godín's last surviving relative out to lunch, me and Charlie and his business partner. If the relative finally agrees to our plan, it'll be a commission of global significance – a four-hour live extravaganza that people will watch around the globe. It's bold and sensational, like Godín's own stunts, with a crystal-clear sense of purpose. It'll make my name. If he says no, on the other hand, we'll have wasted 12 months of effort and tens of thousands of pounds.

The flight has settled and the lights have been dimmed. Most people are sleeping now, or dazed and blank, in long-haul hibernation. I've been talking since soon after take-off to a woman in the window seat. She hates to drink alone, she said, to the steward but looking at me. I said I'd take a bourbon, straight, and she said she'd have the same.

'Where are we now, I wonder?' she says, low and close.

'Over Iceland, maybe. Or the ocean.' It's black as ink outside the window. 'No particular place.'

She tells me she used to live in New York. Moved to London when she got married. It's her first time back since … she says, trailing off. And says instead it's her first time back in years. The first time since her divorce, I think, though I don't ask and she doesn't say. There's an air of excitement about her. An openness that married people lose.

She edits a glossy magazine, the kind you find on coffee tables in the very best hotels. Two years ago she signed a star writer, a novelist on the rise, who had won a prestigious award. Write about anything you like, she said. 3000 words, three times a year. But he'd written barely anything, and then written nothing at all. Finally, he fell out of touch altogether. Now she wants to know why. Maybe there's a story in it?

I think she senses an adventure. A story of her own.

People don't always fulfil their promise, she says. You can have it and lose it. Everyone does, in the end. Even the brightest and best. What matters is making it count when the moment arrives, for as long as you possibly can.

She shivers a little as she says this. I offer her my coat as a blanket. She touches my arm lightly and says, 'You're very kind.' She makes herself comfortable. We order another drink.

I tell her I worry I'll go the same way as her novelist. Last year was a productive one. Lots of commissions. Some of them good. A year of beating the house. Now is the time to capitalize. I'm not sure the moment will last, though, and I doubt it will come again.

'Exciting', she says. 'When the time is now. When everything's to play for.'

We'll be pitching the storage idea over breakfast tomorrow. I still can't think of a title, which probably doesn't reflect well on the idea itself. Is it still too complicated? Titles are easy when you've got the idea right.

'Do you love what you do?' she says.

Her voice is deep and musical, part east-coast intellectual, part native French. It makes her sound both playful and wise.

She thinks her novelist no longer loves writing, or the stuff he writes, or the life that writing requires him to live. Maybe he's found something better.

I tell her about Godín. I tell her I think it's a great idea. An idea that, yes, I love. I'd love to get it commissioned. I'd love for it to be made.

We're quiet for a moment, considering this. I didn't mean to make a speech. Then she turns in her seat. Her eyes look very bright. She says, 'There you go: a $10m idea, conceived and pitched with love. If you're right, and now is the time, it sounds to me like you're ready.'

Cheers to that, lady on a plane. I very much hope you're right.

January 24

It's snowing heavily when we land in New York. Eleven missed calls, number unknown, and four messages.

The first is from Mills, my producer. Rankin might well be a gangster, but he's definitely also a florist, specializing in weddings and funerals, with a sideline in renting out limos. A possible fantasist, then. Or a solution to our problem with the taster tape.

The second message is from Sanderson, the enemy exec from the pub in Scotland. He sounds unusually perky. Big Jim Lovell, the father of all those children might well be a likeable dreamer, he says, but he's definitely also a gangster, a hard man in a notorious firm. And he's just been arrested for murder. It seems he's stabbed someone in the cold concrete stairwell right outside the flat where we met.

The third message is from a detective constable in Glasgow City Police. We understand that you are in possession of a taped interview which we believe may shed light on a current case?

The fourth is from the tabloid I sent packing last week; they're wondering if I'd care to revise my statement?

The missed calls, I'm guessing, are from the office in London and the film's commissioner.

We're queuing at immigration. The magazine editor has disappeared. There's a sign at the head of the line: At all times, tell the truth. Possible with strangers in mid-air, perhaps, where nothing really matters. Conversations there are more like the ones you have in your head. Now it's back to business, and telling the truth is not the business we're in.

CHAPTER TWO:
FEBRUARY

February 2

I'm in an underground car park. It's dimly lit by sickly, yellowish bulkhead lamps. I'm on my knees, head bowed. There's a man standing over me with a gun jammed hard in my ear, which hurts.

'People in your position aren't good at listening', he says. I think he means people kneeling on the floor of an underground car park with a gun in their ear, but it's possible he means TV executives. I'm not sure what he means. I haven't really been listening.

'So I'm going to speak slowly', he says. 'You think you're in charge, but you're not. I am. And don't you fucking forget it.'

We are shooting the taster tape for the gunman idea. It turns out that he is not good at taking direction.

We've been at it for five hours now, and every time I've got close to asking him a meaningful question about his past or his present, he's brushed me off with a boast. It's been frustrating. I still don't really know who he is. He could be someone playing a part.

Then I asked him a question he really didn't like, about two little boys who found an illegal gun hidden in their big brother's bedroom. One of them shot the other in the face. 'Stop posturing and consider the scenario', I said. 'A little boy missing the back of his head. And then when you're ready tell me what you think and feel.'

Now there was anger in his eyes.

'This is how I used to deal with people who ask too many questions', he said, and reached past the camera, grabbed hold of my shirt and pulled me in front of it. And then he moved round and kicked me in the back of the legs so I went down on my knees. And then he pushed his jacket back from his hip and pulled out a gun.

Me and the cameraman go way back. We've gotten into scrapes before. He looked at me from behind the camera, eyebrows raised. 'You want me to shoot this?' I just about managed to give him a look back to say 'Yes, I suppose so' before Rankin stuck the gun in my ear and shouted at me to keep my fucking face down and do as I'm fucking told.

Will this make for a good scene in the taster? It makes him look like the real deal, which is good. But also a bit mad, which is not.

'I feel you've made your point', I tell him.

'Shall I tell you how I feel?' he asks. 'Very fucking indifferent.'

He didn't like the idea of filming him doing flowers for a wedding, which would have been good because we'd have seen him doing something unexpected and creative. Surrounded by happy, smiling faces, you might believe that he's changed, or sincerely wants to. He keeps a clippings book of all the times his guns have been used in shootings. I want him to look at it with me, but he won't. Instead we've filmed him taking a gun apart and explaining how it works. Rhapsodizing about it, in fact. And we've filmed him at a tailor's, where he's halfway through getting a suit made; not uninteresting, but too much like what editors call 'wallpaper' – pretty pictures that don't mean very much. So far, there's been no hint or glimpse of the journey he's on or might undertake. He's having it all his own way.

Rankin helps me back to my feet.

'Did that hurt?' he asks.

I tell him it did, rather.

He says that in some lines of work, pain is unavoidable.

You can learn a lot from making tasters like this one. Much more than from just talking or spending time with someone. Some people just come alive on camera, and you can't take your eyes off them. I think what we've learned from making this particular taster is that my idea is unlikely to work. It's hard to imagine him meeting the families of people who have died. Exposing them to a man this arrogant would be cruel. Maybe Rankin isn't ready to really get to grips with his past or the ramifications of his actions. Maybe he never will be.

But his defences must be built so high for a reason. If we could get behind them, just for a moment, that might be enough. If we could prick his conscience, the results might be compelling.

February 3

My phone rings and wakes me up. It's still dark and the room is cold.

A woman's voice, low and smoky. 'It's Celestine', she says. The woman from the plane. She's just arrived back in London.

'I'm sorry', she says, again.

I tell to her to get fucked, and hang up.

I was in New York for just three days. She called me on the first morning, just after we'd cleared the airport. I was pleased and surprised. She said the office had given her my number. That she'd enjoyed our conversation, and would I care to join her for dinner?

We had dinner every night, in fact, at neighbourhood restaurants that only a local would know. Warm, dark places that felt as old as the city itself. It gave me a front-row seat to the story of her and the writer who writes no more.

The first night she told me about the state in which she found him. His girlfriend had kicked him out, and he'd lost his apartment for failure to pay the rent. He was living in a tiny room above a shop that sells pizza by the slice, getting by on the royalties of his one successful book.

The bed took up most of the room, but still the room was a mess. She tidied it up for him. She felt like his mother.

The second night she told me of her efforts to get him writing again. She offered him every story on her slate. Access to a famous fashion designer, risking his reputation in a bid to revitalize a faded label. An embed with the US army in the world's bloodiest war zone. An interview with a serial killer willing, for the first time, to talk about his crimes. But nothing at all appealed.

It seemed she was right about the guy. He was out of love with writing. He was bored and lost.

The third night she seemed different. The tension she'd had about her was gone. She ate like she was hungry. These things and everything else about her told me they'd been to bed.

We drank some wine.

I said, 'So what happened with your writer today?'

She said, 'My darling, where to begin?'

February 4

I get to the office early. There's a letter on my desk.

It says, 'Sweet boy. All is fair in love and war. I hope you can forgive me.'

On my third day in New York, I received a call first thing in the morning from the relative of Godín, the escapologist. He told me that the family would consent to the exhumation. The project could go ahead.

I told the network we'd sold the idea to, and they expressed their delight.

I told Charlie, and he hugged me tightly. A hug of real significance.

He told me to enjoy myself, the cost on him, and flew on to other meetings.

I went for a walk, and then I went to bed. I'd celebrate in the evening, over dinner with Celestine.

Whilst all this was happening, a second, related set of conversations was taking place, unbeknownst to me.

In desperation, Celestine told her writer about my plans for Godín's remains; maybe he could write a piece to accompany the broadcast? His response was immediate. He loved the idea. Here at last was something he wanted to write about. He called his agent on the spot.

His agent called his publisher, who'd paid a big advance for the writer's second book, then given up hope of it happening. They thought the combination of writer and subject would sell very well.

The agent felt he was on a roll, so he called up a studio boss. Would he like to option the book? The boss said yes, he would.

At lunchtime, Celestine, the writer, his agent, the publisher and the studio boss's sidekick met to formalize their agreement, and figure out next steps.

The agent called Godín's relative and made an offer for exclusivity. The offer was so generous the family could only accept. Then he presented the network I'd sold the idea to with a new, more enticing deal – a night of programmes timed to coincide with the release of the book and the film. Less risky than a live transmission. In fact, with all that free publicity, there'd be no risk at all – as close as you can get to a sure-fire hit. And so the network boss agreed to come on board.

In a little over seven hours, my $10m idea was now worth 100 million and counting. But not to me. Its worth to me now was nothing.

Celestine took the writer off and fucked his brains out, then came to meet me for supper.

We ordered drinks in a very fine mood. Mine didn't make it to dessert.

All in all, quite an eventful day.

'You saved me', the letter says. 'I will do the same for you one day. Bisoux, C.'

February 5

A couple of years ago, a friend asked me to help him out with a project that was running into a spot of bother. The project was about a recent series of coordinated terrorist attacks on London. It had a big budget but was being made on a very tight turnaround. Could I come and help for a few days in the run up to transmission? Maybe help a bit with scripting or re-cutting the opening? I said sure, I'd be happy to.

I like this kind of thing. You get stuck in and meet new people. You grapple with problems and solve them. You help shape a bit of TV. You get all of the fun that comes with that, with none of the responsibility. It's a busman's holiday. Grown-up playtime.

I turned up good and early and someone buzzed me in. It was like stepping onto the Titanic as it finally started to sink. People were shouting and crying, all semblance of order long gone. It stank of sweat and fear, and last night's dinner. My friend looked like a cadaver.

We all knuckled down and sorted it out. We delivered the tape 40 minutes before transmission, two whole weeks after it was due. A dispatch rider took my friend through London on the back of his bike, weaving in and out of traffic, the tape down the front of his jacket. Then we drank ourselves senseless.

The point is that drama and TV go hand in hand. Things are always on the verge of going wrong, and things are always going to the wire. I'm not sure why. I think it's just the way that creative people respond to things like pressure and deadlines. Generally the job gets done, but rarely without some measure of flouncing and bickering. I don't think I've ever made a programme that hasn't involved some sort of major panic.

So long as the show makes it to air, everything is forgiven.

It's a different matter when a film falls down.

I've been summoned to a meeting in the boardroom, tomorrow afternoon.

February 6

Generally speaking, the thing that makes films fail is life. Especially when life – real stuff that's happened and is happening around you – is the thing you're attempting to capture.

I once had a film fall down about Britain's youngest dad when it turned out the baby wasn't his own. Social Services moved in, and that was the end of that. A film about US high-school killing sprees – how best to survive them, based on research by the FBI – was halted by a fresh example in which 20 people died. That made the film timely, of course, but also politically charged. Almost everyone pulled out. Life just gets in the way sometimes.

People forget this, particularly those who spend most of their time in offices, because the processes involved in film-making create an illusion of control. You work out your budget and plan your schedule. You think through the story you want to tell, and plot out the scenes you'll need. It all looks so achievable and neat on paper. But you can't control life. Life controls you.

These are facts. But it's another fact of life in television that someone must always say sorry. Because when films fall down there's always a tab, which no one wants to pick up.

When a series stalls halfway through production, the tab can run to hundreds of thousands. The film about the man with 25 kids fell down before we'd even begun. But still the mood is sombre.

Around the boardroom table, the grown-ups are looking my way.

The money people have spoken. We're 10k out of pocket, and the broadcaster says it's all on us; commissioners will do anything to distance themselves from failure. In the mind of my commissioner it's very clear indeed where the blame for this mess lies.

Now it's my turn to speak.

All I can say is sorry.

'It was a level of risk we never should have entertained', says Charlie.

The money is bad. The damage to our reputation is worse. It makes us look reckless.

'We have to do better than this', Charlie says.

All I can do is nod.

February 7

It's 5 am. I'm giving up on sleep. I'm looking for somewhere to eat.

We wrapped up the blame game in little more than half an hour yesterday. My bad for taking on the film in the first place. We all pursed our lips and went back to work.

But I wonder if my bad stops there.

I wonder if the loss of 10k is really all I'm to blame for?

It's true that life makes things go wrong. Shit happens. But programme-makers are part of life too, not just neutral observers of it. The things we do and say have consequences, the same as anyone else.

The film about the dad with 25 kids went wrong because the central character stabbed someone to death. Who could have seen that coming, right? But would it have happened if not for me?

No one had ever asked James Lovell the sort of questions I did. Interested, thoughtful, sensitive ones. The kind of questions you ask when you're really trying to understand someone. Nor had anyone ever really listened to what he had to say. I think he liked it, as people often do. It's sort of addictive, like therapy. But like therapy, it stirs things up.

He'd started to open up to me. Nothing alarming. Just stuff that he was feeling, and stuff about his life. Stuff that had happened to him. I listened to what he had to say. We had a proper conversation.

'I can never seem to put things behind me', he said.

I told him he should stop trying, maybe. That most people's lives are messy.

He got agitated and he cried. I told him everything would be okay.

And then I fucked off back to London.

Who knows what was going through Lovell's head?

I'm not a therapist. I've had no training. Like most people in TV, my dealings with contributors are mostly a matter of improvisation – just talking and listening and seeing where it leads.

I have no idea really what state he was in when I left him, though on the surface he seemed calm and happy.

The police have cleared me of any wrongdoing. Responsibility, however, is a different matter.

Whatever he was thinking and feeling the night he committed murder, I hope to God it wasn't dredged up by me.

February 9

In some lines of work, help is on hand to deal with problems of conscience.

Doctors are offered counselling. Policemen too, but they have something better – a drink after work, with other people who've been there.

TV, in my experience, is more like being in the army.

It's a much softer, gentler industry now than when I started. You don't often see people throwing stuff around offices any more, or shouting at junior members of staff. You don't often see people coming back pissed from lunch. But one macho relic remains: you don't wallow or wring your hands. You man up and crack on.

So how do you deal with the occasional moment of inner turmoil, or the odd attack of self-loathing?

What I do is try to have another idea.

The comfort of that, of making a new connection or seeing something in a way you never have before, is immense, I think. The start of something. What's a better tonic than that?

In TV you're either soaring or falling. A new idea will arrest a fall. A good one will get you airborne again.

There's a place I go sometimes where I feel completely invisible. Not just anonymous or inconspicuous. It's like I don't exist. No one talks to me. No one looks at me. You go in and the barmaid pulls you a pint. Pints of ale is all there is, so there's no need for words when you order your drink. Pints are £2. Everyone knows that. No need for words there either.

It's a grim old pub a few streets from where I live, at the bottom of the ugliest block of flats you've ever seen, a shade of grey so completely lifeless it sucks the colour out of anything nearby. Soon the block will be gone, demolished to make way for something else. Most of the flats are boarded up. But for now the pub remains, caught in a never-ending wake, its last few regulars stupefied and lost.

I can be entirely alone here, without the emptiness and melancholia that come with actually being alone. I find it a very good place to think.

I'm trying to have a beautiful and imperishable thought. People all over London and Washington and New York will be trying to do the same thing today, in all sorts of different offices and buildings. But today my need is greater. So maybe today will be the day.

February 10

Soon after his death in April 1955, the brain of Albert Einstein was removed from his body. The pathologist who conducted the autopsy wanted to study it in the hope of solving a mystery – the nature of genius.

The brain was measured, photographed, cut into blocks and preserved. 200 slides containing tissue samples were created and sent away to experts in neuropathology.

In the years that followed, a number of studies took place, and various anomalies were identified. One study found that samples of the brain appeared to have more 'glue' cells per neuron than the average brain. Another study determined that the neurons themselves were more densely packed than normal. Another identified an extra ridge on the mid-frontal lobe. Another noticed that Einstein's inferior parietal lobule was unusually wide.

Were any of these features responsible for Einstein's creativity and brilliance? And was he born with the anomalies, or did his brain change as his ideas developed?

Experts now believe that all this effort was a waste of time. Einstein's brain was and is unique, but all brains are. Mine is, and so is yours. Creativity and genius remain as mysterious as ever.

This is a great story. It's full of conflict and controversy, and I think it would make an outstanding film.

What I really like about the story, though, is the lesson it seems to offer. People who have great ideas aren't born, they're made.

February 12

If you give a very ordinary family every possible advantage, short of money – contacts and connections, opportunities, advice, coaching in what to say and how to behave and so on – what would become of them, in the space of a single generation?

I went to enormous trouble to get to university. I gave up all my friendships and the things I was interested in. I gave up having fun. I made it my first and only priority. I wanted it more than anything.

My first tutorial, on classical philosophy, was given by an owlish, twattish old don, who'd joined the college as an undergraduate straight from Eton and never left (or even, I suspect, ventured outside the ivy-grown quads of the college). He spoke of Plato's idea that some people are born with gold in their souls, and others with baser metals. Those with golden souls are born to rule as intellectual philosopher-kings, with everyone else supporting them. He was addressing his comments, I think, quite specifically to me. He felt forced to accommodate people like me – people not widely travelled and not widely read, with huge gaps in their education – by meddling bureaucrats bent on social engineering.

For two years that old man corrected my pronunciation of everyday words, pretending not to understand when I said class instead of *clarse*. When you're young and out of your depth, and probably just grateful to be there, you go along with such things, I suppose. If he tried that now, I'd tell him not to be such a cunt. See how he likes my pronunciation of that.

For pretty much all of those two years I fretted about not having a golden soul. The next level down for Plato was silver. Most of the time I felt part of the tier below that, constituting those with souls of bronze or iron, doomed to labour and never rise. A do-er, not a thinker, no matter how much you might wish to be one.

At the end of the second year I became friends with a supremely posh student studying the same thing as me in the year above. He taught me how the place really worked – how to do well there and get what you want – and he shared with me a life-changing secret. You don't need a golden soul, he said. What does that mean anyway? You just need to be able to convince people that you have one. What you are doesn't matter. It's what you seem to be that counts.

I stopped reading the books on the reading lists, and started reading stuff I was interested in. I stopped spending all of my time in the library, and started talking to people instead. I stopped trying to impress people and got on with the business of *being* impressive, by appearing to be.

I developed a bit of intellectual swagger. I'd leave lectures early, looking bored. I'd boast about all the books I hadn't bothered to read. I'd dismiss other people's points of view, and argue with anyone at the slightest provocation.

Suddenly, the old don stopped correcting my pronunciation of things. He even invited me round to his rooms for sherry. Which of course I ignored, because that's the sort of thing a philosopher-king would do.

I had discovered the power of projecting an image, of telling people what they want to hear and being what they want you to be.

I didn't need to be me any more. I could be almost anyone.

Could we film a team of people doing the same thing for a struggling family as the posh guy had done for me? Teaching them the soft skills that privileged people just absorb from their parents and their parents' friends? Showing them how things really work, and how to go about getting what you want?

One of the biggest broadcasters in Britain has a multimillion pound fund for big ideas. I'm thinking of a series that might run for years and years. The story of our times – of social inequality and social change – unfolding on TV for an hour every six months or so.

It would be a documentary epic, a family saga of aspiration and ambition, full of moments of triumph and heartbreak. We'd grow older and wiser with the characters we're watching, benefitting from a huge amount of takeaway information to help us with our own struggles and frustrations. How to get your kids into better schools. How to land the best jobs. How to move upwards once you've made a start. How to be successful.

And how to cope with the cost, which I know from first-hand experience is both considerable and impossible to avoid. Change your life, and you'll never again belong in the place that you came from. The pisser is that you'll never really belong in the place you've ended up either.

You'll end up spending the rest of your life trying to fit in, whilst living in fear of being unmasked.

Once you start projecting, it's impossible to stop.

February 14

My head hurts.

Last night we did a bit more filming with Rankin, to finish off the taster. An interview in one of his big black cars, with just a hint of honesty and the suggestion of hidden depths. And then we went for drinks, Rankin and his girlfriend, Mills and me.

Then Rankin went off in another big black car, and we carried on drinking.

We went to a sort of private bar down a flight of steps, past a girl in a booth. There were candles on the tables and no other lights at all. Drinks came, which I don't think we ordered or paid for.

I can't remember much after that.

I open my eyes and get a sudden stab of panic at the unfamiliar room. It's okay. A hotel room. Quite a nice one. I half remember checking in.

The curtains are open and the room is bright. It feels like my brain is liquid, sloshing around inside my skull.

Then another stab of panic. Mine aren't the only clothes on the floor.

There's someone in my bed, facing away, fast asleep.

I have no idea who it is.

And then suddenly I do. It's Rankin's girlfriend.

Fuck fuck fuck.

At breakfast Mills is very slightly distant. Not so that anyone else would notice, but it's unmistakeable from where I'm sitting. It's not disapproval. She's not that kind of person. I've never known her disapprove of anything. It's closer, I think, to disbelief. Did you really do what I think you did? I really hope you didn't. Because you really, really shouldn't have.

She looks at me over her teacup, all big green eyes, and I smile back. A *what can you do?* sort of smile.

She keeps on looking, and sips her tea.

February 17

Nothing planned today except a nice long think about Einstein's brain. Maybe we could tell the story by attempting to bring all the fragments together again, for the first time in 60 years?

Mills is checking in with Daisy and Joe, the storage auction traders, while we wait for the network to make up its mind.

The rest of the team is pondering how to progress the social-mobility project. We need to find the right family. But where and how to go about it?

I like quiet, thoughtful days in the office like these. The energetic quietness. The comforting rustle and murmur of people absorbed in their work. The cheerful chirping of phones.

There's a text from Rankin's girlfriend.

'That was a fun night', she says. 'Not much sleep!'

Best to play a straight bat, I think. So I text back, 'Yes, still recovering!'

She says, 'I'm not surprised.'

I write, 'We should all get together again soon.'

Then, 'Say hi to Rankin and thanks for a lovely evening.'

There's no reply.

February 24

Today I'm preparing to pitch, which doesn't involve doing much. Clearing my head of half-thoughts, mainly. Spending time alone.

I've had bosses and colleagues in the past who spent forever doing prep for their meetings with commissioners, carefully considering responses to the questions and objections most likely to be raised. I think this is a waste of time, and fundamentally wrong-headed. You should be prepared to engage in a conversation. Your idea is unlikely to be perfect, and a bit of healthy discussion might well make it better. Defensiveness is very unattractive.

Worse, too much prep fills your head up with little speeches. An unforeseen question could (and often would) unbalance those colleagues entirely, and you'd see a moment of gawping panic on their faces when they didn't know what to say. There's nothing worse for killing off a commissioner's interest. It makes them feel like they've found a fatal flaw in your idea. The flaw might not be fatal at all. It might not even be a flaw. But it's unlikely you'll get another chance to prove it.

Better by far to under-prepare, go in fresh and relaxed and feeling sharp, and trust in the quickness of your wits. The game always goes to the fastest thinker. You're never impressed by politicians who parrot stuff in interviews, are you? You never remember their carefully prepped answers. The politicians you like are the ones who think on their feet, who respond to cuts with a bit of thrust. They're the ones who say stuff that stays with you. And they're the ones who get your vote.

Part of what I love about pitching is how in-the-moment it is. You offer up your idea, and then it's game on. It's a wonderful, addictive feeling.

Who knows what will happen next? Who knows how the commissioner will react and what they'll say? Who knows what you'll say back?

I very often don't. Indeed, I'm very often surprised at the words coming out of my mouth. Surprised sometimes by how clever and persuasive it sounds. Sometimes by how loosely it relates to the actual truth.

February 27

This broadcaster is very different to the one that gave me money to make the taster with Rankin. It's far more image-conscious and much less grown-up. It thinks of itself as edgy and innovative. A pioneering force in TV.

This is mostly bullshit. The programmes it makes are pretty much the same as the ones you see on other channels. They're not edgy in the least. But the marketing around them is clever, and sort of half makes you believe that they might be.

The foyer feels like a bar, all wood and steel and sofas not meant for sitting on. It's full of nervous-looking execs from other companies. They don't think they're cool enough to be here. They feel old and out of touch. They fumble and fiddle with their phones, and wish they were somewhere else. They have about them a general air of defeat and inadequacy, and they'll take that with them into their meetings.

I have a ritual when I come here. I go straight up to the girl on the desk and hose her down with all the charm I can muster, like I'm trying to get her into bed. Like that's the only reason I came here. If there's a queue behind me I'll make them wait. It's all about getting your fuck yous in first. I can feel them thinking Fuck you, you arrogant prick, for making me wait. Fucked you first, sunshine, by not being the least bit bothered.

Then I'll take my pass and find somewhere to sit. Somewhere nice and visible. Legs open, chin up, arms spread nice and wide. Doing nothing at all except having a good look around. A look around intended to say Who the fuck are you lot? And what are you doing in *my* reception area, with your grubby little pitches?

I belong here, is what I'm saying. And I fully expect to leave here today with commissions in my pocket.

If everyone else is just a tiny bit intimidated, their confidence eroded just a fraction more, then that's a good result. Marginal gains matter. I'll carry some of this swagger with me into my meeting, just as they'll carry over their discomfort and glumness. I'll need to. It's fuck or be fucked down here. It's twice as bad when you get upstairs.

This is because, despite commissioning hours and hours of bog-standard programming, the commissioners here genuinely believe they're smarter and sharper than anyone else in the industry. Unless they're just putting it on, like me.

They're all young, which is part of it, and they have no respect for all the experience and knowledge of older execs. I'm just about young enough to be exempt from this generalized contempt. A guy I used to work for, a few years older than me, went to embarrassing lengths to dress and look younger, just to win business from this one particular broadcaster. He started wearing T-shirts, skinny jeans and vintage mirrored shades. I quit one day after giving him an update on various projects and seeing myself reflected back in the lenses, looking like I really wanted his approval. Look at yourself, I thought. Desperate for praise from a man in mirrored shades. But I understand what made him behave that way. There's lots to despise about this place, but its programming budget is significant. If you're serious about making television, it's not a channel you can ignore.

The woman I'm pitching to is easily the worst person who works here. Everything about her is an affectation, from her East End accent to the chunky specs she doesn't need to wear. Recently she dyed her hair the same colour as the flashing lights on an ambulance. I'm pretending I haven't noticed. She is effective, though. Her bosses clearly rate her; she's good at getting ideas across the line, from discussion into commission.

It's clear that the dislike is mutual. But however well-regarded she is at the channel, she still needs a regular supply of good ideas.

She doesn't like any of my first three thoughts, and the conversations I start keep stalling. I'm wondering about calling the meeting to a premature close. Sometimes people are just not in a buying mood. And the ideas I've already told her about are my best ones. They're only going to get vaguer and more ordinary if we continue.

She says my idea about social mobility and social change is far too 'intellectual'.

'Intellectual's not the word I'd use, for me or my ideas.'

She says, 'I can think of others.'

I think one reason she doesn't like me is that she knows that I know that she's fake. All the aitches, not so much dropped as strewn. Not for the first time, I wonder about finding a charming and handsome young man to be Christian to my Cyrano. He would open doors. But they'd close again as soon as he failed to respond in kind to a clever question. How you respond under pressure is what it's all about.

Then the commissioner throws me a bone. Sometimes they'll do that if a meeting's going badly. She says that her boss thinks that the channel might have commissioned and broadcast too many programmes about poor people recently. Maybe it's time to redress the balance?

She only ever refers to her boss by his first name, which is Teddy. I've never met him, but everyone at the channel is terrified of him, because of his volcanic temper. Whenever his name gets mentioned I picture a toddler writing pissy emails whilst being fed mashed banana on a tiny plastic spoon.

I say Ah, posh people. I might be able to help you there. Because I've got a great project on the go about a very posh family indeed.

We've seen lots of entertaining programmes about chaotic families on council estates. And lots of dull and respectful shows about English country houses. Well, this is a programme about a family so posh it's kind of common, living council-house lives in a sprawling stately home.

So it's a show that blurs genres, in a way. It's fresh and surprising, and modern.

She leans forward, suddenly engaged, and removes her pointless spectacles. This is something that might make her look good in front of her boss, which has become the entire point and purpose of her life.

'Do you have the access?' she says.

'Yes. Yes, I do.'

Let me tell you all about it.

Back in the foyer there's a message on my phone, from Rankin. He would like us to get together. It doesn't sound like an invitation.

CHAPTER THREE: MARCH

March 5

Certainty is vitally important in pitching. Pitching is selling, and you'd never buy something that costs £600,000 from someone who seemed shifty or evasive or ill-informed, would you? 'I don't know' or 'Let me get back to you' are fatal things to say when you're closing in on a sale. Which means that you sometimes tell lies.

When you do, you're taking a gamble, which is exciting. You're gambling on your ability to make the lie come true before anyone notices.

So here I am, on a shoot in the heart of the Cornish countryside; £150,000 on offer to make a pilot from the woman with the fake specs, and no access whatsoever to make it with.

I've never picked up a shotgun before, and don't much like the idea of killing things for fun. But I've paid £800 to spend the weekend here, with a mixture of city boys and ex-army types. The shoot is being hosted by Lord Delamain, the head of the super-posh family I pitched to the commissioner. It takes place on their land, and the price of admission includes two nights in a room in their enormous house.

My fellow shooters and I are lined up on the fringes of a beautiful and ancient piece of woodland. There's mist in the valley below us. Being here feels like time travel.

But it's hard to enjoy the moment. I don't know the meaning of the words that people are using – walking-up and flushing and beating and the rest of it – so I don't understand what's happening. I'm stiff and bored of standing around. Everyone is slightly pissed, nipping at hip flasks to keep out the cold and damp. This is good, because it means they're paying less attention than they otherwise might to the fact that I obviously don't belong here.

A gun dog is looking up at me, sadly. In four hours I haven't given him a single thing to do. But soon it will be lunchtime, and we'll go back to the house. With luck, the family will be awake and out of bed.

Their house is really a castle with wings and outbuildings added in the reigns of Elizabeth I and George III. It's full of stern portraits and busts, and books unopened for hundreds of years, if they were ever opened at all. A previous generation lived in luxury here. The rooms are covered in velvet wallpaper, and the furniture is very fine. But now the wallpaper is peeling and the stuffing is coming out of the sofas and chairs. Holes are worn in the carpets and the wind whistles in through cracks in the windows. There's no central heating, and last night I shivered in my sleep.

In the distance I can see smoke rising from the house's Tudor chimneys. Fires are being made in the grates.

The family are truly extraordinary characters. They're like the aristocracy used to be when everyone agreed that they were just better than the rest of us, and therefore entitled to their charmed and privileged lives. These days even the royal family comport themselves with dignity and restraint. They use words like 'duty' and 'service', and always seem to be saying sorry. The Delamains are like Komodo dragons, stomping about on a lost island, sensationally rediscovered. They are creatures from the land that time forgot, sheltered from change by the walls of their vast estate.

This makes them funny and refreshing. Our lives are bound up with rules and requirements. Don't drive so fast. Don't drink so much. Stop smoking and mind your language. About these and similar matters, they couldn't give less of a fuck.

All I need is 15 minutes with the head of the family, to persuade him that making a series is a good idea.

When you gamble on telling a lie to a commissioner, what you're gambling with is your credibility. Lose and you're out of the game, maybe for good if the lie is big enough. So you pick your moments.

I put down a big pile of chips on getting this family on board, partly because the commissioner started talking straight away about a big gap in the schedules that she'd like to be able to fill. A commission to fill that gap might be worth a million or more. But mainly I made my gamble because I'm certain the family will be great TV.

March 6

Personally, I like my television programmes to be as pure as possible. Which is to say, simple and unfussy. A documentary that just observes its subjects, say, and follows wherever the story leads. Or a travelogue that's a journey and nothing more, a happy hour somewhere nice and warm in the company of someone interesting.

In a world of non-stop media bombardment, the purer a TV programme feels, the more it comes across as a premium product. Something that expects and deserves and respects your attention. That's the kind of feeling I want when I sit down to watch TV. Like it's going to be time well spent.

But purity can also make a programme seem old-fashioned. Commissioners are always looking for ideas that appear fresh and modern, which is usually a matter of reinventing existing kinds of television. Observational documentaries, for example, which are time-consuming and expensive to make with very uncertain outcomes, were adapted into factual formats like *Wife Swap* and *Undercover Boss*. In this sort of TV, a bold conceit puts contributors under pressure and reliably produces moments of drama, conflict and redemption. Everything happens within a specific time frame – maybe just a couple of weeks – which reduces risk, slashes costs and makes the whole thing easier to manage. Strong formats produce good shows no matter who is making them. And best of all, for broadcasters and production companies, the format is endlessly repeatable, so viewers know exactly what they're getting; if they like it, they'll keep coming back for more.

This kind of TV was wildly popular for a while, and then started to seem tired too. Factual formats morphed into immersive social experiments, which in turn morphed into documentary-game-shows, scripted 'reality' shows and other genre hybrids.

Now commissioners are again asking, what's next for factual television? What's the next turn of the wheel?

Well, I've always loved situation comedies. I grew up in their golden age, when 20 million people watched them. My big thought for the posh family is to turn their lives into a documentary sitcom.

The reason I think this will work well is that sitcoms depend on repetition – the same characters each week, with the same dynamic between them, stuck in the same place, struggling with the same frustrations. The characters want to leave or change, but they can't.

Generally, the thrust of a documentary series is the opposite to this. The questions you ask of a potential subject are, what is at stake? What will the characters learn as the series unfolds? What moments of realization will we witness?

But nothing is at stake for the family of toffs. Their house and their land have been theirs for 1000 years. The eldest boy will inherit everything, find a wife and produce an heir and a couple of spares, just as his father did, and his father's father stretching back for 50 generations. The course of their lives was set the moment they were born, all of them tied forever to this crumbling house and this rolling patch of land.

I'm pleased with this idea. It's simple and makes good sense.

I came across one of the younger members of the family a couple of years ago, developing a film about a public school, which ultimately came to nothing. We got on well, and stayed in touch. I called him to tell him about my new idea, and he said sure, talk to mum and dad.

That's where I'd got up to before I went to pitch. I wouldn't have pitched it had my meeting at the channel gone better. And if there hadn't been an opportunity to grasp.

I thought the combination of my relationship with the kid and the money that would come their way would swing it, so although the lie was total, I was reasonably confident of getting the access needed.

But when I put it to the boy's mother, she absolutely hated it.

This is partly because of the language I used. I mentioned the word 'sitcom', because I was excited by my big idea and feeling impressed with myself. This was a stupid mistake.

I said, 'I think there's a great opportunity here.'

'I don't care what you think', she said. 'About this or anything else.'

I'm sure I can persuade Lord Delamain, but I need his full attention.

We're sitting at a colossal oak table in the great hall of the house. I'm fighting off a powerful urge to close my eyes and go to sleep. There's a huge blaze going in a fireplace four men could stand up in, and there's a dopey dog asleep on my feet, which are warm for the first time in a day and a half. We've dined on roast pheasant and drunk a large amount of red wine from heavy silver goblets.

Lord Delamain is in a chair that looks like a throne with a knot of grinning sycophants tightly packed around him, like a scene from a tapestry. I haven't been able to get near him.

'I would like if I may to tell you a story', he says, loudly. His listeners cheer, and the knot grows tighter.

I'm at the other end of the table, talking to a very tall, rosy-cheeked chap called Rupert or Toby or something like that. He's as simple and affable as one of the gun dogs, especially now he's tipsy. He's telling me that there's a national shortage of gamekeepers. Dozens of apprenticeships and no applications.

I wonder if there's a format in that? Maybe take young men from inner cities who've been involved in gun crime, and give them a trial on a big estate? Show them a different way of life, healthy and outdoorsy. Teach them patience and respect for guns and other people.

Lord Delamain is happily holding court, telling stories and roaring, oblivious of my presence.

But then his eyes flick my way, clear and focused.

I give him a nod, but he's already looked away.

March 7

We've been up since dawn for a final few hours of shooting, and now we're in the family's kitchen, breakfasting on sausages with coffee and beer. I'm sitting next to Lord Delamain, and we're getting on famously.

We're talking about time, which is always on my mind, and it turns out is always on his. Ever since I was a boy, I've felt that time is short and getting shorter. That the time to act is now, with so very much to act upon. Lord Delamain's perspective is exactly the opposite. He thinks not in terms of hours and days but decades. Aeons even. He's planting woodland now that won't mature for 100 years. But he feels the pressure of time just as much as I do.

'My advice is to do one thing extremely well', he says. 'There's no time for anything else.'

I like him. He's much more interesting than he seems at first. He spends a lot of time alone, walking and thinking. Maybe he's lonely, which would be helpful. Certainly he seems like he wants to be understood.

Now I'm wondering how to bring up the subject of making a TV series. It's a delicate one. I think maybe best to make it appear as though the idea has just come to me? Something about making a record of his time in charge of the estate?

I'm just about to make my move when his wife swoops in, superbly.

'Is there a Truman Locke here?' she says. 'The guestbook says that he's part of the shoot?'

She is Lord Delamain's third consort, and very much younger than he is. Her face is pale and imperious, like a portrait come to life. But faintly exotic, also. Faintly other.

I get up and smile and offer my hand. She's tall. As tall as me.

'Didn't I speak to you on the phone?' she says.

'And didn't I tell you to fuck off?'

Ffack orfff, in fact, as you imagine the Queen might say it. But venomously, like a queen from different age, when queens were often deadly.

'Kindly go away', she says, 'and *never* come here again'.

March 10

It's 11.30 am on a Tuesday, and already most of my team are very drunk indeed.

A piece of research has suggested that drinking alcohol is good for creativity. It bears out the practice of some ad agencies in Korea and the States, which have an all-day free bar in their offices. Drinking is not frowned upon but encouraged. Which gave me an idea for a programme.

We started off first thing with Irish coffees, and a rule that every time anyone wanted to confer with anyone else about an idea or progress with a project, they had to fill up two tumblers with ice, pour out two large measures of Stoli, and hand one glass to the person they want to talk to.

For an hour or so, it seemed to work, in the sense that people were thinking and talking about things in a way they wouldn't usually. It felt like the glory days of Fleet Street, glamorous and transgressive. People smoking cigarettes at their desks, being flirty and funny. Flat-out busy, doing nothing much, enjoying being creative.

Then we moved on to Martinis and bourbon cocktails, and things started to go downhill.

Now they're just eating crisps and talking about each other's sex lives.

My idea is to apply the principle that booze is good for business to ordinary British companies. Maybe companies that are struggling, and have tried everything else. Instead of tea and coffee, they drink wine and G&Ts. We put beer in the water fountain, and jugs of margaritas on the table in meetings. Maybe long-buried tensions would come to the fore, where they could be talked about and dealt with. Maybe people would tell the truth to their bosses. Maybe new solutions to old problems would emerge.

It would sort of be about the stuffy, conformist culture that most companies have adopted these days, in which no one really says what they mean. It would also, you would hope, be cringe-worthy, eventful and funny.

The Einstein film was turned down today, quickly and concisely, by email. Interesting, the email said, but 'not in line with current commissioning needs'.

Fuck it. I pour out a line of shots and propose a toast to good ideas, whatever may or may not become of them.

I get up to go for a pee, surprised at how unsteady I feel on my way to the loo. When I come back, Charlie is standing in the doorway to our section of the office, aghast.

My researcher offers him a freshly mixed Martini.

He turns and closes the door behind him.

March 11

The office is quiet today. Three members of my team haven't made it in.

The receptionist puts a call through to my desk.

'I'm gonna get right to it', the voice says, American, speaking quickly. 'We want to commission your show but we can't.'

I pitched the storage idea rather well, I thought – a montage of auctions to set up the premise, made from footage supplied by Daisy and Joe themselves. Then a live link-up with the couple as they entered a unit they'd successfully bid on, to discover what it was they had bought. For the executives, it was like being out on location, not just seeing the idea in action but experiencing it for themselves.

Daisy and Joe were delighted to find a box of military medals amongst the piles of junk. Joe estimated they might be worth upwards of ten thousand dollars, a profit of nine and a half. Around the shiny conference table high up on Fifth Avenue, there was lots of smiling and nodding.

I say, 'I don't understand: what's the problem?' A little too loudly, so that people in the office start looking my way. Charlie is amongst them.

We checked the characters out. Researched the whole thing from top to bottom. It's a rock-solid idea. Legally sound and ready to go.

The guy says he learned yesterday that another network is onto the scene as well, and the other network learned about us. We called and called you, he says, but you never answered your phone.

'We wanted to announce the series', he says, 'to kill off the other network's idea. A 20-part commission. But there were questions we needed to ask you. A few simple facts for the press release.'

Then the other network played the same trick themselves. Now any commission in that field would look like an imitation: late to the party and second best.

He sends me a link while he's talking. The idea is exactly the same as ours, commissioned not as 20 but 40 hours.

'Thanks anyway', the guy says, half rueful, half pissed off. 'I hope we'll get to work together one day.'

I send the link to Charlie with a note that says simply, limply, 'I'm sorry'. I see him read it and wince. We were banking on this, and Godín. Now both are dead in the water. My ears are ringing, like after a car crash.

Be ready when the moment arrives, Celestine said that night on the plane. One month later, it already feels like the moment has gone. Seized by others, not by me.

March 13

Big occasions always make for good TV. Weddings, of course. The birth of a baby. Buying a house and moving in. You're guaranteed emotion, and there's almost always drama. And most importantly, everyone can relate to what's going on.

Today I'm out looking for an engagement ring, with Mills.

Buying a ring is a big deal, not just because rings cost a lot, but also because it marks a point of no return. Hand over £2000 and you're committed. You haven't asked her yet, and she hasn't given you her decision. But you've decided that you will, and you're confident that she'll say yes. You've thought it through. You've imagined yourself down on one knee. You've decided that you want to get married, and your life is never going to be the same again.

I like it that all this complex emotional stuff is temporarily focused on a tiny thing that you have to choose, from a huge range of very similar items. It means a lot, so you have to choose very carefully.

Is there a fact ent show about men choosing rings? They come into a shop that we've rigged up with cameras. I read that most men make three visits to the same shop before they buy a ring, so we'd have an opportunity to get to know them quite well. And choosing a ring is about finding one that suits your girlfriend and her personality, and sort of fits your relationship. A good salesperson will strike up a conversation that draws out all sorts of personal information about the guy and the girl. Watching this unfold, you'd get a sense of what their relationship is like, and whether they're a good match.

If we follow three men choosing rings in the same shop, we'd be able to cut between their stories. And you'd stay watching, because at the end you'd see all three of them propose, and you'd finally meet the women the men had been describing and discussing. You'd be rooting for them, and 90% of marriage proposals are accepted, so there'd almost always be a happy ending.

Mills never usually says she likes my ideas. She says that she likes this one.

We're in an old-school jeweller's shop, in the ancient jewellery quarter of a city 60 miles from London. The area is a magnet for people choosing engagement rings; there are 100 shops to choose from, and prices are keen. We chose this particular shop because it's low-lit, with an intimate, conspiratorial sort of feel, and it's quite busy for a Tuesday morning. There are two young men on opposite sides of the shop, each bent over a case of rings, examining them closely. One of them is with a mate, who is laughing. The other is with an older lady who is probably his mum. She looks like she's having the time of her life.

Mills is looking at a simple, flower-shaped diamond-cluster ring in an antique display case, moving her head to and fro slightly to make it catch the light.

'They *are* beautiful', she says, mostly to herself, like she's trying to persuade herself that it's okay to think so.

The sales assistant says that most young men come to choose a ring with someone to help them. Sometimes a friend. Sometimes their dad or uncle. Or even their granny, or a colleague from work.

This is good for the show we're researching. More relationships mean more variety and more texture, and more of a reason to come back week after week.

The sales assistant looks from me to Mills and back again, trying to read the relationship. She does it badly, and asks if we're brother and sister.

Mills says no, we're doing research. The sales assistant looks confused and wary. Whatever we're researching, it's clear she wants no part of it.

In the next shop, we agree to just go along with whatever assumptions the sales people make.

The assistant in shop two tells us that buying a ring is a rite of passage. It's a transaction that turns a boy into a man. That's a good line. I make a mental note.

But she also says that it's not just young men who come shopping for rings. She tells us about romances that have blossomed in old-age care-homes, women choosing rings for themselves to marry their partners in prison, and heartbreaking deathbed proposals.

Shop three is newer and brighter than other shops in the area. The woman behind the counter has a spectacular smile.

We look at a few rings. The woman is very likeable and easy to talk to. She tells us that she set up the business with her fiancé last year. Both of them are from old jeweller families. They're planning to get married in the autumn.

Mills asks to see her ring, and says something so heartfelt and lovely that she makes the woman cry. They hug each other, friends already.

It's a side of Mills I've not seen before. Girlish and unguarded.

All of the staff in the shop are young and lively, except for a glamorous older lady who, the woman explains, is her mum. Sometimes nervous customers like to feel that they're in the hands of someone more experienced.

Maybe this is where we should set the series? I like it here. I feel at home.

We meet the woman's fiancé who's been out to get coffee. He's handsome and charming and cheeky.

The staff tease and flirt with each other. I think viewers would like it here too. They'd enjoy spending time in the company of these people, and I think it would work as co-viewing. For men, it's a friendly and funny guide to a life-changing choice. For women, it's a privileged peek at a process they'd never normally get to witness.

We'd probably want to format it lightly, to give it shape and clarity. But I think the feel should be observational. We could cast grooms-to-be into the shop, but I'd rather not. Authenticity tends to be a key ingredient of successful shows in factual entertainment. Best to make it as honest and real as possible.

The woman says that over 200,000 people in Britain get engaged every year. In this shop alone they sell ten or twelve rings every week. So we could produce the show in volume. As a series, it could run and run.

The woman tells us some stories. About a couple who came shopping for their ring together, and the girl manoeuvred the guy into spending three times what he wanted to. About a guy who spent £80,000 on a ring and had it thrown back in his face on the day of the proposal, because the diamond wasn't big enough. About a guy who came in to buy a ring with his girlfriend's best friend, and it was painfully obvious that she was the one he was really in love with.

I'm feeling excited. I can tell that Mills is too. This could be great. An uplifting, celebratory snapshot of love and relationships in modern-day Britain.

The woman says that figuring out people's relationships is her favourite part of the job. She's clearly much better at it than the woman in the first shop we went to. She's a sort of love detective, she says. She can always tell when it's going to work out.

'And can I just say that you two make a very lovely couple.'

March 14

People think it's strange that I don't have a girlfriend, or a partner or a wife.

I did have one once. Quite a long time ago now. We were together for just short of two years.

Actually, not together as such. She was with someone else throughout. But we were good together. I made her feel known. She made me feel like all things were possible. But also like I had nothing at all to prove. I loved her ferociously.

I think at the beginning she wanted to somehow mend me. And at the end came to see that this wasn't going to happen. It must have felt like too much drama. Too much stress and strain. Too much sneaking about.

It would have hurt too much to break up the night she said that we would have to, so we gave ourselves a month to say goodbye. We had a few last adventures. Bits of stolen time here and there, and a weekend away where no one knew us, holding each other's hands in public, in a fragile little bubble. I spent a long time looking at her beautiful face. I fretted that one day I'd forget it.

On our very last night, I fought hard not to fall asleep. Then, just before I finally did, I found myself wishing never to wake up. That I'd spend forever in that moment, arms wrapped around her, face buried in the warm, safe place where her neck and shoulder meet, feeling like a little boy.

The next day we avoided words like goodbye. She said 'try to be good' and kissed me on my head. I said 'see you later' or something like that. But I never did. I haven't seen her since.

March 15

Mills didn't react at all to what the woman in the ring shop said. Not even a flicker. Neither did I. It's not the first time either of us has heard it. People are always assuming that men and women working together in TV are actually an item. There's a closeness that comes with making programmes that you don't much get elsewhere. You're creating something new together, often against all odds. It's intimate and all-consuming, in the same way that sex is.

This morning we went back to the shop and came clean. The woman was fine about it, and excited to be talking to people from the telly.

Now we're shooting some footage to show to potential commissioners, Mills charming the customers, me operating the camera. Both relaxed and efficient. We've done this together many times before.

There are moments of spontaneous joy and loveliness. A young man comes back to the shop with his girlfriend, now fiancé. 'She said yes!' he says, and there's hugging and tears all round. They keep bottles of fizz in the back for times like these. It becomes a celebration.

There's an energetic, optimistic vibe about the place, which is coming through on camera. It makes me feel calm and happy.

March 20

Today is day two of a major documentary festival.

The festival takes place across five days and 15 venues. 10,000 people attend, from a dozen different countries. The first few times you go it feels chaotic and confusing, but it's not. There are three different sorts of things happening here, all at the same time.

The first sort of thing is what you'd expect from a film festival – documentary films from all over the world being shown and discussed. Some of them will be premiering here. A handful will go on to play in cinemas. Most of them will be very bad and boring, way too long and appallingly indulgent. The only airing they'll get will be on the festival circuit. No one in their right mind would ever put them on TV.

Many of these films will have been self-funded and shot over many years. People aspiring to make their own documentaries come to watch films in large numbers, mainly for the Q&A sessions that follow, in the hope of picking up tips. No one in these Q&A sessions ever talks about the one thing that enabled them to make their film, which is not tenacity or daring or flair but a generous parent or trust fund.

The second sort of thing that happens is a mirror image of this largely amateur gathering – a more formal and organized coming-together of industry professionals to talk about new trends and developments. There are briefings by commissioning editors and upcoming shows are revealed.

Lots of young people making their way in TV come to the festival to attend these sessions. If you're used to getting your information second- or third-hand, from the head of development or a series producer at the company you work at, it feels like a revelation. You get a sense of both how big and how small the television industry actually is, and you can start to see where you might fit in.

The third sort of thing that happens is a function of the second. TV executives like myself are encouraged by the companies they work for to attend the festival, to make sure they're up to date with industry news and gossip. Your pass is paid for, and your travel to the festival, and your accommodation. It's like a mini-holiday, with all expenses paid, so pretty much everyone comes. And there's only one decent hotel, which pretty much everyone stays in, including all the commissioning editors. What this means is that in every corner of the hotel, at all hours of the day and night, there's a conspiratorial conversation taking place, or a piece of high-level schmoozing.

This is how big series get commissioned. They'll have been well-developed and well-pitched, but broadcasters need to feel a lot of confidence to spend, say, £2m on a single idea, and that confidence comes from relationships.

You need to get lots of people on board with your idea, because the commissioner you pitched to doesn't commission programmes in isolation. He or she is part of a team, and once a week they sit around a table and talk about the best new ideas they've received. This is a vulnerable time for ideas, even really good ones, and even ones that an individual commissioner loves, because his or her colleagues might hate it, which would probably kill it off for good.

There are all sorts of reasons why a commissioner's colleagues might hate an idea, only some of which are to do with the idea itself. They might hate the commissioner rather than the idea. They might think that he or she has been doing too well recently, and needs to be brought back down to earth. They might have their own similar idea, which they'd rather see commissioned instead.

A smart producer leaves nothing to chance when the stakes are high, which means canvassing support from as many of the people who will be sitting around the table as possible. That way, when the commissioner you pitched to starts talking about your idea, there's a general murmuring of approval. They already know about the idea, because you've taken the trouble to explain it to them, and encouraged them to see its merits.

That's basically what all the producers are doing in dark corners of the hotel bar – buttering up commissioners, building relationships, smoothing the progress of their big idea. And that's basically why I'm sitting in a booth, listening to a big man with a small voice talk about his many insecurities.

'You can't turn the clock back', he says, of a piss-poor show he commissioned that no one watched.

I tell him, 'Of course you can.'

I've bought him lots of drinks to get him relaxed. Now he's certainly that. I need to stop buying drinks soon, or else he won't remember anything we've been talking about.

He's worried that people in the industry don't have enough respect for him. And that people would rather pitch their ideas to one of his colleagues. This assessment of his situation is entirely correct.

It's good that he feels friendless. It gives me something to work with. I'm pretending to be his friend so that he'll make enthusiastic noises when his much cleverer and more popular colleague pitches my idea.

Now his eyes are starting to look unfocussed. I tell him that his colleague will be pitching my idea next week, and tell him all about it – the jeweller's shop and the rings and the men and their mums.

But I tell him that's not my biggest idea. I tell him I'm saving that one for you. And then I pitch him something vague and ambitious, mostly making it up as we go. Something about a new take on survival, that's also about immigration – ten people in a boat, adrift on the sea, like the poor, desperate souls in the news, risking everything for a better life on the other side of the ocean. What's that feel like? How would you cope from day to day? How do people survive it?

Very simple, very pure. Like a movie.

'That could work', he says. 'Or maybe the ship that's adrift is a ferry. More relatable that way. Or a cruise ship, even. Everybody loves cruising.'

Ferries and cruise ships make the idea much worse, in my opinion. They turn it from a series about something into one about nothing, a reality show, adrift in every sense. No matter. So long as it makes him want it. I tell him, 'Great thought', and write it down in my notebook.

Once my big ring idea is up and running (small pause and a glance so he catches my drift), we should get together to talk about that, my *really* big idea.

He nods sadly and smiles. He'll support my ring idea in exchange for something – anything – of his own to pitch upwards, even a half-baked idea like the one I just sold him. Commissioners are nothing without ideas to commission, and the best producers have stopped sending theirs to him.

He says he's excited to pitch the boat idea to his boss. But he won't be at the channel long enough for that to happen. Everyone knows it. Everyone, it seems, but him. He's a dead man walking, which is why I picked a booth at the back of the room, where no one can see us. He's just not cut out for commissioning. He's far too honest, his vulnerabilities too clear, a dolphin in a shark tank.

March 21

This morning an assistant producer on my team is taking part in one of the festival's pitching contests, aimed at emerging talent.

I strongly advised him not to.

But he's young and ambitious and doesn't give a fuck what I think, even though he's always asking me. He's clever and he has charisma. And he's very good with ideas. I'm sure he'll be a success in TV. But I'm equally sure that today will not be part of that story.

It looks like a great opportunity. You're invited to pitch your idea to a panel of industry experts in front of a large audience. They ask you questions about your idea and about yourself. And at the end of it, someone is declared the winner and given a budget to make their first full-length film, for one of the main broadcasters.

That sounds good, right? But you have to ask yourself why it needs to unfold as a spectacle, in a packed auditorium. The channel wants people to see how seriously it takes its responsibility to develop the next generation of programme-makers. It so badly wants you to see this that it doesn't care in the least how painful and damaging the process might actually be for the people taking part in it.

The panel consists of some of the most vain and egotistical people in all of television. The person organizing the event would have been pleased to get them on board; it makes him look well-connected, which is his sole motivation for taking it on. The panellists have agreed to take part because it's important to them to maintain a certain profile in the industry. This is a thousand times more important to them than supporting and encouraging new film-makers.

The audience is tired and hungover, because it was up till very late having fun on expenses. At another festival venue this morning, there'll be a formal debate about how the BBC should be funded, which will be both noisy and dull. This event, on the other hand, promises entertainment. The kind you should be ashamed of enjoying.

And there's an extra incentive: should any of the candidates turn out to be impressive, you can approach them afterwards and hire them. It's hard to find good young people. The person who wins will be very much in demand, not least because they'll come complete with a free commission.

The first two people give a reasonable account of themselves, but the ideas they pitch are indifferent. They won't win.

Then it's my AP's turn.

'We all find ourselves living lives we never expected', he says, by way of introduction. 'Doing things we never expected.'

His idea is a good one. It's about a wig shop he's found, the last one in the country, and the men who go there. Which makes it about male vanity and sex and relationships. He pitches it clearly and concisely, and he's made a short taster to bring it to life. It's funny and the characters are good. He's doing well.

But then one member of the panel starts picking on him, I think because he's coming across as so calm and confident. There's a crackle of excitement in the room. My AP wasn't expecting this. He doesn't know what to say.

The guy asks him if all the people in the shop were really looking for wigs. And my AP says yes, indeed they were. Emphatic words, but he says them with the tiniest hint of doubt.

The guy says really, all of them? And my AP says yes, he cast them from the shop's own register of customers.

The guy says, 'What about the one in his twenties?'

The one in his twenties is the stand-out character. He's upset about losing his hair, and speaks about it directly from the heart. He's laughable but also totally genuine. As a viewer, you can't help rooting for him. You really want to know what happens to him next.

My AP hesitates, and the guy asks him again, 'What about the one in his twenties?'

My AP looks my way, then admits he found the one in his twenties somewhere else, and bussed him into the shop.

'Ah', says the guy on the panel, theatrically.

Now I remember the young man on the tape. He's from another development we did, about people with autism learning to drive.

Now there's blood in the water. People in the audience have stopped fiddling with their phones. All eyes are on my AP, shifting his weight awkwardly from one foot to the other.

The guy on the panel says that this undermines everything. 'How can we trust you?' he says. 'If your characters aren't who and what you say they are, how can we believe anything else in your film? If the film is fundamentally untrue, how can anyone learn from it?'

There are answers to all of these questions. All documentaries are 'produced', to some extent. Especially ones that set out to entertain you. The important thing is that the man in his twenties is genuine in how he feels and honest in what he says. So long as that's the case, any truths the film might reveal will be authentic and worthwhile.

But my AP doesn't say any of this. Of course he doesn't. He's young. Young and humiliated, in front of a fucking audience.

He looks at the guy on the panel, and then down to the floor, shaking his head, desperately trying to summon a thought.

Game over.

The chair of the panel intervenes to say thank you and introduces the next contestant.

March 22

Day four of the festival.

Last night was the last of the big festival parties. The booze was free, so everyone got drunk.

I saw lots of people I used to work with. People I liked (and still do like) a lot but gradually fell out of touch with. TV makes so many demands on your time. It's hard to maintain friendships.

I saw the editor I made my best film with, and the cameraman who taught me to shoot, and someone who used to be my researcher. She's a commissioner now, which made me feel very old.

Then I saw a guy who runs a company I used to work at. I didn't feel so old after that, because he looked truly ancient. Not just aged, but tired and worried and out of place.

When I first met him, he talked about his plans for the company. It was a boutique business, known for making films of high quality in extremely small numbers. He wanted to build on that, he said. Diversify and grow the business. He said he wanted to assemble a new young team, and was excited to see what that team would achieve and where it would lead the company.

None of this was a lie, as such. I think he genuinely wanted to do those things. It's just that he found that he couldn't. He was too old and stubborn to change.

In the years since I left that company, TV has changed a lot. Smaller companies have come together to form much larger ones. Large companies have come together to form media leviathans, with hundreds of employees in dozens of different countries, bigger sometimes than the broadcasters they supply. A company that once looked charmingly old-fashioned now looks like a relic from a different age.

We had a drink and wished each other well. I'd be surprised if I see him here again.

I saw a glamorous producer I used to work with and have always been very attracted to, and a famous director who was kind to me at the start of my career.

And then, at the end of the night, swaying slightly and full of piss and white wine, I saw the guy from yesterday's panel, heading towards the loos.

I followed him in.

I said to him, 'You were on the panel?' He grunted in the way that people do when they want to shut a conversation down.

I said, 'The wig shop was the best idea by far.' He grunted again. And then he said, 'That cocky little prick needed taking down a peg or two.'

He was standing at a urinal when he said this. I shoved him into it, hard, and kept him there with my shoulder. He felt heavy but soft and boneless. Then I pulled back his head by his hair. He was jabbering now, his fat cheeks quivering. His eyes wide open, like a cow at a slaughterhouse.

'Maybe you need taking down a peg or two?' I said. 'But I don't need an audience to help me. In fact I'd rather no audience at all.'

Then I put my face very close to his. 'If I ever see you treat anyone that way again – or hear that you have, or even think you might have – I'll fuck you up so bad you wouldn't recognize your own fucking face.'

Then I went back to the bar and left him there, cock hanging limply, trousers soaked in piss.

This morning rather more delicacy and tact are in order.

I'm at the hotel bar again, drinking strong coffee and trying to ignore another message from Rankin. There's no indication of what he wants. No clue at all in the tone. I've got my hands full today. I'll call him later this week.

The woman I'm meeting is Jools, a colleague of the guy from the booth, the opposite of him in every way. She's confident, attractive, sharp and well-liked. Her career is on the up and up. And she's exactly the right age to really understand what the ring idea is about. She's been with her boyfriend for four or five years now. Maybe he'll propose soon. I bet she thinks he might.

She loves the idea. Doesn't just say so; it's clear she really does. She says she'll pitch it as soon as possible. I know she'll do it well.

March 24

Relationships are important in TV. It's important to get along with the people around you.

I pulled out of a film I'd agreed to make once, because I felt the company hadn't been honest about the situation I'd be walking into. The exec was apoplectic. He said he'd make sure I'd never work again. I said get fucked. He said you'd better hope we don't run into each other. I said I hope we do. 'In fact how about I come round your office right now?' He said, 'Are you threatening me?' I said, 'Yes. To be accurate, threatening you back. But unlike you, I mean it. Unlike you, I would and I could. And now you've got me wanting to.'

I had a wonderful sense during that conversation of suddenly being let off the leash. Of having stepped from a world that I've had to learn the ways of – a world in which you rarely say exactly what you mean – into a world I know well, the world I grew up in, where things were very clear and tangible. There was no 'passive' aggression when I was a boy, wrapped up and disguised. Aggression was unmistakeable. A challenge you have to respond to. It usually came with the promise of pain, and you learned very quickly to respond in kind.

I know how to do this, I thought. I grew up doing this. Posturing, intimidation and fighting. This is second nature. I know how this goes down. And for 30 seconds it felt good. Better than good. It felt great.

Then I hung up, and had an immediate crushing sense of having done something ruinous. Something stupid and very bad. You'll never recover from this, I thought.

But there was nothing to recover from.

The commissioning editor on the film, who I'd worked for a lot, called me ten minutes later. Here it comes, I thought. He said 'Did you invite a leading industry figure out for a fight, like some oik in a pub?' I said, 'Yes, I did.' He said, 'You don't want to make the film?' I said, 'No, I don't.' He told me this will mean a huge amount of disruption and annoyance. I said nothing. He said, 'When I've sorted this shit out, I'll take you for a drink and we'll talk about what you want to do instead. So long as you promise not to punch me.'

There's a lot of anger in TV, because there's a lot of rejection and a lot of frustration. And anger gets things done. It cuts through all the bullshit and paralysis and makes things happen. It galvanizes and demands a response.

Don't be fooled by the grace and bonhomie you see on TV at the Baftas and the Emmys. The most successful people I know are marked by rage. They might suppress it most of the time. They might even devise a way to use it as a sort of toxic fuel, like depleted uranium. But stick around long enough and you'll witness some sort of meltdown.

One of my old bosses had a tantrum in the canteen of a major broadcaster. He hadn't got what he came for, so he swept everything on the table onto the floor, and sat back in his chair, fuming. Everyone looked, of course. But what they saw was passion, from a man with a vision. I was still young and felt shock. I think everyone else felt sympathy. Yes, their faces said, I know *exactly* how you feel.

Another boss smashed up a cutting room, when a film failed to match his expectations.

Anger is fine, because it's an entirely appropriate and reasonable response to working in TV.

But never, ever make enemies.

March 27

No one at work knows where I live. None of my friends either.

Which sounds odd, I know. I don't have anything to hide. I just like the idea that my home is a place that's separate to everything and everywhere else.

When I first came to London, having grown up in a small town, I loved the anonymity. The way you could just disappear in plain sight, and move around freely with no one to deal with or avoid. I felt able to think very freely. I felt entirely at ease.

I lived in a flat-share initially. There was far too little space, which made for pettiness and resentment. After work, I'd go out and wander around the city. I'd only go home when everyone else was asleep.

When I could finally afford a place of my own, I wanted the same feeling I got from my evenings out roaming. So I bought a flat in a very impersonal block, on a dark and unfriendly street, in a rough and unfashionable neighbourhood. Whenever someone wanted to know my address, I'd give them that of a rundown cafe two miles away. It serves cab drivers so it never really closes. I used to go there sometimes to read at night, waiting for my flatmates to stop bickering and go to bed. I got to know the owner and helped his daughter once when her landlord tried to double her rent. I called him up pretending to be making a show about Britain's worst landlords, citing all the ways in which the girl's flat failed to meet regulations. I told him I was giving him a right to reply. I told him that, in his shoes, I'd get myself a lawyer. He dropped his demands the very next day. Now the cafe owner saves my mail, for collection once a month.

The day I got the keys to my flat and stepped inside, it felt like going off-grid. The vendor had stripped the place of everything, including light bulbs. It was a big space that seemed vast in such an empty state. It felt like being nowhere. Which as far as I'm concerned is a comfortable place to be.

There was no cooker or fridge. No shelves even, or blinds. Just bare floorboards and bare brick walls, and big, half-rotten windows that rattled in the wind. Coming from a fully furnished flat share, I had no furniture of my own, and no possessions beyond one big bag of clothes and another full of books. I bought a bed and a rail for the clothes, put the books in a pile and left it at that.

In the hallway were ghostly outlines of pictures that had hung there. I wondered about hanging pictures of my own, but decided in the end that the ghostly outlines were probably more interesting than anything I might have chosen myself.

I think some people would find it rather barren and sad. To me it feels full of potential. And why give up something as precious and exciting as that in exchange for things as dull as scatter cushions and pot plants?

There's a knock at the door. Safe to ignore it, because no one knows I'm here. That's the whole point of what I've been telling you.

Then someone shouts, 'I know you're there, Truman, you dick. Open the fucking door.'

I recognize the voice.

Mills is on the doorstep, looking flushed. 'You weren't answering your phone', she says.

I turned it off for some peace and quiet. I have no idea how she could have found me. The trouble I've put her to has made her bad tempered.

She pushes past and looks around. She seems both appalled and unsurprised.

I'm about to explain, though I really don't want to. Being found has made me bad tempered as well.

She says, 'There's a problem. Rankin has been arrested.'

I say, 'Okay.' It was always a possibility; he's clearly a long way from the straight and narrow path. Not necessarily bad news, either. Might give us a story to tell, and bring the film to life.

If not – if it's serious and Rankin gets put back in prison – that would probably be okay too. It might actually be a relief.

So I say okay again, and pour us both a drink.

But Mills is shaking her head, slowly, like a teacher. 'Not okay', she says. 'Because now the police are looking for you. Rankin says you're his alibi.'

CHAPTER FOUR: APRIL

April 3

There's been a robbery, in a close-set and historic part of London. It's an area that has always had criminal associations. There are posh boutiques and bakeries now. A new shop made up to look old, selling vintage vinyl records, cassettes and VHSes. But the pubs and snooker halls are still rough and rowdy. At night it's easy to picture prostitutes standing under glowing gaslights, and thieves looking out from darkened doorways.

The police have put tape across the road, and a fresh-faced detective constable is trying to control a rabble of reporters and TV news crews. They're here because it seems that the robbery wasn't a simple smash and grab. Overnight, an ill-advised interview given by a security guard on duty when the robbery happened made it sound more like an inside job, and everybody loves a heist.

I'm here not so much because of how the robbery happened. Rather, I'm interested in what was taken. The target was a safe-deposit facility. 600 little boxes in a basement vault, containing God knows what. But *I* know what was in them – hundreds if not thousands of secrets and stories. Missing treasures. Photographic negatives and memory sticks. Letters and scratchy notebooks. Confessions to be opened in the event of death.

I've got two coffees. Black for me, and the other one frothy, made with skinny milk, but with chocolate on top. That's how I imagine the fresh-faced officer takes her morning cup. She's the enemy as far as the news people are concerned, and she looks close to tears. I'm guessing she got the short straw this morning, as the newest member of her team. My plan is to make friends with her, and to see if she knows what was stolen.

Any one of the boxes raided might contain a gripping story, the raid itself just the opening scene, the event that sets the story free. I have the same feeling I get whenever I open a newspaper, or set foot inside a bookshop, only more so – a squirt of excitement in the pit of my stomach, a cold prickle of fear on the back of my neck. Excitement at the sheer number of storytelling possibilities. And fear that I'll miss them all, so overwhelmed by the countless opportunities that I'll fail to grasp a single one.

Across the street from the press cordon is a small, anxious knot of people. Mostly, but not all, men. Mostly, but not all, grey. Customers of the deposit facility, silent and watchful, waiting for news. What fears have drained the colour from their faces? I need to find a way in.

The police officer takes the coffee and tells me to get fucked. Perhaps not as new to the job as she seems.

Tomorrow we're having a company away-day, at a country-house hotel in the countryside. The heads of department like me will be giving presentations on the programmes we're making and the projects we're developing. Then we'll move on to six solid hours of brainstorming, with not just my own small team, but all the people who work at the company. I want to remind the company's smartest and sharpest that the smartest and sharpest of all is me. Which means that, as ever, I'm in need of a good idea.

April 4

It's 11 pm, and I'm sitting at the hotel bar. Around me are all the people I work with, three or four drinks down now, and starting to speak the truth.

There's a wiry-haired production manager beside me at the bar.

'You know what I thought when I first met you?' she says. 'Who *the fuck* does this guy think he is?'

Her tone suggests that I've failed to win her over since then. She's looking at me like she's expecting me to answer the question.

I'm trying to think of something charming to say, that won't come across as such. But that particular cupboard is bare. It's been a very long day.

Being present at the birth of a good idea is a wonderful, transcendent thing. It makes you feel not just alive, but almost immortal. It makes you feel like your time is now. And like you're doing exactly what you ought to be when your time arrives – reshaping the world through imagination and the power of creativity.

The feeling I get from away-day brainstorms is the exact opposite of this.

Beyond the small team of people I work with – hand-picked to get along and make each other think good thoughts – are maybe 20 other individuals. Big egos and fragile personalities. Practical people and dreamers. Bullshitters so skilful you'd believe anything they say, and people so straight and honest you can't believe they're for real. Some of them specialize in current affairs; others, in history, arts and factual entertainment. Generally, we do our own thing.

Charlie, my boss, thinks he'd get better value from the salaries he pays us if he could persuade us all to pull together. To support each other, and improve one another's ideas. And so we gather for a biannual jamboree of resentment, hostility and suspicion, in a cold and echoey ballroom under over-bright orange lights.

A man who won a major award ten years ago, and has done little more than talk about it since, proposed the same idea he always proposes, wafting away every suggestion offered to him, in the way that he always does. Once he was short and boyish. Now he's short and fat. He resents the success of people he regards as lesser talents. Those lesser talents resent the fact that he does so little and talks so much.

An enthusiastic horse-faced woman in her early thirties explained that many of Britain's former territories around the world are now more British than Britain itself. A simple (and not particularly original or interesting) observation that doesn't need unpacking, but she did so anyway, doggedly and in detail. She thinks there might be a programme in this, but has no idea what that programme might be.

Most people in TV are very bright. This girl is a notable exception, which never inhibits her from loudly expressing her thoughts and opinions. You can overthink TV though, and she is capable of brilliant insights into what viewers want from a night in front of the telly.

She noticed a few years ago that the pleasure and appeal of food shows, which were all over the schedules at the time, isn't to do with food as such, but rather things being made. Most people don't get many opportunities to be creative, but that's when people are at their best. And when they're really concentrating and savouring something, people are mesmerizing to look at. She got a commission off the back of that observation, for a slow-burn carpentry series that was cheap to make but enormously popular. It's still running – now in series ten – and has made a lot of money for everyone involved. She resents the fact that other people at the company – cold, intellectual types, from her point of view – patronize and ignore her. The cold intellectual types resent the fact that the odd aperçu seems to be enough to keep her in a job; the rest of the time – like today – it's like watching a puppy running into a mirror.

A twitchy, beady-eyed exec, who looks and sounds like a lecturer in Women's Studies, put forward an idea about the different ways we've thought about rubbish and refuse through history, and what it says about us and our changing values. Proposed changes to the laws on recycling, fiercely opposed in parliament, make the subject timely and important, she said.

No one was interested, but she felt very strongly that we should be, and carefully set about telling us why, like a comedian explaining a joke to an audience that's failed to laugh at it. I noticed that she sometimes gets a startled look when she's expostulating, as though her mind has wandered off (like everyone else's) and then turned back in, and she's realized with a start that the droning sound that's annoying everyone is emanating from her. The dim, horsey woman correctly pointed out that people watch TV to escape from grubby, complex and controversial things they don't fully understand and would rather not think about.

After that, it turned into a free-for-all, a constant white-noise hiss of non-ideas and pointless discussion that made it impossible for anyone to think their own thoughts. A junior member of my team has looked aggressively, mutinously bored all day.

The wiry-haired woman at the bar is still talking, but she's out of focus now. I'm looking at Mills, further down the bar, placing an order. She's speaking slowly so that the barman can understand her over the din of raised voices. I can read her lips. Two Old Fashioneds. My all-time favourite drink.

She showed up briefly at the start of the day, then vanished as soon as she figured out what sort of day it would be. Rules and expectations only really exist for those who agree to follow and meet them. Mills doesn't even pretend to.

Now she's heading this way.

She slides into the space between me and the irate woman with the wiry hair, and puts her drinks on the bar. One in front of her, one in front of me. And then leans into the bar with her back to me, and starts talking to the woman like she's picking up an established conversation. Truman, you're dismissed.

Rescued, in fact. And not for the first time.

April 7

TV – especially factual TV – exists to reflect, interrogate and understand the world around us. The real world. But plenty of people in the industry only know the real world through other TV shows they've seen. Some successful shows are copies of a copy, the bright colours and sharp lines of the original faded and blurred over time, no longer relevant or true. Some successful executives have never crossed paths with the sort of people that feature in the ideas they pitch and the programmes they're responsible for.

I'd half like to be one of those people, because they seem happy and make it all look so easy. I'd half like to be able to do what they do, but I can't. I've tried to do it, and failed. It's harder than it looks.

The other half of me feels very strongly that glib and ungrounded 'concepts' produce the worst sort of television, all surface sheen and no substance. That the value of an idea is related to the work that goes into it, and the right way to have ideas – the *only* way, if you're serious about TV – is to go out into the world and find them. To meet people and experience things. To go on safari, hunting for stories, and err on the side of adventure.

So here we are in Maidenhead, in the county of Royal Berkshire. Rankin, the Delamains, the engagement ring shop and everything else on my slate is on hold, at least until tomorrow. According to a recent report, Maidenhead is the infidelity capital of the British Isles.

I'm sitting in the window of a freezing-cold supermarket cafe with Mills, sheltering from the pissing rain. A mug of instant coffee is keeping my hands warm. Outside, the light is fading. The rain and the yellow street lights are dissolving our view of a cab office and empty car park. 'I'm sorry', I say, for the third or fourth time.

We – which is to say, I – had a tip-off that tonight is unofficially hook-up night at the supermarket. They're all at it, my informant said. Exchanging glances in the aisles. Exchanging numbers in the car park. Exchanging STDs in the budget hotels by the airport. But not tonight. If the married people of Maidenhead are out pursuing sexual adventure, they're certainly not doing it here.

We're trying to figure out a conundrum. Could you film an affair from all three sides as it begins and flourishes, and then fades and fails, or comes to light and implodes, or steps into the light, bravely, whilst other relationships fall apart? That would mean filming at least one person – the husband or wife at home, washing the car, ironing shirts, putting out the rubbish – whilst he or she was in the dark. And you'd have to keep them in the dark, participating in the lovers' lies. How could you justify that, morally? Would the lied-to husband or wife ever consent to be included in the film? Or even be happy enough not to want to sue you? Would the film feel brave or cruel? Or maybe just depressing? Would anyone want to watch it?

Mills says that affairs always seem unique from the inside and clichéd from the outside.

'No one on the outside knows anything', she says.

I realize I know nothing at all about Mills' personal life. I think she must have a boyfriend (or girlfriend), but I don't know for sure. One of the things I love about documentaries is the licence it gives you to ask questions – pretty much any question to pretty much anyone you might be interested in. But I don't feel able to ask Mills.

It's okay. I don't need to know about her love life or where she lives or where she went to school. I feel like I know her anyway.

Mills says everyone assumes that it's better to be in a relationship. That when affairs happen, the loser is the one who ends up alone. But some people want to be. Some people are happier and better that way. So maybe the trick in filming an affair would be to find a loser who's actually a winner – someone set free by a pair of liars who deserve one another. Maybe that's the twist – two fingers to people's stupid assumptions.

'Happy-ever-after is bollocks', she says. 'It's an idea that makes people unhappy.'

I tell her I've heard of a company that provides fake girlfriends and boyfriends for people who want to be by themselves. Cover, I suppose. A product of those assumptions. It sounds remarkable – so much so, I can't believe it's for real.

Mills says, 'Let's find it and go see.'

I haven't told her yet that a Frankenstein's monster of an idea that came out of the away-day – a factual format that opens a fully kitted-out free-for-all workshop in the middle of a deprived estate – has been snapped up by a major channel; 200k to put it to pilot. Residents will be invited to bring along things that are broken and learn how to mend them, thereby boosting their skills and self-respect, as well as saving themselves money. Amidst all the away-day's tension and bitterness, this one idea carried the floor, with something in it for everyone: a hands-on quality the horsey girl liked; a critique of our disposable society for the beady-eyed lady with the passion for rubbish; and high-minded social purpose for the man with the Bafta. Charlie is delighted, of course. And I'm pleased for him. I'm not sure where it leaves me and my approach, though.

Sitting in a cold cafe, I guess. A dozen projects neglected, a hundred emails unwritten and unread. Sitting here with Mills, and feeling alright.

April 11

Today I'm in Dover working on a long-term project, a difficult and delicate piece of access requiring lots of patient negotiation. I was up early, and over the Dartmouth Crossing into Kent just as the sun was rising. By 8 am I was drinking coffee with long-distance lorry drivers at a roadside burger van, listening to their stories of dirty and desperate people clinging to the underside of their trucks in Calais, hoping to make it through the Channel Tunnel to Britain, with its benefits and its NHS.

By 11, I was standing outside the gates of a controversial immigration processing centre, wondering once again what it must be like to have nothing at all, and to be so far from home, friendless and afraid.

By 11.30, I had passed through security, my phone and ID checked in at the desk, patted down and scanned. Then through the four sets of double-locked doors, the smell of sweat and tension getting stronger all the time.

And by 12, I was on the inside, meeting my contact.

The nature of the project means that I can't mention names, you understand. And I had to sign a personal confidentiality agreement, so I can't tell you much about the cases I came across and the things I witnessed. And of course the thing with the phones means I'm out of contact all day – no calls or emails or texts. But it's rich and exciting territory – perfect for a big state-of-the-nation series. The sort of thing that wins awards. Certainly worth persevering with.

In the creative, business-winning bit of TV, no one cares or monitors how hard you work. You can never have enough good ideas. You can never bring in enough business. You can drive yourself mad, or burn yourself out, and no one will blink an eye. No one will ever say, 'Son, you look tired. You should take the day off. You should go freshen up. Have some fun. Empty your mind. Come back next week, and we'll begin again.' The only person who can and will give you a break from the endless pondering and wondering and scouring the world for ideas is you, yourself.

Which is why I am not in fact in Dover at all.

To be entirely frank, I've never been to Dover in my life.

Dover is the place I visit when I'm very hungover, or worn out or depressed. I find the imaginary sea air, and the total lack of contact with any of my colleagues, most refreshing.

I am in fact in the midst of a movie marathon at the most featureless multiplex in London, out in the badlands of the ring road. It was built in the 1980s, I think, judging by the carpets. The out-of-town shopping mall beside it closed down years ago. The cinema remains open only because of a clause in the development deal signed when this was a vacant brownfield site, an eyesore that the council was under pressure to do something – anything – with. The clause says that if the cinema closes, the land reverts to the council. And so it never will, while the developer reworks the abandoned mall, and makes millions for its investors. No one in their right mind would come to this cinema. On Dover days, I have the place to myself – a 700-seat private screening room. It makes me feel like the last man left alive.

The police politely asked me to attend an interview today, about Rankin and his alibi. I politely told them I'm busy, so they'll have to wait. You should never let yourself be summoned to meetings, and policemen are much less scary and impressive than they seem when you've dealt with them once or twice.

My phone rings – not my own phone, which I left at home, but the phone I use for special projects, now and then. There's no one to disturb by answering, so I do.

It's the policewoman from the robbery the other day. I wrote my name on her coffee cup, like they do in Starbucks, and my special-projects number. Her name is DC Lockwood.

'You're probably just as cynical and greedy as the rest of them', she says, 'but I was having a shitty day, and the coffee was nice. Exactly how I like it. So I'm choosing to believe that you might be okay … I have a piece of information that you might find of interest.'

Most of the opened boxes at the depository belong to known associates of a criminal firm that was big in the '60s all the way through to Thatcher, run by two brothers by the name of Nelson. Prior to the robbery, none of the boxes had been opened in over 20 years. A lot was taken, but gems and jewels worth millions were left behind on the floor.

'So it seems like the thieves were after something else', she says. Something specific, perhaps.

I ask, 'Any clue what?'

She says 'No clue at all, and not a single thing to go on. Not a single print or fibre. The whole place has been wiped clean.'

Interesting.

'A mystery', she says, with pleasure in her voice.

DC Lockwood doesn't want anything in return for the tip-off. Nothing tangible anyway. But if anything happens with the story, she wants in. She's bored of coppering. She wants to work in TV.

April 14

People tend to think of a placebo as being the same as nothing; there's no medicine in that pill, it's just a placebo. If they're aware of the placebo effect – whereby someone's health improves despite being given a pill with no medicine in it – they tend to see it as a sort of con, whereby doctors trick you into feeling better. Or perhaps into revealing that you were never really all that ill.

But the placebo effect is fascinating and mysterious, traced in scans to the most primitive parts of the brain. It's part of what has kept us alive for seven million years and more, and its impact can be transformative, giving strength to the lame and bringing people back from the very edge of death.

I read a theory this week about how the placebo effect works, and I really like it. The idea is that your brain is hard-wired to keep some of your body's strength and energy in reserve. Say you're a caveman being chased by a sabre-toothed tiger. It's very important that you escape, and your brain channels significant resources into doing that. But not *all* your body's resources, because, having evaded the first sabre-toothed tiger, you might run into a second. Being entirely exhausted under those circumstances would be very bad.

Now, let's assume that you evaded the first tiger, and the second one never materialized. You make it back to your cave, bleeding from your wounds. Your wife or mother hugs you and kisses you and puts you to bed. A pot of your favourite stew is prepared over the fire, and brought to you as you lie recuperating. You know that you're safe now.

You feel spent from your exertions. But you're *not* spent; you still have the resources your brain set aside as insurance against the second tiger waiting in reserve. Now you're safe, your brain authorizes the use of those resources to get you well again. It's important that you recover quickly, because without a husband or son to go hunting, the survival of the whole family is put into doubt.

The placebo effect is the release of those hidden reserves of energy and determination – of life force, you might say. And in the caveman scenario, what triggers it is the hug or the kiss, or being put to bed, or being fed. Being looked after, in other words. Knowing that your flight or fight moment of crisis has passed. Feeling like you're in safe hands.

The theory is that in the modern world the placebo effect works in the same way. We're ill and our bodies fight the illness, but always with something in reserve, because it's unclear what else you might have to deal with. Then a doctor tells us that it's okay now – we're under his or her care and, like the caveman back in the bosom of his family, we're in safe hands. So our bodies release the reserves, and our condition suddenly improves.

Tests have shown that the more authoritative and expert a doctor appears to be, the more dramatic the placebo effect, suggesting that our bodies release those reserve resources on a sort of sliding scale. If you feel *quite* safe, you get *some* of the reserves. If you feel entirely safe, you get all of them.

It's not clear what proportion of all our energy and determination and will to live is kept in reserve. It might be 5%. It might be 30%. It might be more.

Two days after I read about this theory, the newspapers were full of stories and opinion pieces about people on long-term sickness and incapacity benefit. Figures show that around 2.5 million people in Britain claim incapacity benefit, costing somewhere in the region of £13 billion a year. Now a new piece of research has suggested that 2 million of those people have been on these benefits and notionally unable to work for two years or more. But the welfare state was never intended to carry such a burden; the idea when it was established was that it would provide a safety net for the times when we might stumble and fall. A period of respite while we get back on our feet. Politicians and pundits have been queuing up to express outrage. How did Britain get into this state? And what can be done?

Mills and I are in a jolly cafe at the centre of a parade of shops in a town close to where I was born. There's lots of chatter and clatter and the windows are steamy. Huge plates of old school northern food are being put down by two kind-faced middle-aged ladies in faded brown uniforms – chops and gravy, gammon and mash, cream horns and sticky buns. There's a strong smell of stewed cabbage. Almost everyone looks unwell. I'm no waif, but I'm the lightest man in here by five or six stones, at least. Parked outside are three mobility scooters. There's a big black bin by the door for umbrellas, and another for walking sticks and crutches. One newspaper has published a list of the ten places in Britain with the highest number of people claiming long-term incapacity benefit, and this town is on it.

Mills is looking around her, taking it all in.

'You should call in and see your family', she says.

I tell her I won't be doing that.

My family was solidly working class, and so was my upbringing. My life now – or at least my lifestyle, in so far as I have one – is middle class. I get my groceries from a middle-class supermarket. I do middle-class things, like pick up coffee every morning on my way to the Tube. Most of my friends are middle class. I've learned to speak and behave in a middle-class way to get on in TV, because that's what people expect. In truth I don't really feel part of either the working class *or* the middle class. To be more precise, I feel equally not at home in both. But then I don't feel especially at home even when I'm at home. I'm happy to get on and fit in wherever life takes me, which is a useful thing in my particular line of work.

I feel painfully out of place here, though. Not because of the way I'm dressed, which is similar to everyone else, only with better brands. And not because there's a gulf between my experience of everyday life and theirs; we can easily get to know each other and find some common ground. Rather, I think, my awkwardness is to do with feeling uncomfortable about the idea that has brought us here. I might not see myself as a middle-class TV wanker, but I'm worried that my idea is exactly the sort that a middle-class TV wanker would have.

Could we make the placebo effect work on a whole town? I wondered. Open a gleaming new surgery, and let it be known that some of the world's best doctors would be coming to work there. Maybe say that they'll be using expensive, cutting-edge medicines and techniques before they become available elsewhere, and that the town has been selected from hundreds that applied for the honour. Around it we'd create a sort of theatre of care and well-being, an irresistible sense for anyone visiting the clinic of being looked after and in good hands. But none of the treatments would be real.

How many of the town's inhabitants would we be able to get back to work that way, with all the myriad improvements to life that working, striving and earning money can deliver?

One of the broadcasters wants to commission some big social experiments. Maybe this would fit the bill?

I ask Mills what she's thinking.

'Paying my wages doesn't give you a right to access my thoughts any time you please', she says.

I'm about to disagree with this, but she's not finished yet.

'You never ask the boys what they're thinking.' She means Conrad and Skinner, two APs on my team.

'True.'

'Exactly', she says.

'Because I'm not very interested. I *am* interested in what you think, though.'

In the first rush of excitement that always accompanies a new idea, it seemed like a winner. Maybe even like something that could be taken up by the government and rolled out around the country. Maybe we could change the world! Now it seems horribly patronizing. The people in the cafe aren't in need of cleverness. They're suffering from decades of being told they don't matter, and feeling worthless and disposable.

Mills says that sure, the placebo effect won't last, but at least we'd be drawing attention to the problem, and pointing a way forward. I don't agree and I don't want to discuss it. I dragged us up here and wasted our time. I feel angry and upset with myself.

An old lady comes and sits next to us. 'Haven't you got a lovely face?' she says to Mills. She looks at me and says nothing. Then she starts to tell her story, like we've known one another for years. She fell in love with a man she met during the war and he died. She dreams about him always. Talks to him sometimes, when she's on her own. One of the waitresses passes our table and rolls her eyes; we're not the first to hear this. The old lady sips her tea. She never found anyone else; she only ever wanted him. Not long now, she says, happily, and smiles again at Mills.

In a long slow traffic jam shuffling out of town, we're sitting saying nothing.

I can hear Mills thinking. Breathing more shallowly. Preparing a little speech.

She says she thinks it's a good idea and that people would understand and relate to it. 'Everyone needs to feel loved and safe', she says. 'Everyone needs to belong somewhere and to someone.'

There's silence for a moment while the thought settles.

I'm about to speak when she continues.

'Everyone needs a bit of looking after', she says. 'It's a universal longing.' Even mobsters and loners. Even spacemen and drifters.

'Even someone as fucked-up as you.'

April 15

It rained hard all the way back to London. The traffic was slow moving because of the spray coming up from the road.

We stopped at a service station to fill the tank, and got cold and wet picking up coffees to drink in the car. Then we settled in for the journey. It would take five hours, I reckoned. Maybe six.

I like the monotony of long drives. The same scenery for mile after mile. The buzz of the car, like an aeroplane. I like not being able to do much. It's dead time, which always makes me feel like my mind is unwinding.

I was thinking half-thoughts about the wages people earn (what if we pooled all the earnings of an average street, and then divided the money up and handed it out again according to what's fair and what people deserve?), about job interviews and employability (could we film every job interview in a single week in a single town like the one we just left?), and about all the self-employed van drivers racing up and down the motorway (what if we brought them all together to form a white-van army? What might that army achieve?). Nothing very interesting or useful. As the beginnings of ideas, too much like the placebo one. Too clever and trying too hard. Insufficiently real.

Mills was wrapped in a picnic blanket I keep in the boot, looking out of the window. I could see the expressions on her face changing in her reflection, her brow rising and falling. She was thinking about something too.

'All these people are in worlds of their own', she said, gesturing at the cars all around us. 'In their own little bubbles. All talking and listening. All trying to make themselves understood.'

April 20

There's something about long journeys – especially in cars – that makes people open up. It's not just the time spent together. It has to do with the fact that you're both facing the same way, and not really looking at each other. And with the fact that you're nowhere, really. You're on your way from one place to another, on a stretch of anonymous road. You're in a sort of no man's land. A neutral place.

It feels a bit like what you might say in such a place doesn't matter. Unlike, for example, an office. Or sitting opposite someone in a restaurant. Or lying next to someone in bed. Different rules apply.

'You think you don't need people, but you're wrong', Mills said to me again, halfway back to London. 'You think you don't have anyone, but you do.'

It's given me an idea for a programme.

We've been looking for people who travel along the most congested road in London every day. The idea is to rig their cars with tiny cameras, and to record their conversations every morning and every night for a month.

We're hoping to capture conversations and moments that feel uniquely honest and revealing, intimate stories unfolding over time like a novel.

But it's perfectly possible that we'll capture nothing much at all. A study in boredom. And there's nothing so boring as people who are bored.

All the grown-ups in the office are predicting a waste of time and money, which makes me feel like we might be on to something good. Tomorrow the first of the footage will arrive into the office for us to view.

April 21

'Shall I be mother?' Rankin says.

We're in a dingy cafe near King's Cross, with yellow net curtains and old china plates displayed on the walls. Opposite us, two old ladies are sitting in perfect silence.

Us being Rankin, me and a small thin man with a runny nose. Rankin's solicitor.

It's so quiet I can hear the old ladies breathing.

One hour from now, I'm due at Paddington Green police station to give a statement. Rankin wanted to meet beforehand, to offer me some advice.

'Nothing to worry about', he says. 'No need to answer questions. Just say your piece and leave.'

'My piece?'

'We were together all day, right?'

We were.

'And drinking all night?'

'Yes. Most of the night, anyway. Didn't you have to go somewhere?'

I tell him that after a certain point I don't remember much.

I remember waking up the next morning, though. I remember that very clearly. I'm hoping that bit doesn't come up.

The lawyer hands me a phone. On the screen is a message from me, to Rankin's girlfriend. What a great night. Lovely to spend time with you both. We should all get together again soon.

Ah.

One of the old ladies sighs. A tube train rumbles by.

'So what's new', Rankin says, 'in the glamorous world of telly?'

I tell him about the safety-deposit boxes, and my tip-off about the Nelson brothers. I ask him if he knows what the thieves were after.

'Who do you think I am?' he says.

But I can see he's pleased to be asked. Pleased to have me recognize the strength of his criminal connections.

He's interested in TV. Everyone is really. And now he owes me one.

He smiles and pours me another cup of tea.

April 22

What makes documentaries stand out is the characters that appear in them, and the things they say and do. You can happen upon characters, if you're both very lucky and very attentive to what's happening around you. But that sort of thing is rare. Mostly you have to go out and find characters. Documentaries based on a format or conceit generally need to be cast.

Mills is amazing at casting. She's found some very good people for our experiment with the cameras in the cars, and the footage is extraordinary.

One set of rushes features a father driving his daughters to school in the city. He seems very down to earth. They seem quite proper, in uniforms with straw hats. He's trying to communicate with them. They're not really listening. He keeps talking about when they were little, which embarrasses and annoys them. He's not teasing them; he's just saying what's on his mind. I think he feels like he's losing them. Maybe he did well at work and made money, and married someone more cultured and refined than himself. He wanted the best for his girls, of course, and paid for their schooling. Now he feels like he doesn't know them. Or maybe he knows them perfectly well, and doesn't like what he sees. Or maybe he just wants them to know him, as a person rather than the guy who pays the bills and drives them about. I find the silences and the look in the man's eyes almost too moving to watch. While the girls are gossiping about their friends and boys they know, their dad looks ahead at the road, thinking about when they used to rush to the door when he got home and he knew everything about them, wondering what he can say or do to get that feeling back.

Another set of rushes features a smart young couple in a Porsche. On first appearances, you envy them deeply. They're good-looking and well-off. They always seem to be running late for something fun and glamorous. Then you start to get a sense that maybe they're not quite as happy as you imagine they should be. On their way back from parties, they seem to be occupying entirely different spaces. You can see them wanting to speak, but not really knowing what to say. You get the sense that all the dashing around is a way of avoiding these moments. You're watching them fall out of love with each other, and it's terribly painful. Neither seems to want it to happen. Neither of them is a bad person, or a guilty party. There's no anger or resentment. They've simply run out of road. You wonder if on one of these tapes, perhaps in a week or so, you'll see them have an honest conversation, and the sad process of disentanglement will begin. Cameras are a sort of stimulant; just knowing they are rolling can sometimes prompt people to face up to things they normally run away from.

A third box of tapes features a gang of Polish builders, all in their twenties save for their gaffer, who's slightly older and wiser. They're all recently arrived in Britain from a small town near the Ukrainian border, travelling every morning from west London into the heart of the city to work on a prestigious new building. They're innocents abroad, spending their time together in their van trying to make sense of their new lives in a vast and confusing city. Why do people walk so fast? Why does everyone look so frowny? And where does all the money come from? They're utterly charming to watch – affectionate with each other, bewildered, frank and funny. A band of brothers. You want to be in their van with them. They make your own humdrum world seem beguiling and marvellous.

The material will make for a terrific taster, and it's the sort of idea I know I'll pitch well. I'll talk about how commuting isn't just dead time to be endured. It's inspired poets and writers and even Albert Einstein, who was looking up at the town hall clock on his way to work when he wondered whether time might be relative. It makes you think in interesting ways and feel unusual emotions. It can make confusing things seem clearer, and bring hidden things to the surface.

I'll tell stories of conversations I've had in cars myself, that wouldn't and couldn't have happened elsewhere. The time, not long after I learned to drive, when I took my great-granddad away on a day trip. He told me about his life and disappointments. He told me he was proud of me, and that he didn't want to see me again; that I should leave and not look back. The time I told my little sister that I'd be doing exactly that. I couldn't stand to see her face. The time I was making a film that was dying on its arse, and my central character suddenly started to speak and told me all his secrets – things he'd buried that made sense of all the confusing stuff I'd filmed up to that moment. We drove way past our destination, talking, and the film went on to win an award.

'You think you don't really need looking after', Mills said, that day on the road in the rain. 'But you really really do.'

'You think that you've got no one', she said. Then we looked at each other, for the first time in hours. Her eyes said 'But you've got me.'

Then her phone rang and she spent the rest of the journey talking to a contributor, probing and listening, reading between the lines and mapping things out in her head. Warm and funny and gentle. She looked at me once more, at the start, and we both looked back at the road.

April 25

I'm making my way to the front of a small cinema against a stream of deflated TV executives heading for the exits. I know most of them, and I'm trying to say hello without starting conversations.

We've been listening to the commissioning requirements for the next six months of one of the major broadcasters. The talking has gone on for two whole hours, and I can't remember anyone saying anything remotely meaningful. The last thing commissioners want to do at a channel briefing is identify an actual commissioning need; that would only trigger a deluge of bad ideas, each of which would need to be read and considered to be properly rejected. One moment of accidental specificity could bring about weeks of unwanted work. They do have to say something, however, so they say the same things that all commissioners say, which turns the event into another long litany of jargon, cliché and bombast. I don't know why so many people bother coming to these things.

I know why I'm here, though. I want to talk to Jools, the commissioner I pitched the ring series to. It's been with her for a while now. The long-expected exit of her bumbling, lumbering colleague has held things up. He was finally sacked three weeks ago, happily not before getting a chance to enthuse about the idea when Jools pitched it to the head of their department. That night at the festival was time well spent. The rest of his colleagues agreed with his assessment; I'd done the same thing with each and every one of them, just to be on the safe side. A full house, Jools told me that night, which hardly ever happens. Everyone around the table loved it.

Not much has happened since. I thought we'd have a commission by now.

'I've been meaning to get back to you', she says, embarrassed. She looks away, composing herself, thinking what she'll say. And her eyes settle on something over my shoulder.

'Let me introduce you to my new colleague', she says. 'There's been a reshuffle. He's heading up popular factual now.'

Have you met? she says.

He says no, but we have.

The last time I saw him he was close to tears, with his dick hanging out of his trousers.

'It's a pleasure', he says. Eyes cold and dead.

Jools says the announcement will be made next week, but the guy has already started work.

'I've reviewed all the ideas on the table. Including yours', he says, studiously sympathetic, like a vicar at a wake. 'And much as I like it, I'm afraid it didn't quite make the cut.'

Two million pounds worth of business. Gone in a vengeful swipe.

Jools pulls a what-can-I-do? face, and says let's meet again soon. Then she's off to speak to someone else. Good commissioners always have other promising projects on the go. Four or five more, probably. She's too smart and ambitious to waste time fighting for something a senior colleague is dead set against.

Telling Mills will be hard. She loves this idea.

The new Head of Popular Factual shakes my hand politely. 'I'm sorry', he says, and smiles.

CHAPTER FIVE:
MAY

MAY 2

I'm in a meeting with a guy I don't like.

We know some people in common.

I say, 'How's Bill?'

I love Bill. He was my first boss and mentor.

The guy says, 'Bill's dead.'

This is my first meeting with the guy, and we're only five minutes into it. I knew for sure two minutes into it that I don't like him, which includes 90 seconds of giving him the benefit of the doubt. His hand was sweaty when I shook it, and his eyelids fluttered when he said he'd been looking forward to meeting me, because he was lying.

He works for the company I started out at. I left after a year or so, to take up a job in London. He joined as a young man also, and works there still. I don't really know anything about him, except that he's in possession of a piece of footage that I'd really like to get my hands on. He seems to know rather more about me, and apparently finds all of it distasteful.

He says, 'Bill used to talk about you all the time. Made us watch all your programmes on the night they went out.'

'Very entertaining', he says, his eyelids fluttering like a geisha.

I don't care what his problem is. He can get fucked. He's done nothing of any worth in his entire 15-year career, which is why he's still at the same small regional company.

Bill started out as a cameraman, shooting on 16mm film. He loved film – the whirring noise the shutter made, and the deeper purr of cogs and reels turning inside the camera. Like the camera was alive, he said to me once. He was head over heels into the romance of it all. All those tiny moments, trapped in little canisters, set free when you put the film through a projector. When he stopped filming and started directing, he began a collection – any old bits of film he could get his hands on. By the time I met him, he had hundreds of aluminium cans full of footage on shelves in a room at the back of the office. I asked about his collection, and he showed me, picking out reels at random and threading them into his ancient Steenbeck editing machine, with its tiny, flickering monitor. We spent a few evenings like that, with beer and pizza, and one slow summer with not enough work to keep me busy, he asked if I'd like to catalogue them.

After I left, he carried on collecting. He bought a job lot that turned out to include early footage of the Beatles and other rarities. Now his collection could make money, and he put the man sitting in front of me in charge of it.

Most of it has no value, though. Much of it has never been developed and probably never will be now, because developing film has become expensive.

The particular roll of film I'm interested in – a negative, ghostly roll of Super 8 that I last looked at over ten years ago – was worthless then, but might not be any longer. A changing set of circumstances has put the contents in a different light.

TV is mostly about getting on with people. I need to find a way of getting on with this guy. But I'm not really listening to what he's saying, because I'm thinking about Bill.

Bill was astonishingly generous and kind. He was volatile, but only ever angry for a moment. And then he'd smile at you, and you'd find yourself smiling back. He was often infuriating, but you could never hold it against him. He could be embarrassing and inspiring in the space of the same conversation. The same sentence, sometimes. He was affectionate and tactile. He loved people, and he always told the truth.

He taught me lots of things, but one thing above all – that TV is not something you do for a living but something you live. That TV is an adventure.

I feel crushingly sad that he's no longer part of it.

I want to be alone and think about Bill. My eyes feel hot. I should have thanked him and never really did.

The guy's mouth is moving still, and then it stops.

It doesn't matter what he was saying. I need to take charge now. I feel angry that he had nothing more to say about Bill than a few sparse facts about when and how he died. You'd have to be a cunt to know him and not love him as much as I did. But I need to keep that anger in check. I really want that reel.

I tell him I'd like to acquire a roll of film from his archive for a project I'm developing. He says, 'What about?' I say, 'I'm sorry, I can't say. But I'm looking for original archive from the period, which is hard to find, and I think I remember Bill having a few feet of film that might be suitable. The label on the can says "party". I wrote the label myself.'

He looks suspicious and uncomfortable.

He says he could license it to me. I tell him I want to own all the archive, because I want to keep the rights position with the project simple. When you own all the archive in a film, it's ten times easier to sell.

I can see it cross his mind that there might be something on the roll of real interest and value. Something he could use to win his own commission, perhaps? But then there's a tiny slump in his shoulders. He's too lazy and incurious to do the work and the thinking it would need. And years of failure and frustration have taught him that he doesn't have what it takes to get ideas commissioned. That's a hard thing to know, and his mouth draws up like he's tasted something bad. He needs people like me – people with ideas and relationships with commissioners, that he can peddle his bits of archive to. He thinks that TV is run by venal, pretentious, metropolitan wankers. Which it is. And that I'm one of them, only worse, because we started out the same.

He steeples his fingers and puts them to his lips. Now he's thinking only how to value the reel. He's a bottom feeder, making ends meet, out for what he can get. I couldn't be happier about that. Bottom feeders are so much easier to deal with.

He starts talking about what unseen archive can bring to a film. The difference it can make.

I say, 'Look, undeveloped reels change hands for £50. You might license it at £50 a minute. I'll never use more than that. And it might be another ten years before anyone is interested again. But we're connected, through Bill, so I'll make you an offer. A generous offer. £300 for the reel.'

Which is hopefully low enough to convince him that it features nothing of great interest. But high enough to make him engage.

He shifts in his seat and licks his lips. We're almost there.

'Cash', he says.

Which means 50 to the company, and 250 in his pocket.

I say, 'Okay.'

He says, 'You've got a deal.'

May 3

So now I have four and half minutes of 8mm film, and I'm £300 out of pocket.

I'm back at the company where the guy works, only now there's no one around. It's 6 am. I bribed the security guard to let me in.

The place is much smaller than I remember it. And less colourful. It's muted and dull now, made over by someone with suburban taste. It had a garish 1980s' colour scheme when I was here, which felt entirely right. Downstairs, the paunchy middle-aged journos who worked at another TV company, specializing in current affairs, would smoke at their desks and pour out Scotch into unwashed coffee cups. I used to hang around down there just to listen to them on the phone, establishing the when, the where and the why. A wonderful old lady with dyed black hair used to come round in the afternoons with a tea urn on a trolley and plates of fat home-made buns.

Bill's office is in the same place it used to be. It doesn't look like anyone has been in it since he passed away. The air inside is heavy and still. There's a stone paperweight on his desk that he had in my day, brought back from a mountain he climbed and nearly died on, and a picture of him in his heyday, receiving an award and looking fit to burst. I put both of them in my bag.

He stood at the door of his office once and called me over from my desk. He was angry about something and everyone could tell. As I got to the door, he grabbed me round the back of the neck and shoved me inside and slammed the door. I'd written a bad and lazy treatment, partly because the idea I'd been given to write up was lame, but mostly because I thought I was too good to write it. I wasn't long out of university. I had an academic way of thinking and writing, and I tended to look down on the noisy language of TV treatments, long on promises and short on detail. The treatment I'd written was snooty and boring. Bill ripped it up and threw it in my face. And then calmly explained to me what TV is and what it's for, why treatments exist and why learning how to write them would be a passport to anywhere I wanted to go. Crack treatments and you'll crack TV. He didn't need to do that. Most bosses would just have sacked me. He countered my arrogance with patience and kindness.

For over a year he taught me how to think like a TV producer. And then as soon as I was good and grown-up enough to actually be useful, I fucked off to a better-paid job in London.

I told Bill on a Friday night after everyone else had left for the weekend, and he bear-hugged me and said he knew that I would. And that he knew that I'd make a success of it.

The company will certainly die now. Only Bill's personality kept it going. The guy who sold me the reel will soon be out of work.

In my position Bill would have helped the guy out. Landed the commission and then offered the guy a job on it.

But I'm not Bill. He was a much better man than I am.

May 6

In the US a few years ago there was a spate of phone calls from policemen to chain restaurants and takeaways in small towns in rural areas. The phone calls always followed the same pattern. The policemen would instruct managers to detain young female employees and strip-search them, on the basis that they were suspected of committing a crime. Sometimes the policemen would induce the managers to do rather more and worse.

To be more accurate, it wasn't policemen making the calls, but a single policeman.

And to be completely accurate, it wasn't a policeman at all, but seemingly an ordinary guy pretending to be a policeman.

He was able to manipulate, bully and cajole respectable, law-abiding people into doing things they never normally would, against all their better instincts, because of the fear and cowardice that go with working in strict and petty hierarchies.

I learned all about this kind of manipulation and bullying during a miserable spell working at a big broadcasting corporation. You probably know the one I mean.

I joined imagining that someone with energy and initiative would cut through the organization like a hot knife through butter. In fact I found my energy and initiative just annoyed people. No one wanted to upset the apple cart. Energy and initiative were not how things got done there.

I'd be summoned to a dozen meetings a week, and sent scores of emails, all to do with procedures for managing creativity. We monitored creativity, documented it, and plotted it in graphs. We analysed it in long weekly meetings led by a pinched and sorrowful man, who'd sniff and shake his head at us. We designed systems for facilitating creativity. We listened to lectures from guest speakers about harnessing and refining creativity. We spent entire days attempting to define creativity. We were told again and again that we were part of the world's most creative organization. But of course this was untrue. Because talking about creativity and being creative are not the same things. They are not even slightly similar.

For almost two years the most creative thing I did on the average day at work was find ways of evading corporate controls, like a captive airman in Colditz, waging war on the Germans through childish non-compliance. I'd stand near entrances and exits and pretend to be on the phone, and then sneak in or out by following other people, to avoid having to use the little plastic swipe card that monitored our whereabouts. When the novelty of that wore off, I paid the stand-in IT guy to fix my card, so that whenever and wherever I swiped it, every gate in the 40-hectare site would beep and open up. I was everywhere and nowhere. But mostly I was shuffling from one meeting to the next, obedient, oppressed and despairing, like everybody else.

My boss was a nervous, colourless man who smelled distinctly of soap and was always in favour of everything. In favour of having cake. In favour of eating it. In favour of the quietest possible life of the deepest mediocrity.

Eventually, before a big corporate meeting with this guy, and his boss, and other bosses of bosses lined up like Russian dolls, I had a moment of clarity. Suited and booted, and thoroughly prepped for the presentation I had to give, I was standing near a zinc fence, having a cigarette and coffee in the sunshine, waiting for the meeting to start. A security guard was watching me. I'd normally look away, but this time I didn't. He spoke into his walkie-talkie and kept watching. And I kept looking back. 'Who are you?' he was saying with his eyes. 'Yes, who am I?' I was thinking, at first. And then I remembered. Now, as he was saying 'Who are you?' with his eyes, I was saying 'Fuck you' with mine. The next thing I knew, I was climbing over the fence.

I almost had a change of heart as I got to the top. It was a long way up, and I felt like a dick in my suit. I could see people looking out of the windows on the floor of the building where I worked. I could hardly climb down again with an audience. And then the guy who ran the coffee cart in the mornings, who I'd got to know and who was kind and wise, did a sort of black power salute, and I did one back. I wanted to say something rebellious and incendiary, but I couldn't think of anything. Then I climbed down the other side, a fugitive.

The coffee guy was clapping and whooping. People were staring, some of them on their way to the meeting I was supposed to be speaking at. The security guard was busy on his walkie-talkie. Another security guard came over, and the first one pointed in my direction.

I put my swipe card, work phone and tie in a bin, and went shopping for books. Not very rock and roll, but that's what I felt like doing. Before joining that company I'd steer clear of bookshops, because the sheer volume of ideas stacked up within them – ideas old and new, good and bad – often felt overwhelming. But that day it felt like stripping off and diving into a cool pool on a hot and humid day. I stayed there until closing time, bought a dozen paperbacks and caught the night train to Edinburgh, like a character in a novel. No one would know me there. No need to pack anything; I'd buy what I needed when I arrived. Four weeks later, now back in my flat, I was invited by post to attend 'an urgent performance review'. I was already making a film for someone else.

The people who flourish in such places are, like the man pretending to be a police officer, entirely psychopathic. They know how to dupe and manoeuvre. They play on the insecurity and paranoia that come with multiple levels of management. They're able to detect the tiniest trace of weakness across vast open-plan office floors – your secret worries and frustrations, the particular type of vanity or shyness you work so hard to hide – like sharks can taste a bleeding wound across miles of open sea, then use your shortcomings to torment and control you. They drip gossip like poison in the ears of their bosses, and lay traps through hints and feints, but are never less than charming. They're thick-skinned and devious and immune to disappointment, sustained not by creativity and moments of joy but politics and connivance, by getting their way and winning, whatever the game might be. They thwart and destroy for the fun of it, but nothing is ever their fault. They're assertive, clear-thinking, calm under pressure, and entirely focused on their own agenda. The more toxic the environment, the more effective they become.

Today and for the next couple of days, the skills I learned in my time at this place – hard-earned fuck-or-be-fucked skills of survival – are going to come in useful.

There's a psychopath in my cutting room.

May 7

The biggest and best part of my job is finding ideas. The toughest part is getting them commissioned. The worst part is turning those ideas and commissions into television programmes.

The reason this is the worst part is that it's inherently disappointing. The moment an idea is green-lit is the beginning of the long process whereby it ceases to be a perfect, crystalline, gleaming idea, and it becomes real, with all of the compromises, misunderstandings and missed opportunities that reality always brings.

To mitigate this, you hire the best people you can. Which is to say, clever, inventive people who share your creative vision.

You don't always get it right. In the case of a film I got commissioned last year, currently in production, I got it spectacularly wrong.

On paper, the director of this film was a decent choice. In reality, she has spent the last several months telling pointless lies, humiliating and mistreating the people around her, and making grandiose claims about the quality of the footage she's been gathering.

In the end, the crew didn't want to work with her. Nor did the contributors. The film limped into the edit, and whenever I dropped in to say hello and ask how things were going, the editor, sitting at his desk next to her, would say 'everything's fine', with the same blank tone and facial expression you get from hostages forced to make videos denouncing the decadent west.

I finally saw a rough cut last week, and was utterly appalled.

The idea behind the film is simple – access to a prison visiting room, every week for three months. Between visits, we film with the prisoners on the inside, and their wives and kids at home. We see what prison does to relationships, played out in tense, dramatic and emotional exchanges across little Formica tables.

The commissioner loved it. If the film delivers, a series might be possible.

But the director has imposed a narrative on events instead of listening to the characters and responding. She wants the film to be a story of female emancipation, but it's not. None of the wives wants to break free. Rather it's the story of several women who've fallen for the wrong sort of man, trapped in a miserable situation by love.

Her direction is terrible as well. Fussy and intrusive. She's taken great access and good characters and made the whole thing about her.

Now it's clear that the film is a mess, it's my job to sort it out. If I don't, it will be very hard to sell ideas to the same commissioner. Maybe even the same channel. All mouth and no trousers, people will say. He promises you champagne and gives you fizzy piss. You can be the world's greatest salesman, but if people lose faith in the product you're selling, you won't get very far.

So it's very important the film gets fixed.

It's personally important too, because it's Mills' pet project. She worked exceptionally hard to win the access and build relationships with the wives and kids. The film is important to Mills, which makes it important to me.

The director knows all this. And being a psychopath, she sees it as my secret weakness. The more politely I ask for changes, the more difficult and evasive she becomes. The fact that I'm right is irrelevant. It's a game to her, and all she wants is to win.

May 11

I'm in a cab on the way to the cutting room. It's not particularly early and I'm not particularly hungover, but it feels like it. My head is heavy and thoughts are coming slowly. I'm not particularly tired but I'd love to go to sleep.

That's what pointless power struggles do to you, I suppose. They wear you down, which is how come most people try to avoid them. They weigh up the personal cost and decide that it just isn't worth it. But avoiding power struggles generally means giving in and losing, and that's just not something I can allow. There's the matter of my reputation with the channel. But it's not only or even mainly about that. I have a strong personal aversion to being fucked with.

Good execing is all about psychology. Boosting fragile egos. Getting the best out of people. But none of that has worked.

Nor can I simply sack her. Like all psychopaths, she never gets caught misbehaving, and always has reasons not to do the things I ask. In any case, sacking her wouldn't be smart. It would only reflect badly on me.

Now my plan is to fight fire with fire.

The director has made it very clear that she doesn't much care for the commissioning editor. She regularly says patronizing and disparaging things about his height and lack of intelligence. But the same commissioner and his department give the director all her work.

The last time we spoke, her comments were particularly withering. I'm listening to them now, on the Dictaphone on which I recorded them.

Thinking it through, I can feel the fog in my head beginning to lift. Get through this morning and everything might work out. I think I can put the film right using all the stuff in the rushes she's ignored. The stuff her AP and cameraman shot on the days she didn't turn up. Patient, observational stuff she was too grand to film herself.

And then the same fantasy I always have at times like these comes over me. It's like a dream I only have when I'm wide awake. I'm putting a camera in the back of my car, and the bag I keep ready with tape and batteries and useful things, and a rucksack with a change of clothes. And then I'm heading off somewhere, at the start of something new.

If you're successful in TV, every step leads away from this, towards the kind of situation I'm in right now – none of the adventure, with all of the worry and stress.

On the radio, they're talking about a missing kid in the Midlands. Her mother has six kids in total, all by different dads. She's been pictured drinking beer from a can in the street outside her house. Is this any way to carry on? the people on the radio are saying. She looks like she doesn't care. One caller says it's because her brood is so large, as though she'd hardly notice if one or two got mislaid. He says that's how it is with people like that.

Absent-mindedly, mostly to pass the time before the battle of the cutting room commences, I type out a text to a commissioner I know.

'Have you heard this shit on the radio? It's like this poor woman's not human. Who's to say what's right and normal under circumstances like that? The girl is probably dead, or worse. Someone should go up there and film this. Compassion and some truth-telling are what's required, not vitriol and condemnation.'

I send it off and settle back. I'm thinking about the cutting room. I'm composing my opening salvo. Start on the front foot, and stay there.

My phone chirps with a text.

It says simply 'You?'

I hadn't really expected a response. That's what tends to happen with messages like the one I just sent – semi-serious punts, sent from the back of a cab. No response *is* the response. No response means absolutely not, and don't bother me like this again.

I write back, 'You offering?'

He texts me again to say, 'Yes.'

May 12

I'm in a black van with my cameraman Luke, laden with kit and supplies. We're on the motorway out of London.

I love this time on the road, the hours full of possibilities and expectation.

The woman lives on the sprawling Brightwell Estate with the father of her six-month-old baby and the rest of her children, and two of his from another relationship. I called them up last night. Can I come and meet you and film what's happening? She sounded wary and exhausted. A dozen broadcast news crews are camped outside her house, men in suits taking it in turns to stand at the gate and record their reports.

'We're not like them', I said. 'They're on the outside looking in. We want to come inside with you, and see things through your eyes.'

'People think we're scum', she said.

I said, 'Yes, but not me.'

'I can't imagine what it must feel like to be you right now', I said. 'I don't think anyone can. So why don't you let me in and tell me?'

And she said, 'Okay.'

So here we are, at the beginning of a new adventure. A mystery to unravel.

May 13

We're inside the house, drinking tea, filming out of the window. A man is standing on the patch of grass at the front of the house, holding a poster with a picture of the girl on it, talking into a camera wired up to a truck. Luke pans right to a TV in the corner of the room. The same man is on the screen, his face studiedly solemn. A newspaper has offered a reward for information leading to the recovery of the girl. One of the kids lifts the net curtains and flicks a V sign at the camera.

Yesterday we filmed non-stop, till the hour was very late.

The only place still open when we left was a tired-looking Indian restaurant. We sat in the corner, buzzing, and ordered some beer.

Filming actuality – a story that's unfolding around you – is always addictive. That day, it felt like smoking crack. We couldn't change over the tapes fast enough. All the emotions were supercharged. Every moment seemed worthy of capture.

You can't really communicate with your crew when you're filming. Not about your impressions and private thoughts, anyway. You focus your attention on your characters. You don't want them to feel analysed or observed. Now we were off the clock and alone, I could finally think aloud. I talked about my excitement. The amazing tension in the family's house. The sense of being at the centre of something that everyone is talking and thinking about.

I was suddenly conscious of talking too much. I asked Luke what he made of it all.

He thought for a moment and said that something seemed odd.

I said, 'Of course it does, their child has vanished!'

He said, 'Not that, something else.'

The woman is in pieces, but always looking for the camera, he said. Flirting with it, is how he put it. Like a star performer. Courting the lens, desperate for attention.

I said, 'Flirting with you, maybe.' (He's very tall and good-looking). 'Remember how strange this must feel to them. Two strangers up from

London, camping in your house. Studying and recording everything you say and do.'

He shrugged and went back to his dinner.

Outside, the reporter hands back to the studio. On the TV in the corner, the programme moves on to other news. The reporter comes up to the house and knocks on the door. The woman lights up a ciggie and ignores him.

I ask her how she's feeling, and she starts to cry. 'Nobody understands', she says. 'I just want to see my little girl's face again.'

May 14

The girl has been missing for ten days now. Experts say that after just two, there's little chance of a missing child being found alive.

The police have been conducting a house-to-house search. I've made friends with a senior officer. The details of the investigation don't much matter to me; my focus is purely on the family. But it's interesting, of course. I think he appreciates a chance to talk freely, off the record, with someone invested in the case.

Like lifting a stone, is the phrase he used today. The search has uncovered drugs and weapons and child pornography. But not a trace of the missing girl.

And last night, something horrific. A man found howling in scrubland nearby, his arms outstretched and nailed to a piece of wood.

Crucified, in other words. A local loner.

Frustrated with the police's lack of progress, a group of men took matters into their own hands. They dragged the poor guy from his house and tortured him. Nobody tried to stop them. But the man had no information to surrender.

Police helicopters are buzzing around the sky today, and sniffer dogs have arrived from a neighbouring force. Some are search and rescue dogs. Others are specially trained in 'victim recovery', known to the police as 'cadaver dogs'.

At the house, a middle-aged lady in a bright red coat comes to the door. Luke picks up the camera and starts filming once again. The woman says she's had a vision. The mother of the missing girl invites her inside.

The woman says that the vision is of the missing girl. She's in a derelict building in a wooded area, with a body of water nearby.

The mother presses her for more details. 'She is partially clothed', the psychic says. 'And I'm sorry to say she's not moving.'

The atmosphere in the house is febrile. It's the same outside on the street. People are becoming desperate.

May 15

We're in the house, in the missing girl's tiny bedroom, talking to her mum. As in the rest of the house, the paint is peeling off the walls and there's a smell of damp and cigarettes. It's cosy, though. Full of teddy bears and pink stuff, but there are posters of pop stars on the walls too, and a diary with a lock on it. It's the room of a little girl, but one who's growing up fast.

I'm asking her mum questions, gently, about what sort of person she is. Twice I almost say 'was' instead of 'is', but catch myself just in time. I'm trying to give the girl a presence in the film, so viewers will feel her absence.

'Tell me about the things she likes?'

'I don't know', her mum says. 'The usual stuff, I suppose.'

The diary was taken away by the police when the girl disappeared, but returned soon after. Her mother unlocks it and reads us a few lines. It's typical little-girl stuff about her friends and her brothers and sisters, but it makes her more than a face on a poster. This modest space, where she would have felt safer than anywhere else, is heartbreaking without her and it makes my eyes sting.

We've been filming for four hours straight, and we're running out of tape. I go out to the van to get more.

The fresh air tastes clean and reviving.

A journalist from one of the tabloids wants a word. I hold up my hand and say sorry. It's what I have been doing from day one. All the reporters want to know how come we're inside the house, and what's going on in there. What do we know that they don't? But I've got nothing to say. Just doing my job, same as you. But that's not going to wash today. Not with this guy at least. He steps into the path in front of me, and puts his fingertips up to my chest.

His voice is low and growly.

'Help me out', he says. 'We've got to print something.'

I say again that I'm sorry, and look down at his hand, his manicured fingernails still touching my chest.

He says, 'If we can't find a story about them' – glancing back towards the house – 'we'll have to look elsewhere'.

He delivers the last line slowly, like he's been out here rehearsing it, and looks me dead in the eye.

A camera shutter flutters, *clack clack clack*. His photographer is across the road, his lens pointed at me.

Now's not the time for a confrontation.

I say, 'Excuse me', and make my way to the van.

May 17

I'm going to make this easy. All you need to do is shut up and fuck off.

You can claim the credit when it's done. But get in my way – even slightly, ever again – and I'll make sure you're fucked, permanently.

You belong to me now. You might even be useful one day. My own pet psychopath.

That's roughly what I said to the person directing the prison film, that morning in the edit.

I asked the editor to give us a moment, closed the door and gave it to her straight. Calm and clear, like a doctor with bad news.

She just smiled and shrugged. No recriminations at all. No anger or bitterness. Just a look of recognition. Admiration, almost.

When the editor came back we were chatting happily. He looked completely bewildered. She'd already packed her things. She said a quick goodbye and then she was gone.

The mother of the missing girl has asked for some time to herself today.

I've been watching a new cut of the prison film in a cafe on my laptop, and I love it. You can see the editor and AP have gone about their work with glee. There's a freshness and vibrancy to it, a sense of something wonderful emerging.

It's rough still, but full of warmth and humour. Gentleness, also. But above all empathy, something I doubt the director has ever felt. Now you see a sorority emerge in the cafe outside the prison, of luckless, downtrodden women helping each other through. Their marriages are strained, but they want to stay together, all hoping for a fresh start when their husbands are released.

It's inspiring to watch, and I think it will be a very fine film.

May 18

One of the newspapers has run a story featuring the grandparents of the missing girl. They allege that her mother has always been a bad and neglectful parent. The woman gives the piece to her partner and asks him to read it aloud, listening closely. By the time he gets to the end of it, she's furious, her eyes wide with rage. The journalist behind the story comes to the door to ask for a response. He's the guy from the footpath three days ago, the one with the snapper and the manicured nails. The mother makes a scene, all of which we film. Her partner asks the journalist to go away and come back later.

Now the mother is working on a response to the piece in the paper. Her partner is writing down her words. It's rambling and garbled and full of serious accusations directed at her own mum and dad. When they're finished, she shows it to me and asks me what I think.

There aren't really any rules in documentary-making as such, whatever academics and moralists say. The strength of documentary as an art form is that it's so flexible. It's forever being adapted and reinvented. My advice would be not to listen if someone tries to lecture you on documentary dos and don'ts. You do what's appropriate and necessary to tell the story that's in front of you. But there's one principle that I've always tried to stick to, especially when the story is a sensitive one, with important stuff at stake: don't become involved.

Care, of course. Sympathize. You have to do that. But don't get mixed up in events.

The events in this case are front-page news, and have been for weeks. Every evening the broadcaster has got me reporting back to a team of lawyers, who scrutinize every decision I make to ensure I do nothing wrong. Imagine if some small thing were to impede the investigation, or assist the people who took the girl, or result in her being lost forever. So their advice, underlined every evening, is to observe and nothing more.

But the page they've written is incendiary stuff. And now the journalist is back at the door.

He reads the page and I swear his eyes light up. This is dynamite, he's thinking. A family feud.

The camera is still rolling.

He says, 'Great, thank you', and turns to go, but the mother tells him to wait. And then she asks me again for my opinion.

I think the journalist is scum. I think these poor people don't stand a chance against people like him. I think a social worker should be here to help them.

I consider asking Luke to cut the camera, but decide against it. Saying whatever it is I'm about to say – and I still haven't settled on what that will be – on camera might be safer. My own record of what happened, in case things turn nasty.

It's been quite a long pause now.

I take the page, and look at the childish writing. I say, 'I wouldn't give him this if I were you. Nothing good will come of it. I think you should focus on what really matters.'

The mother nods and smiles, and folds up the page and puts it away. The journalist scowls and wants to know my name. Her partner shows him to the door.

The mother looks delighted. Someone's on her side.

Outside, the journalist is talking to a group of other reporters.

Luke puts down the camera to change a tape. He says nothing but looks my way. His face says You're in charge, but that was a mistake.

May 19

It's early evening. The light is beginning to fade. A march is about to start around the neighbourhood, organized by community leaders tired of the way locals have been portrayed. As scroungers and layabouts, one of the leaders says to me. 'We're not bad people. We just don't have any money.' Their placards and banners say 'Find This Girl'.

They set off and it starts to rain. News crews line the route, men in suits brightly lit and reporting live as the procession slowly files past. We're at the centre of it, behind the mother of the girl, cradling her baby, and her partner with the rest of the kids. It's a moving and dignified event.

I spent the whole day with them again today. There was a constant stream of neighbours and well-wishers asking if the family needed anything. And a visit from the police, updating them on the search. It has become the biggest manhunt since the days when Britain's most notorious serial killer was at large, several decades ago now.

The kids ran around and wanted to be fed and played with. Life goes on, especially when small children are involved. We chatted about how fast they grow up, and how they're doing in school. I helped the oldest kid with his homework, and read the rest of them a story.

'You're a natural', the mother said.

In the afternoon, she asked me for help moving an old wardrobe from the house of a relative to their own. I couldn't see any reason why not. We have a van that's mostly parked up doing nothing. She was pleased with the wardrobe, and gave us tea and biscuits to say thanks.

She seemed optimistic then. Now, in the half-light, in the midst of the sombre march, all trace of that is gone. Her eyes are dark red and sunken. It feels like we're part of a funeral procession.

Surely we soon will be.

May 20

Today I was supposed to be at a wedding. It completely slipped my mind, until a phone call first thing asking where I was.

Luke, my cameraman, has gone back to London. He had an excuse, but a weak one, and couldn't look me in the eye. He hated it here, more and more every day.

A replacement has arrived, and we go together to the house. But there's a problem. The family are inside, but no one comes to the door.

We walk slowly back to the van. The journalist from the other day smiles and nods his head. The family are not picking up their phone either. I don't understand what's happening.

I call up a writer I know on a local paper. We've helped each other out in the past. He's much more likeable than the journalists up from London. He grew up just a few streets from here. He knows this place and the people well.

We meet at the covered market in the centre of the town, and buy tea from a lady in a hatch.

He says that something is going on for sure, but as yet he doesn't know what. The police have gone quiet too.

Back at the house, we're on the street with the rest of the press, filming nothing in particular. On the outside now, looking in.

May 21

I'm out with the new cameraman on the hills above the street where the family live, filming wides. It's a harsh, dramatic landscape. Out there somewhere is the missing girl.

Early this morning, her mother appealed again for information, then walked her kids to school. Photographers and cameramen followed every step. Us too, at a distance, filming the filmers as well as the woman herself. I wondered how and when it will end, this frenzy of attention. Whether it will fade and fizzle. Or if one day everyone will leave en masse, moving on to the next sensational story.

The clouds are racing. It's a blustery day. Half the sky is full of rain and half the sky is blue.

My phone rings. It's the writer from the local paper. Come quick, he says. You won't believe it.

The wind changes and blows up towards us. I can hear shouting and cheering from the street below.

We arrive, camera rolling, struggling to make sense of it all.

Outside the house, there's a huge celebration. People are smiling and dancing in the street. People are hugging and crying.

A neighbour comes up to us. I ask him what's going on.

'She's been found', he says, again and again.

He looks entirely shell-shocked.

'The best news', he says. 'The *best* news. The little girl's been found.'

But the mother and the rest of the family are nowhere to be seen.

May 22

This morning the street is deserted. The news trucks and vans have all gone.

It's blowy still, and discarded home-made posters featuring the little girl's face and a number to call are whirling about and taking flight. We film it, because there's nothing else to do.

The family's house is quiet and still, but their neighbour is sitting out front on her doorstep. She's wearing a thick towelling robe and drinking from a mug that says World's Best Mum.

She's looking off up the street, to the hills and the clouds and the sun.

I ask if we can talk to her on camera, and she nods. There's no need for questions. Speaking softly, she says what's on her mind. All the chaos and the questions and the searches, all the stuff the police stirred up and all the stuff in the papers, had made her think hard about this place. What sort of people she lives amongst. What sort of person she is herself, and how she's raising her children.

But people pulled together, like they always do.

She heard someone on the radio say there's nowhere worse for a child to live. Now she thinks there's nowhere better.

I ask if she knows where the mum and the girl are now, and she shakes her head. She hasn't spoken to them either.

I need to, I think, to finish off the story.

But there's a message from the commissioner. The channel wants to rush the film to air. 'What an astonishing story!' he says. 'What an amazing twist!'

The girl who was found. Ten days at the eye of a storm. What the people concerned were really thinking. And how it really felt.

They've already scheduled it, for transmission in just four days.

A car is already on the way, to bring me and the rushes back to London.

May 24

Ordinarily an hour-long film gets seven weeks of editing – six weeks to put the story together, and a week to polish and finish it off.

That's about 50 days in total.

Compressing that work into *four* days requires extraordinary measures. Today is day two.

Four cutting rooms are running simultaneously, around the clock on 12-hour shifts, so not a single minute gets wasted. I spend my time shuttling from one to the next, directing the editors to the best and most interesting moments, and writing commentary to make sense of it all.

There's no time to go home, or even to a hotel. My cutting rooms are in the basement of a big West End post-production house. They don't have windows, so it's hard to know what time of day it is. I've been napping on the sofas in reception, and drinking gallons and gallons of coffee. It's hard to think of anything but the film.

Mills arrives to help run things. We find a cutting room that's not being used, and sit down to discuss what needs to be done. All sorts of legal processes need to be followed, and clearances sought for the archive footage I'd like to use. We need to arrange a voice-over artist to read the narration, and put together a list of credits. Now she's here I feel very much better. The room is cool and still. The big leather sofa we're sitting on is swallowing me, slowly. I can feel the lights going out in my brain.

But there's a phone call.

It's the police, with a single question they'd like to ask me.

'You helped the family move a wardrobe, is that right? Can I ask you, sir, was there anything about it that struck you as strange?'

May 26

It's 9.15 pm. The film is on air, right now.

The last 12 hours or so have been nothing but a blur. Hundreds of questions and decisions, faster and faster as the time went by, till finally we ran off a tape and the thing was finished.

There's a party down the road for everyone who worked on the project – all the editors and runners, the loggers and transcribers, the production managers and the channel execs.

I'm in the suite where the last few checks were made, just a couple of hours ago. It's silent now, except for the buzz of the decks and the air-conditioning. I'd like to leave but I can't think of anywhere to go, and it's an effort just to sip my drink. My body feels like it's made out of marble.

I've thought of nothing else but this film for 16 days now. But at the same time, I don't feel like I've really thought about it properly at all. All the oddness and loose ends, and what the whole thing means.

My phone is chirping so I turn it off.

I'll find a place to stay in town tonight, and use a fake name to check in. Nobody will be looking for me now the film's finished, but that's not really the point. I'm tired of other people's voices, and my own. Tired of the sound of my thoughts. For the next several hours, I don't want to even exist.

May 27

I slept ten hours without stirring, and woke with my body aching.

I take a long shower and pad about the room for a while. I don't have any plans. Soon I'll need to get back to the things I've ignored and neglected. But not yet. Maybe I'll walk to Mayfair for an old-fashioned breakfast. Maybe I'll ask Mills if she wants to come too.

There are 23 messages on my phone.

The first 15 are from last night. Well done and congratulations. Most are polite and dutiful, from friends and people I work with. Two or three are from people I respect and admire, directors and executives at other companies who wouldn't say nice things unless they really meant them. This feels good.

The rest are from this morning.

The ones from this morning are all short and to the point. They all say a version of the same thing. Essentially, 'Jesus Christ, have you seen the news?'

The big old TV in the room has only seven channels. Breakfast shows are still playing on the main ones. The rest are devoted to news. All of them are preoccupied with the same single subject.

The missing girl was never really missing. Several arrests have been made, including the girl's own mum.

May 28

The messages and phone calls came thick and fast for the rest of the day. The police wanted to view all my rushes. The channel wanted a meeting, to help them devise a response. Charlie wanted to know what fresh fuckstorm was this that I'd brewed. Mills wanted to know if I was feeling okay. I ignored them all.

I rented a car and got straight back on the motorway, surfing radio stations for news bulletins to try to make sense of it all.

How could I possibly have missed such a gargantuan lie?

The girl had been kept in a house just two miles away from her home, by a relative in cahoots with her mum. Analysis of the girl's hair suggests she'd been heavily sedated, and it looks as though she'd been restrained.

It was mid-afternoon when I arrived back on the street. A policeman was standing guard outside the girl's house, the door sealed off with yellow and black tape marked 'Crime Scene, Do Not Cross'.

The press were being held at the far end of the street, away from the police's comings and goings. They were restive and noisy, impatient for news.

I parked up and hung around for a while without learning anything new, and then went down a side street to the corner shop. It had been a day and a half since I'd eaten, and suddenly I felt famished.

The guy from the other day was there, the one who told me the girl had been found. I said hello and asked him what on earth had happened. He lunged forwards, suddenly, like he'd tripped, and swung a big clumsy punch my way. The shopkeeper came out from behind his counter and put his arms on top of the guy's in a bear hug, to restrain him. But there was no need for restraint. There was never any fight in him, and he wilted in the shopkeeper's arms, like a small boy being cuddled.

Now it's very late. Another day in fact. Most of the press have given up and gone back to their hotels. Most of the lights on the street are out.

But not at the house next door.

The neighbour lets me in, still in the same thick towelling robe, and I follow her through to the kitchen. She's a kind and sensitive woman. She knows why I'm here. Not for news, but for answers.

She looks dazed and worn out. Broken. She put her life on hold to lend support, she says. Gave all her savings to the campaign. Sat up night after night talking and crying with the little girl's mum.

Why? The little girl's mum, I mean? Why did she do it?

The neighbour shakes her head. For money. To claim the reward for finding her. And then the reward kept climbing.

Then the police were everywhere, and the newspapers came and stayed. Then there was no way out.

I say, 'She fooled me completely.' But I'm worried that she didn't really. Maybe I just ignored the signs, too wrapped up in the brave and honest film I wanted to make to notice what was really happening.

'She fooled herself', she says. 'As in believed her own lies. Really believed that her daughter was missing. Really believed she might never come home.'

Now her daughter never will. She's been placed in care, along with the rest of her kids.

The woman herself is in prison, and probably will be for some time to come.

'It was a good thing you tried to do', the neighbour says, and puts her hand on mine.

May 29

It's a bright blue morning in a park near Mills' flat. We're drinking instant coffee out of polystyrene cups, sitting on the grass and leaning back against a tree that's coming into leaf.

Last night, as I drove back to London, we talked for hours on the phone. Actually not talking so much as hanging out, keeping me company as the miles slipped by. In the end I think she fell asleep.

This morning there's not much left to say, but there's no need to speak. The silence is easy-going. Perhaps everything will be okay.

Two young mothers are sitting on a bench on the other side of the park. One baby is sleeping. The other is in his mother's arms, looking up at her, full of love. Then one of the women starts to cry. They hug each other tightly, and then one of them says something funny and they both laugh. They're laughing and crying at the same time. Exhausted probably. Overwhelmed with it all.

Mills says there's never been a documentary about people in parks. But good stuff happens in parks. Important stuff.

So maybe we rig up a park somehow and film ordinary people, living those important moments?

Kids and the dad they only see at weekends. Old people remembering things. Friends discussing their problems. Couples falling in love. People talking honestly. But mostly not speaking at all.

'It's the opposite here to people in their cars', Mills says. 'People come here to just be.'

'So maybe we could film that?' she says. 'The stuff that's between people, that doesn't need to be said. Stuff that's there, if you look. Obvious even.'

No one will ever commission this, but they really should.

Mills says, 'Let's develop it anyway.'

New ideas always make things better. The start of something new.

People come and go in the park, and we try to guess who they are and what's happening in their lives.

Mills says that everything *will* be okay, as though she's reading my mind. People aren't really so bad.

May 30

Through work, I've met many people *in extremis*. People dealing with loss and despair. People coming up short. People facing ruin. I used to think that each encounter taught me a little more about the human condition.

I'm back in the office today, comforted by familiar rituals. A big pot of coffee and the papers. People arriving one by one.

'What did you learn?' Charlie says.

I'm really not sure.

I feel numb, mostly. And when I'm not numb, ashamed.

CHAPTER SIX:
JUNE

June 2

I collect facts from day to day – arresting pieces of information that might some day serve as sources of inspiration. Today I've spent hours combing through them.

There are 1000 missing Picassos. 3000 people go missing in the UK every year. Most of the tigers in the world are privately owned. There are 6.5 billion 1p coins missing and not in circulation. A government report into domestic accidents has revealed that 3000 people a year in the UK go to hospital after falling over laundry baskets and 2000 after running into tree trunks, 13,000 people are wounded whilst peeling vegetables, and 10,000 are injured in the act of putting on socks. On Good Friday 1930, the BBC cancelled its evening news bulletin, on the basis that nothing in the world had happened that day. They showed a piano recital instead.

I feel listless and exhausted. A whole day of foggy-minded pondering has produced nothing of use or value.

It's dark now. I'm sitting in my study, feeling invisible. I never got round to putting up blinds, so with the lights off and the windows open, I can see into the flats across the road. There's a young couple making dinner and arguing, as they often do. I hope they work things out. Two guys, labourers, still in their work clothes, are sharing a pack of beers from the shop downstairs. They look exhausted and sad. There's a nice, professional-looking lady I sometimes say hello to, in bed alone, reading a novel with a glass of wine. And a guy my age is trying and failing to put a wide-awake toddler to bed. There's never a woman. I wonder what happened.

There's a text, from Mills. Just two words: 'You okay?'

A moment later, there's another. But this one's not from Mills.

The sender calls himself You Know Who.

The text says, 'I know about Monroe'.

Last year I spent two days at a big council tip in west London, fascinated by what people throw away, thinking there might be a film in it – the story of the way we live and the things we care about, told through the things we discard. There were couples moving in together and shedding possessions, and couples parting and doing the same. There were families clearing the houses of dead relatives, or preparing to move elderly ones into nursing homes, flinging boxes of mementoes and trinkets into the void. And ashen-faced parents, finally letting go of their children's childhoods, depositing boxes of forgotten toys. All of them quietly living their lives, like the people in the flats opposite. All with some sort of story to tell. None of the stories large enough to be worth putting on TV.

Another text from Mills. Three words this time: 'Fuck you then'.

At the tip I saw a man in pinky-red trousers throw away a magnificent throne-like chair. When no one was looking, I climbed into the dumpster and rescued it. I'm sitting in it now. The upholstery – silk I think – is stained, torn and worn thin. The varnish is chipped, the legs grazed or maybe gnawed. It's been restored who knows how many times. Who knows how many people have sat in it and talked, read letters and remembered things? And then, finally, it was abandoned. When I sit in it, trying to think of ideas, I imagine summoning the spirits of all the people who ever sat in it also.

I wish they'd help me tonight. I need some renewal and refreshment, to start up some new projects, if only to get myself back on my feet.

One more text from Mills: 'I hope that you're okay'.

All day, through the white noise of fruitless thinking, one clear notion has recurred. What if I've already had all of my ideas? What if I never have another?

June 3

I'm on the Overground, heading to work, looking down on the streets and the houses. Everything looks slightly different today.

I text back to You Know Who: 'You have the wrong number I think'.

The reply comes through before my phone is back in my pocket. It says, 'I think not'.

I type back, 'I don't know what you mean'.

You Know Who says, 'I think you do'.

June 4

When I was a boy I used to play a computer game, the aim of which was to build your own virtual city. You'd begin with just a couple of huts. Then you add a well, and start growing crops. Then other huts spring up, and you add a market, a smithy and a school. Before long, you're building aqueducts and fountains, temples and libraries. If you stick at it long enough, your city might look like Manhattan.

It helped me through a long summer of exams one year. I played the game to relax and let my mind unwind. Its USP was that you couldn't pause it. The city remained alive, even whilst you were absent, which made it perfect to come back to for a break in endless revision; you'd see how your choices and decisions had played out, and then have a chance to respond.

By the end of the exams, my city was a gleaming metropolis, vast and efficient. Then I went on holiday. When I came back the city was in ruins.

This is what my slate felt like this morning – the fruits of so much careful cultivation, now crumbling and fallen, choked and overrun, slowly returning to a natural state of chaos.

The editor we'd lined up for the car taster has taken a job elsewhere. The contributors feel in-the-dark and angry at the lack of contact. The lady from the ring shop has left a message: she's assuming that the project is dead. Everything has stalled.

Momentum is so important in developing ideas. Once it's lost, you can huff and puff for months and never get a project moving again. It feels infinitely more appealing to start again from scratch, despite the challenges that entails. But the grown-up thing is not to moan and shirk; rather, stick with it and reinvest. I'm not good at grown-up things, but Mills is here, calm and reassuring, patiently making a plan.

The commissioner for the posh family series calls, asking for an update. I tell her it's all going swimmingly.

June 5

Several years ago I made a film about a much-loved celebrity. He was, at different times, a comedian, actor and singer, but tended to call himself 'an all-round entertainer'. He was on TV all the time when I was a kid and, unlike most famous faces from that era, he never went away. Now he's a national treasure.

The secret of his longevity lay in the fact that he never had an act, as such. He was really just himself – down-to-earth and brash, somehow both ordinary and larger than life. He seemed always to say and do exactly what he wanted, a super-confident, perma-tanned rascal, shirt undone four buttons down, barrel chest covered in bright white hair.

Success came early, and his lifestyle was flamboyant from the start, a working-class fantasy of champagne and oysters for dinner, a villa in Marbella and a gloriously vulgar bright red Rolls. By the time I met him he'd been married three times to women who all looked the same. They were always there in the background, smiling, never speaking, referred to not by name but as 'the old ball and chain'. As he got older he'd quietly trade them in, so that the woman by his side seemed miraculously ageless.

He'd been filmed without his knowledge doing an after-dinner speech. The speech was peppered with references to 'the gays' and the 'the blacks'. A torrent of criticism followed. He apologized profusely without appearing to mean it.

I approached him as the criticism reached its peak. I wanted to make a film about the passing of a certain age, and the passing of a certain sort of man. I asked if I could follow him about with a camera. To my amazement he agreed.

His name was Ray Monroe.

My thinking was that a comedian would be a good subject for a film about changing times because comedy relies on a common set of assumptions, and it seemed to me that finally, after 30-odd years of success, the assumptions Monroe relied upon could be relied upon no more.

We spent five or six months together, and out of it came a film that was funny, insightful and sad. It was watched in huge numbers and went on to win more than one award. Monroe came on stage with me to collect the most prestigious one, pretending to trip on his way up the stairs. He took the mic – no question in his mind who'd be giving the speech – and gently mocked the pomposity of the occasion whilst appearing genuinely humbled to be there. He joked about his agent, which got big laughs, and rounded it off with a heartfelt plea for forgiveness and courtly little bow. He turned and put his hand on my shoulder in a way which clearly said 'trust me son, you've got nothing to add', and steered me off the stage, waving, the audience cheering wildly, completely under his spell.

There's a new message from You Know Who.

'Here's the deal', it says. 'You tell me everything you know about Monroe – everything, on the record – or the story becomes about you.'

Only journalists worry about things being on or off the record.

The journalist from the Brightwell Estate, whose scoop I managed to ruin. The one with the manicured fingernails.

'If we can't fill the paper with stories about the family', he said that day, 'we'll have no choice but to look elsewhere'.

Now he's back, as good as his word.

June 7

TV is full of clever and creative people. Entertaining audiences and making them think is a good way to spend your working life. You're involved in what's going on in the world. You're part of the cultural conversation. But as a medium TV is here today and gone tomorrow. The film that you spent a year making exists for barely an hour and then is gone for good. Tomorrow, everyone will be watching something else.

Past a certain age, perhaps having made a certain amount of money, you start thinking about your legacy. About how people will think of you when you're gone.

The truth is that they won't.

Most TV careers dwindle out. Look back at the names of the directors and producers who won Baftas or Emmys 20 years ago, and you won't recognize any. Almost all of those people, so relevant and central then, have left the industry now, their considerable achievements part of television history, mostly of interest to academics.

But two or three names from each passing generation of TV producers do linger on. The guy who made the first ever reality TV show back in the 1970s, a fly-on-the-wall series about a working-class family, that told the truth about their lives. Each episode was the story of what had happened that very week, an amazing achievement at a time when films were literally cut together, with scissors. Or the guy in the 1980s who made a documentary series with and about the police that was so honest and raw that it led to changes in the law.

What these people have in common isn't their cleverness, though all of them undoubtedly were. Or their boldness or vision, their charm or skills at self-promotion. It's the simple fact they made a show that people loved to watch.

It's amazing how few of these shows there are, when you consider how much TV gets made every year. And this is because most TV sits on a spectrum that runs from ordinary to disappointing. It's primarily a way of passing the time. The shows that people genuinely love somehow emerge out of this, through an elusive and perhaps unrepeatable combination of luck, timing, rising talent and lots of other factors. Usually not even the people who made them know how to do it again.

I don't think you can set out to make a show like this. But you can respond accordingly when the vague chance of doing so presents itself. You need to seize that opportunity. You need to do what needs to be done.

Lord and Lady Delamain and their kids could be the basis of such a show, I think. Something to be remembered by.

June 10

One day I will be old, I suppose. But I can't imagine ever being as old as the people in the room I'm in right now. They smell of soap and meat, and their dusty clothes and paleness make them look like a gathering of ghosts.

It's cosy and serene here, though, and I can't help wishing to be part of it. I envy these old men their sense of belonging, and their ease in each other's company. So much at ease, in fact, that some of them are sleeping.

I'm not part of it. Not at all. But I'm trying to look like I might be. I came in my fustiest clothes, and I'm pouring a drink from a decanter on a trolley in the middle of the room. Nothing makes you look so at home and self-assured as helping yourself to a nice big glass of something.

The room is the library of a gentleman's club in the wealthiest part of London. It's a place of perennial fascination, because it's a closed and mysterious world. Every decade or two, it finds itself back in the headlines, when someone proposes that women be admitted. The rest of the members are forced to rise from their leather armchairs to defend tradition and see off the threat. If we admitted women, they say, we wouldn't be able to relax. We'd have to sit up straight at lunch, stand when a lady leaves or arrives, and mind our Ps and Qs. The vote won, they sink back into their armchairs, safe for another few years, as the rest of the nation tuts and shakes its head.

I wrote to the secretary to ask if the club might consider collaborating on a documentary, to give the members' side of the story. What do rich old men get out of spending time in one another's company? What are they taking refuge from, in the hushed, wood-panelled rooms of the club? What do they make of the modern world?

The film would be fair, I said. I even hinted that it would be more than fair. That they'd like the film. I suggested that I was on their side.

You'd never do this ordinarily, of course. Documentaries should be balanced; film-makers cool and impartial. I could afford to make promises on this occasion, because I have no intention whatsoever of making a film about the club.

I've been hanging around and asking questions, which the members have found vexing – even laughably inoffensive ones, designed to disguise my true purpose in being here. I suppose the point of this place is that no questions need to be asked – it is what it is and always has been, unlike the rest of the world, where everything is subject to question and nothing stays the same.

The members of the club are former politicians and diplomats, judges, military men and professors of this and that. A rich, entitled tribe. Among them, one Henry Albert Cecil Montague IV, Lord Delamain of Somerset.

I'm pouring myself another drink, and starting to relax. An old man with white hair to his collar gets up to do the same. He looks like a teenager in old-man disguise. His face is impish and his eyes are twinkly.

He says, 'Why are you really here?'

I set about telling my story again. I've repeated it so often today it's starting to sound convincing. But he shakes his head and interrupts: 'I think you've come to cause trouble.'

I protest, but he shakes his head again and says in a loud stage whisper, 'It's okay, young man; me too!'

So we sit in the corner and talk. His name is Frederick Bingham. He likes you to call him Bing. He's the one who keeps proposing female members, mainly, I suspect, out of mischief.

Now he's leading me through the club as his guest, up an elegant staircase and down a squeaking corridor to a colonial-style bar full of plants, huge mirrors and frowning portraits.

Fans are turning slowly on the ceiling. There's a breeze from a set of French windows. And buried in a book, with papers spread all around him, is Lord Delamain, looking like it's 1865.

'Ahhh', he says, as though he's been expecting me.

He offers me a drink – gin, the same as him – and I tell him why I've come here, to persuade him to let me put his home and family on TV.

'But discussing business is against house rules', he says. 'This is a temple of philosophy and thought. So what is your philosophy, young man? What are you about?'

I start to tell him that I have none. His face says 'Come now, you can do better.'

I can't think of anything clever to say, so I end up telling the truth – that I believe we were put on this earth to explore and do interesting things. That one should always take up an opportunity or invitation to do something of interest. That it's more important to be interesting than it is to be good, not least because people will forgive you for being bad so long as you've been bad in an interesting way.

'What of the world's great faiths?' he says, with a flourish. 'What of the world's great thinkers?'

'I don't care what other people believe. So long as it doesn't make them dull.'

'Harrr', he says, nodding, then tells me at some length about the book he's writing, about a nineteenth-century sea captain, explorer and drawer of maps. A relative, of course, fingers in all manner of pies.

'You'd have been a good Victorian yourself', he says.

Then he announces he'll have to be going. He collects his hat and is gone, as the bar steward hands me the bill.

June 12

These days, there's only one place to get a single roll of exposed Super 8 film processed professionally. And professionally isn't really the word. You send your film off to a guy in Germany, who develops it in his bathtub. I've heard of rolls gone missing, wiped negatives and developed film so dark and blurry that it could be footage of almost anything.

Today my reel came back in the post.

Now I'm threading it into a projector my granny left me in her will. She used to shoot Super 8 of my sister and me when we were very small.

The film shows six young men in dinner dress, standing on some steps, smirking. Then it flickers and glows, and they're standing in a circle, shoving a terrified girl back and forth, groping her breasts. One of them puts his hand up her skirt. The girl's eyes open wide in shock, and the young man's eyes narrow, lasciviously. Then the film glows again, and all six young men are seen smashing up a dining room.

In the midst of it all is a man we've suddenly all become familiar with. The events depicted happened more than 30 years ago, but he's unmistakeable, a good three or four inches taller than the rest, and handsome, with a thin and cruel-looking mouth. He became an MP just last year, having increased his already-substantial fortune in the city. Now he's a leading figure in the party he represents. Sometime soon, I'm sure he'll be running the country. In the footage, he looks as though he always knew that would happen.

It's no secret that he was part of a notorious dining club at university. But seeing it in action is a different matter. The sense of superiority and untouchability is appalling.

The camera pushes in to the tall young man. He tips back his head and empties a bottle of red wine into his mouth and over his face and hair. He looks into the lens, monstrous, silently roaring in triumph. Then the image burns yellow and gold, the projector whirrs, and the film runs out.

June 13

I'm juggling two coffees – black for me, and the other frothy with chocolate on top – and peering at a map drawn on a napkin in the murky orange glow of a street light. I'm trying to find an address on a side road. The man in the coffee shop thought I'd struggle: a towering grey warehouse, he said, unmissable in the daytime, invisible at night.

It's late. There are no passers-by to help.

The road bends and dips, and then, suddenly, there's no need for help or the map. A dozen police cars and vans are bunched together tightly, their light bars flashing a silent howl, casting everything blue and black. Pale faces are peering from the windows opposite. One or two bolder locals are standing in the street and staring. I've found the place I'm looking for.

Outside the warehouse, the police are busy. They're tired and preoccupied, heads down, following protocol and filling in forms. Some are starting to pack up.

I'm wearing an old suit and a proper pair of shoes, as DC Lockwood said I should.

She takes her coffee without a word and holds up the strip of blue and yellow police tape outside the warehouse. I duck underneath and follow her in.

The warehouse has been converted into flats. The one on the top floor is a vast open space with double-height ceilings. There's barely any furniture. No photographs or books. Not much of anything at all, in fact. But still it's a terrible mess, ransacked so thoroughly it looks like the building has been lifted up and shaken.

Neatly taped to the back of a giant piece of art – a blown-up frame from a superhero comic – the police have found plans and photographs of a safe-deposit facility. The one that was robbed in the spring.

And in the centre of the room, a big black stain on a huge white rug, gaping like an opening to the underworld.

Outside, DC Lockwood says, 'The item I told you about that day on the phone – the item we're assuming the depository heist was staged to obtain – it seems that other people want it as well. May now have it, in fact.'

'There are lots of interested parties', she says: 'The police, the people who killed the guy in the flat, who was presumably one of the thieves who stole it, and the rest of the thieves who stole it, who are either going to want it back or be extra-determined to hang on to it, depending on what happened here today. And you, of course.'

She pauses and looks at me intently, her face blinking on and off, black and blue.

'Have you made enquiries of your own?' she says.

It's something they teach trainee police officers, I think: the value of a good long stare.

I look back and say nothing.

'Do you know what it is?' she says. 'The item? Do you know what they were looking for?'

Now it's my turn to use a searching look.

'Do *you* know?' I ask her.

Then it's her turn to say nothing, and we each take a sip of coffee.

June 15

I'm in a launderette, feeling calm for the first time in what feels like weeks. People are quietly attending to their washing, or reading books and magazines while the machines churn and spin. I've been walking since breakfast, trying to have an idea, or at least find a place where having an idea feels possible. I'm perfectly well, but I feel like I'm coming down with something. My bones ache but I can't stay still.

It's not just a lack of inspiration that makes me feel this way. It goes much deeper than that. It's a sense that I've had my hands on something priceless and somehow mislaid it. A perfect, flawless, idea. Finding it again doesn't seem possible. But at the same time, finding it is absolutely all that matters, to the extent that having ideas which are merely acceptable doesn't seem possible either. It feels like I've forgotten how to think.

The feeling comes upon me every few months, and is torture every time. It's never been this bad before, though. If I could, I'd disappear.

Some people's minds are immaculate factory floors, everything in its proper place, everything ticking over, calmly supervised, smoothly efficient. Mine is like an ancient junk shop, full of broken bits of stuff, crammed into tiny, warren-like rooms. There's no organization to it at all. There's no system. It's not even clear why it exists. Thoughts and ideas have been dumped wherever there happened to be space at the time. The torturous feeling is that somewhere in one of those junk-filled rooms is a masterpiece, or a once-mocked invention whose time has finally come.

So I walk about aimlessly, feeling better for being on the move, trying to find my way back to the room in my mind that might contain the misplaced treasure.

Over the years I've found myself in all sorts of places. A waiting room at a train station, amidst all the daydreams, and the comings and goings, and the little human dramas. A field of council allotments, things hissing as they sprouted and grew. Places that somehow help open rooms that I'd forgotten about. Then time slips away while I root around.

Today, the mechanical sounds of the laundrette and the oddly studious atmosphere seem to be helping. The ache is slowly receding.

I'm pottering around the junk shop now, picking things up and putting them down. I can feel my thoughts getting clearer, possibilities taking shape.

A new message comes through, from You Know Who.

'I'm waiting', it says. 'Do not ignore this. This will not go away.'

June 16

Today has been very hot. I'm sitting in a stuffy waiting room with half a dozen other people. We're here for an interview. Every one of us wants the job.

'Why do you want to be a cleaner?' the interviewer asks.

I tell her it's because I'm heading back to university, to finish a course I dropped out of aged 19. I want to pay my own way. I want a physical job with not much responsibility, a simple set of tasks that I can do well and then go home. And I want to work in the evenings, to give me the days to study. And I just broke up with my girlfriend. I don't want to be alone in my flat, thinking of how things used to be. I really miss her. She was beautiful and special.

The interviewer didn't look convinced through most of that, but she smiled at the last bit. That's the bit that got me the job.

The real reason I want the job is because bankers – specifically young bankers – are very much in the news. They ruined the national economy. They took greedy and foolish risks. They're the reason the rest of us are struggling to pay our bills. But still they're paid huge salaries, and take bonuses every year worth hundreds of millions.

Who are these young bankers, already rich in their early twenties? What motivates them? What do they believe in? And above all, what would it take to get them to take part in a documentary?

They're hard to reach, suspicious of the media and protected by the banks that employ them. We've tried approaching them in swanky bars, and been immediately asked to leave.

So I'm trying a subtler approach. For the rest of the month, I'll be cleaning the offices of one of London's biggest banks. I'll be handing my earnings over to a cleaner already at the agency, in exchange for advice and information. He's taking the month off to visit his family in Lagos. I paid for his ticket.

June 17

Charlie has asked us all to gather in the meeting room.

'This is Sam MacLean', he says. 'He's a brilliant ideas man. And he's coming to work with us. Here's to more commissions!'

I don't know anything about this guy.

His hands are smooth and free of calluses, but his handshake is firm and manly.

He's clean-shaven and he's wearing grown-up, polished shoes. And he smiles a lot, without detracting from an air of education and authority. The production manager who instantly disliked me when I started has taken an instant shine to him.

He's calm and self-possessed. I doubt very much that he spent last night pretending to be someone else.

In TV, companies only make hirings when they've got a problem. If you want a job, you have to figure out what the problem is and offer a solution. At the moment, the problem at our company is me.

June 18

A number of rumours about Ray Monroe have surfaced since I made my film about him. Lurid ones, in the main. Tales of parties at his house in the '70s and '80s. Stories of girls brought to his dressing room, arriving full of excitement, leaving full of tears.

A new rumour has emerged in the last few days, about a nightclub Monroe used to frequent, run by a close friend who is also the subject of much gossip and speculation. It's suggested that Monroe would arrive at the club in his big red Rolls, pick a girl, bombard her with flattery, drinks and promises, then offer to drive her home. Home being generally her mum and dad's house, because mostly the girls were still at school. The rest you can imagine.

Today Monroe's lawyer has called a press conference. He's a round-bellied, confident man in a boxy light brown suit, his hair slicked back, a sheen of sweat on his brow. A man from the same era as Monroe. A man cut from similar cloth. I'm watching him on TV.

He shushes the journalists packed inside the conference room, and looks around waiting for silence. 'Mr Monroe categorically denies the rumours and allegations made against him', he says. 'They contain no truth whatsoever. Mr Monroe will not be commenting further at this time.' Then he turns and leaves amid the clatter of a hundred shutter releases and a roar of unanswered questions.

One day, during filming, I turned up to Monroe's mansion unannounced. He came to the door looking flustered and dishevelled. More than dishevelled. Distorted, somehow, like he'd hurriedly put on a wig. It hinted at a less brash and bullish figure, someone vulnerable and vain. Other hints followed, but nothing I managed to catch on camera. Monroe never stopped performing. The material I was gathering was great. It was funny and heartfelt. But by the end of our time together, it seemed to me that a whole layer of the film might be missing. I worried it would feel like a failure. So I asked Monroe if I could shoot some footage of him relaxing with some friends. No researchers or producers or crew. Just me and a little handy-cam. An intimate affair. Would he perform less with close friends? Or would he perform more? I thought either would be revealing.

He invited me to a house party thrown by one of his oldest friends. It was uncomfortable from the beginning. He turned up tipsy, and made a beeline for his friend's youngest daughter, who I learned was just 15. He talked about how grown-up she'd got, enquired about boyfriends, and asked her to sit on his knee, which she did, bright red with shame. Her father was deeply awkward all night, fawning on his famous friend, avoiding the eye of his wife. The couple rowed quietly in the kitchen. I stood in the corner and filmed everything that happened.

I took a break for a bite to eat, and then couldn't find Monroe. I caught a glimpse of the girl, though, her eyes pink and swollen, her mother leading her off to bed, furious and protective, her father a picture of impotence, pathetically unsure where his priorities lay. Then Monroe reappeared and announced that he wanted to leave. We drove home in silence, Monroe in the back with a bottle of Scotch, me at the wheel of his ludicrous car, acting like his chauffeur.

We arrived at his house and I opened the door, but he didn't get out of his seat. He sat for a moment, eyes dead ahead, then said, 'It's a weakness. I've battled it all my life.'

I picked up my camera – openly, not surreptitiously – and Monroe proceeded to confess. To 'behaviour he wasn't proud of'. To a predilection for young women.

'Girls', he said, correcting himself.

He asked me not to judge him too harshly. It was fine when he was in his twenties, he said. He was pretty open about things then. Less so into his thirties and forties. At the time of filming, he was 65.

I asked him 'How do you feel?' The one question documentary-makers couldn't live without. The most important thing, always. Especially in moments like this.

He deliberately misunderstood and told me he felt fine. Emotions weren't up for discussion.

'How many?' I said.

'Too many … Too many to count.'

He was very drunk but entirely lucid, in the way only heavy drinkers can be. He didn't mention it the next day and we carried on filming. A few days later I asked him, can we talk about the things you said that night in the car? He claimed he couldn't recall very much at all about that particular evening. That he couldn't hold his drink any more, the way he always used to.

So it's true I know a thing or two about Ray Monroe, as You Know Who suggests. The question is, how to respond?

Ten days after the party, we brought the film to a close. I shook Monroe's hand and thanked him, drove back to London, and handed over my tapes to be ingested for the edit.

Early the next day an assistant at the editing house called me.

'I'm so sorry', he said, 'but one of your tapes – tape 59 – appears to have gone missing.'

June 19

Mills said that today would be a mistake, and I ignored her.

A mum and dad, roughly the same age as me, are arguing. As they have been for several hours now. Arguing and then clinging on to each other, as though the world is ending.

Which, for the two of them, it is.

The room we're in is small and dark. The walls are bare and there's only one piece of furniture – a bed, upon which lies their son, caught between life and death.

You wouldn't know it to look at the boy. He appears to be sleeping peacefully. The various machines attached to his little body are steadily marking time. But he will never wake up. Earlier today, he ran into the road outside his house, and was hit by a speeding car.

I've been interested for a long time in organ donation. Removing the heart or lungs or liver from one person and putting them inside another are near-miraculous procedures that have become routine. The surgeons who perform them are practical people who are good with their hands. In their spare time they do DIY and restore old cars and motorbikes. They talk of transplant operations in terms of plumbing, but the levels of skill involved are mind-boggling.

It's not the medical dimension that fascinates me, though, so much as the questions of life and death the whole business raises. Seeing inside the human body – the heart muscle still pumping, the lungs rising and falling – makes you wonder what people are, fundamentally. What a person is. What it means to be alive.

The little boy is present, but he's also gone for good.

He's a candidate for a multi-organ donation. If donated, his tiny organs might save the lives of half a dozen other people.

In one hour's time, the doctors who have been looking after the boy will come back and ask his parents for their decision. If they agree to donate, the machines that are keeping his heart beating will be switched off. His organs will be gathered and rushed to critically ill recipients all over the country. Surgeons and couriers are standing by. The people at the top of the relevant transplant lists have been informed that tonight is possibly the night their transplant will finally happen.

A scene in a documentary might last two or three minutes. Maybe five minutes at the most. I have filmed every moment of the parents' deliberations, because there never seemed to be an appropriate time to put the camera down. Indeed it felt as though stopping filming might seem disrespectful, as though as I was somehow passing judgment; now your pain is less interesting than it was, so I'm going to pause and rest for a while. I was filming when they got into bed with their son, to cuddle him and say goodbye. And when being close to him broke their resolve, and the woman sank to the floor in utter despair, and the man fell to his knees beside her, and together they cried their hearts out.

Cameras are heavy, and I'm suddenly aware of my face being wet. I'm not sweating, though. If anything, the room feels cold. My face is wet because of tears of my own, shed without knowing it. I can honestly say that I haven't cried since I was a little boy. I remember the last time I did, and then deciding that I never would again. A girlfriend once said that she thought I was no longer able, or maybe had forgotten how. But here the intensity of the emotion is overwhelming.

We want to tell the story of a single multi-organ donation. Mills' feeling has always been that we should focus on the potential recipients of organs, because this is where you might witness joy and lives transformed, which for an audience would be a less gruelling and more rewarding watch. The questions asked are much easier to contemplate. Not what would you do, if you were told that your son or daughter would never regain consciousness? Rather, what would you do if you had a second chance at life? What would you change? What sort of person would you want to become?

Either way, you'd want to kiss your kids and ring your parents at the end of watching the film. But with a film about donors, Mills maintains, you'd be doing so out of fear. With a film about recipients you might do so out of a determination to be better and kinder, and more appreciative of the life you've got.

We met dozens of people on the transplant list, all of them terribly ill. Some old people, some young men and women, in their thirties and forties. One thing they had in common was that I didn't very much like them.

That's quite a thing to say about people who are dying, I know. I'm ashamed to admit it, but it's true. It seemed to me that most of them had wasted their chances, and had lived their lives selfishly. Their spouses and parents and children all bore the scars of living in close proximity to them. Their lifestyles and choices – their addiction to drink or drugs or even tobacco – had wrecked the lives of others. And crucially, none of them – not one – really wanted to change. They just wanted to carry on living.

(Not everyone on the transplant list will be like this, of course. I'm aware of that. I can only speak from my own experience. That's the point of getting out and actually meeting people, rather than making assumptions.)

The people who decide who gets what organ say they do so purely on the basis of medical priority. In other words, whoever is closest to death gets the first chance at life. Moral matters have nothing to do with it.

My feeling is that viewers will dislike the characters we've met as much as I do, or at least fail to sympathize with them. Which will fatally undermine the film, and perhaps even have the opposite effect to the one we're hoping for, making people less inclined to join the organ-donor register than they were at the beginning of the film.

To make the characters likeable, I think we'd need to 'produce' them – to manipulate things, to get a performance out of them. Which is to say that we'd need to minimize or ignore the objectionable bits, and play up their best qualities and redeeming features. This is fine if you're making a reality TV programme, and not fine at all when you're dealing with a subject as serious and sensitive as this one. Whatever goes in the film, it needs to be honest and true.

Mills and I have quarrelled over this. She thinks it's unreasonable for me to want ordinary people to suddenly gain wisdom and nobility simply because of being close to death. And that, just because someone is unable to articulate profound thoughts and feelings, it doesn't mean that they're not experiencing them. Typical of me, she says, to obsess over words. The value of someone's life doesn't lie in how articulate they are, but in what their life means to others.

I think that the people who donate their organs are heroic. Which goes double for people who take the decision to donate the organs of a loved one, even as they're coming to terms with the sudden loss of that person. Heroic in a pure and straightforward way that doesn't require any manipulation for an audience to understand and appreciate. These are the people I think we should celebrate, however difficult it might be to witness people making the decision. Mills says that viewers at home on their sofas, at the end of a long and taxing day, will switch over, or not tune in at all. No parent wants to imagine the death of their own child.

In the dark little room, the mother and father have talked and cried themselves out. They are sitting on the floor, entirely numb.

The reason Mills and I quarrelled about whether to focus our attention on the recipients or the donors is that in the case of organ donation, you can't film both sides of the equation. Donor families and recipients rarely meet. Hospitals will arrange for letters of thanks from recipients to be forwarded to a donor's relatives, if the relatives are receptive to the idea, but that is generally all. If and when meetings are allowed to happen, they take place years and years after the donation occurred. This is to protect both sides, and give everyone the best chance of getting on with their lives. To tell the sort of story we want to tell – the story of a single multi-organ donation – you either film with a donor family, and reveal at the end how many lives the donated organs saved; or you film with the recipients, and reveal at the end that the lives of all of them were saved by organs from a single donor.

There's just 15 minutes left till the doctors come back to ask for a decision. And now comes the moment that I had dreaded from the start. A moment that my non-stop filming was an attempt to avoid. The mother looks to me and asks 'Do you have children?'

I say that I don't.

She says, 'What do you think we should do?'

Just a simple question. The same question the mother of the missing girl asked me, when the pushy journalist came to their house.

This time it's hard for me to answer.

I've never loved another person this much. Or been loved by anyone the way they love their son.

A film-maker, making the film we hope to get commissioned, might want to make the decision him- or herself about which end of the donation process to focus on. Mills and I are only developing the idea at the moment. But development involves more than exploring a subject. It's a process of refining your thoughts and ideas into a clearly defined proposition. A commissioner will ignore a vague wish to make a film about multi-organ donation, however well-informed you might be. A clearly stated ambition to examine one part of the subject in depth stands a chance. You have to make choices.

Mills thinks that I've made a poor choice in making the idea about donors and their families. But that wasn't why she warned against me coming here today.

She knows me better than anyone. 'It'll fuck you up', she said. And it has.

June 20

The idea of big-bang creativity – the notion that good ideas can form suddenly and unexpectedly in your head, out of nothing – is nonsense, a myth peddled by movies, because it makes for good stories and scenes. A writer called Erich Von Däniken posited in the 1960s that revolutionary inventions and groundbreaking ideas might in fact be memories of wisdom taught to us in the ancient past by spacemen. I think this is more likely to be true than I am likely to have a brilliant and fully formed idea whilst in the shower or riding my bike.

Ideas have to come from somewhere, and in the main they come from within, the product of things that shaped your personality and the ways in which you think and interact with the world. This is why particular producers tend to have particular sorts of ideas – about justice, say, or victories against all the odds, or loneliness or escape.

A theme that I've returned to again and again throughout my career is that of family. Which is a good theme to be obsessed by, because everyone has a family of some sort. It's one of the few universals in life, which means that everyone can relate to it on one level or another. It's a much better thing to be obsessed with than justice or loneliness.

I've made a film about women trying to clear the names of sons and husbands serving time in prison, deluding themselves, often, putting their own lives on hold. And a film about children up for adoption, whom no one wants to adopt.

I didn't have the happiest childhood, and a psychologist would probably say that I've been trying to make sense of that by returning so often to the theme of family in general, and to stories about dysfunctional families in particular. It's true that documentary-makers are often complex people – outsiders who became accustomed at some point in their lives to watching from the margins, perhaps attempting to learn the rules of belonging. Making films allows them to use skills assembled over a lifetime of trying and failing to fit in.

We are currently developing a project that views family life from the point of view of a newborn baby, by means of a cute little hat with a camera in it. The baby gets the hat the moment it's born, and with luck we get a simple, celebratory film about the joy a new baby brings to its parents and grandparents, and the ways in which it changes their lives and relationships. And we're negotiating access to something called a child contact centre, which provides neutral ground for kids to see the parents or family they no longer live with. They're important places, full of heartbreaking stories, and many are closing down through lack of funding.

The mother and father in the small dark room decided in the end to put aside thoughts of their son's body being cracked open and disassembled, bit by bit, to give their consent for the donation of all his organs.

The films I've made and the ideas I've developed have taught me that families should be and generally are sources of huge comfort and happiness for people. That's what we expect them to be. But they go wrong sometimes. Occasionally quite badly. And when they do, because of our rosy expectations, it's terrible and traumatic. They're the best thing and also the worst.

I can't imagine having a family of my own. Which is probably a very good thing.

June 21

It's late. I'm watching the posh boys again in their dinner jackets, smashing and sneering and shoving that poor girl around like a doll.

What did the owner of the place say? And what would he say now, looking back? What would the boys in the film say? What does the film say about them?

The details are compelling. The pecking order. The gestures and expressions. The total and utter confidence that nothing bad will ever happen.

But something bad *is* about to happen.

This is a piece of film that everyone should see. To judge the behaviour it depicts, and hold these thugs to account.

Putting it on TV is the right and proper thing to do.

June 22

When I was a boy, still quite small, my grandfather took me to sea.

Technically it was a kidnapping. It certainly felt like one.

We were on a family holiday, on the north coast of Scotland. We were staying in a cottage in the same fishing town we went to every year. I don't know why this place rather than any other. There must have been a reason for it; it took eight solid hours to drive there, in my grandad's battered old van.

It was so far north it would stay light until midnight, and the locals sounded more like Vikings than Scots. My memories of it look like the Super 8 film my grandmother used to shoot on these holidays, five- or six-second fragments of small characters in big landscapes, and weather that was always wild.

My grandfather would gamble and drink with the fishermen. We never really saw him much. I'd spend time with my mother and grandmother. I liked to draw and read, and spend time exploring on my own. Then one year my grandfather decided he needed to make a man of me.

I went with him to the harbour and we climbed down the slimy ladder to a trawler boat. Everyone was busy, so I just sat on a crate and looked around. The next thing I remember, we were moving. We slipped out of the harbour, and I watched the land gradually recede. I was scared. I'd never been out on the ocean before. I couldn't stop thinking about all the dark space under the boat, and what might be in it. But I'd been places I didn't much like before. I'd just wait it out. I reckoned I'd be back in the harbour in two hours, tops.

We stayed at sea for four days.

My grandfather used to say that he'd been taught to swim by being thrown into a canal. I have no way of knowing whether that's true. But I also have no reason to doubt it. He tended to behave very much like someone whose father had tried to drown him.

I didn't eat for the first two days. I was too upset, and sick. At night I'd pretend to be asleep whilst the men drank Scotch and played cards. I had no change of clothes. I had no books or toys. Nothing comforting or familiar.

These days, in the vanilla-scented psychotherapy rooms of Kensington and Chiswick, this kind of thing might be called immersion therapy. My grandfather intended it as a cure for softness. The industrial world that he had grown up in was disappearing, and he looked upon my clean fingernails, my shyness, and my 'book learning' (as he called it) only with despair. It must have been heartbreaking to see all of the structures and certainties underpinning your life start to crack and crumble. So much worse for the values of this alien, post-industrial world to seep into your family, and make a stranger of your own flesh and blood.

This is real life, he wanted to say. This is real work. And these are real men.

On the third day, as the rest of the crew were busy hauling ropes and gutting fish, a tall gruff man with a thick red beard came below decks to where I was sitting on my bunk, reading an old newspaper because there was nothing at all else to do. He reached into his yellow overalls and pulled out a handful of toffees. The taste of them after two and a half days of puking and starving was indescribably nice. I felt warmth come back into my body. It was the first piece of kindness – by anyone, to anyone else – I'd encountered on the boat.

'Don't mind the others', he said. 'They don't know any better. They're not as bad as they seem.'

He told me that he'd been taken to sea at the same age as me, and he remembered how it felt. He told me that he had a son of his own, and hoped he'd do something better with his life.

He put his sou'wester on my head, gave me his penknife and said that I could keep it. He said he'd take me to the wheelhouse, and that I could steer the ship.

On deck, he told the rest of the crew that he'd made me first mate. One of the other fishermen – the guy who made the food – cut up a set of wax chest-waders and sewed them into something that fitted me. I was too small and weak to help with the endless tasks, but I discovered something that I could do, and indeed was good at. Which is, ask intelligent questions. The fishermen liked explaining what they were doing, and how it felt to be out in the sun and the spray, hunting fish.

That night, I sat with them as they ate, and took a nip of whisky when they passed around a bottle. Dinner was usually whatever they'd caught but couldn't sell – octopus and ugly fat fish. But that night the cook took a sea trout from the ice store and roasted it just for me. They told me stories that made me laugh. When they'd say something I didn't understand – about women, mostly – and I'd ask them what they meant, they'd laugh too, and do their best to explain. We stayed up late, sitting around the table in the galley in the warm yellow light of a paraffin lamp hung from the ceiling.

My grandfather watched me, proudly, but fuck him. I was doing this for myself.

I still think of that night, but now when I picture it I see the boat from far away, silhouetted against the not-quite-dark sky, rising and falling on the huge black sea, the windows of the galley glowing with the light from the lamp. It would probably look to someone else like an image of vulnerability. It looks to me like an image of survival, and it makes me feel strong.

I don't know if that trip made a man of me. People I know would probably say they're still waiting for that to happen. But I did learn how to adapt and get by in pretty much any environment, no matter how foreign it might feel at first.

Tonight I'm at the top of the second tallest tower in London, looking down on the city. From here, the scale isn't human at all. All you can see is buildings and lights, blinking in the haze coming up off the streets. If this was your view every day, you'd start to feel like a god.

I've been cleaning for a couple of hours, enjoying it. I like the way it makes my mind wander. I like the drone of the air-conditioning and the hum of the machine that polishes the floors. I like the calmness and concentration of one or two late workers, not rushing now, the whole night in front of them.

I've had a look at the things on people's desks. No personal stuff or photos. Printouts of graphs and numbers. Nothing telling or useful. Nothing I can even understand.

When the fishing boat finally came back to the harbour, I was standing on deck, with the rest of the crew. My mother was waiting on the sea wall, crying and trembling with anguish and rage. She hugged me and kissed my head and took me back to familiar and comforting things. But now those things felt less familiar and comforting. I had changed.

June 23

I told an older colleague my story once. Her background was in journalism, and she was good at listening to people, and not interrupting. I can't remember why I was in the mood to talk. It was probably just one of those mornings when you want to be known and understood. It was early and we stood in the kitchen, nursing cups of coffee. She listened intently, smiling with her eyes and encouraging me to continue. When I finished she said, 'Forgive me, but I don't think I believe you.'

'Forgive me.' I don't think there's a more aggressive way of beginning a sentence.

I've never told anyone in TV about myself since. Fragments of information maybe. Shows I like. Places I've been. But nothing really about me.

I have a friend who tells people about himself all the time. In essence, the story he tells is one of a working-class boy who fought his way into a middle-class industry, overcoming significant odds. It's similar to my own story, the one that my colleague didn't believe.

My friend's story is utterly compelling. It's funny and moving, full of dramatic and funny scenes and memorable details. I've heard him tell many times the story of the job he took cleaning toilets at a TV company, just to make a start. And the story of the weeks he spent secretly sleeping on the floor of a production office when he finally got his break as a researcher, paid too little to afford a proper place to stay. And the story of how he sneaked a camera out of the building at night, and taught himself to use it. And then made his own film about a night bus that was always full of homeless people travelling round and round a circular route in central London, enjoying the warmth and safety and one another's company, relaxed for a while before the sun came up and they had to disappear. A film which won an award.

The thing you need to know about this guy is that his father worked in advertising, and was brilliant at telling stories. One of the very best. The sort of person who would attract an audience at parties. My friend learned to tell stories at the knee of an absolute master. How to engage people. How to draw them in and get them onside. How to make them laugh and make them cry. He used these skills to concoct a backstory for himself that is utterly winning, but not even slightly true. I mean *none of it*. The whole thing is a sort of advert. A plausible but entirely bogus narrative designed to connect you emotionally to a product, like the idea of the Ploughman's Lunch, invented by admen working for an organization called the Cheese Bureau to help them sell more cheese.

Everyone believes the story he tells, because he tells it so well. And because it's a story that middle-class people in TV are happy to hear. It doesn't contain any of the troubling moments or disconcerting notions that you'd get if the story was true. It's a story with a positive ending – here I am, at the end of my travails and peregrinations, safely and nicely middle class like you, and available for work. No resentment or anger. No broken relationships. No chip on the shoulder. None of the ugly scenes that are a feature of my own, bumpier narrative.

I love my friend for inventing such an elaborate lie. It's a sort of fuck-you to all the clueless middle-class liberals in TV. Only someone from a very comfortable middle-class background would have the confidence to make it up and tell it so brazenly.

We liked each other immediately when we met. Perhaps we recognized something in each other. I think it's probably true that you can't kid a kidder.

So here we are in a nice dark bar, a working-class boy who's learned how to look and sound middle-class, and a middle-class boy who's pretending to be a working-class hero, both of us doing whatever it takes to get on, neither of us quite what we appear to be.

I'm telling him about the roll of film.

'It's a get-out-of-jail-card', he says. 'And one day you might need it. Maybe literally, in your case.'

'Meaning what?'

'Don't pitch it or show it to anyone.'

He pulls a face that says 'pay attention, because this is really me. These are words I mean and believe.'

'A commission is just a commission', he says.

June 24

I'm back in my flat after five hours of cleaning at the top of the tower, following a ten-hour day in the office.

My body is heavy and tired, but it seems unusually noisy outside. Or maybe I'm just more than usually aware of it. I've too much on my mind to sleep.

I'm scrolling through the last few days' texts from You Know Who. It feels like he's tormenting me now, the voice of my conscience, speaking through my phone.

'You'll have seen the charade on TV this week', he says. 'Didn't it make you sick?'

June 25

Tibetan monks produce works of art known as mandala. They involve vast amounts of work and attention to detail. Coloured stones are crushed into granules, which are then applied to a surface using tiny tubes, in complex geometric patterns. Often the monks operate in teams, and enter a trance-like state as they work. Each mandala can take several weeks to complete.

When it is finished, it is ceremonially offered to others for viewing. And then, in a gesture symbolizing the transient nature of life, the whole intricate and beautiful thing is simply thrown away.

This is mostly what writing treatments for programmes is like.

Treatments are as hard to avoid as they are dull to produce. I have not much referred to them in these pages, because I can't bear to think of them when I don't absolutely have to. So far this year I must have written a hundred or more.

Some people write a treatment for every idea they ever have, and then send it off to one or more commissioners, with a covering email. This is a clueless way to carry on. Such treatments are simply never read. Commissioners groan when they receive them. At best they get printed out and put on a pile, which to a commissioner feels like doing something about the treatment, whilst simultaneously condemning it to be forever ignored. I've seen piles of treatments in commissioners' offices that reach from the floor to the tops of their desks and beyond. The bigger the pile, the more awful the prospect of ever doing anything about it. As a producer, the last thing you want is for your idea to end up on that pile.

I much prefer to talk than write. Talking – or rather conversing – is a much better way of explaining what something is, and what it might look like and what your ambitions for it are. You can work with the person you're conversing with, to reach a level of understanding that works for both of you.

That's how I like to pitch. But successful pitches always end in the same six words – 'Could you write me a treatment?'

For the last two days I've been trying to write a treatment for the organ donation film. I've been finding it difficult. I don't know where to start, so I haven't. Two days of effort with nothing to show. It's made me feel bad-tempered and restive.

I always find requests for treatments difficult to fulfil, because as an exercise it feels just as pointless as writing an idea down and speculatively sending it away, to add another thin layer to a teetering pile of doom somewhere. Maybe even more pointless than that, because you've *already sold* the idea to someone. That person will need to sell the same idea internally, at the channel he or she works for, but that will probably happen verbally as well. It's very likely that your treatment will never be read by anyone.

But it's also possible that it will be read by just a single someone. And the reason the treatment needs to be good is that this single someone might be the person in overall charge of the channel. Reading your treatment might be the last thing he or she does before finally commissioning your programme. Or, as the case may be, not.

After your tenth good idea has progressed at a channel but failed to reach this final stage, summoning the motivation to perfect a treatment is hard.

Lazy writing stands out a mile, and transmits a terrible message; you're vague and unprofessional, and your thinking is ponderous and dull. You are, in other words, a very bad choice of person to hand half a million pounds to in the hope of getting back a well-made and interesting piece of television.

So you need to distil your thoughts into the most concise form possible. You need to be crystal-clear about what your idea is and why your show will be arresting, entertaining and informative to watch. You need to bring your characters and locations to life, and conjure a world that your reader will want to spend time in. You need to be creative, but without including anything that is obviously a lie. You need to showcase your originality and the freshness of your vision for the programme you want to make. All in a page or two at the most.

It's hard, and some very bright and talented producers I know are unable to do it. Some very bright and talented producers I know think that writing in the way you need to is beneath them, because the language you use needs to be the language of selling, colloquial and to the point. Here's why this idea is good, and here's what you'd get out of buying it. You need to make a channel controller *want* it.

The people I know who think that selling is beneath them write long, dense treatments, as thick and formal as Russian novels, designed primarily to show off all the research they've done. Their ideas become so encrusted with information and detail you can no longer see the outline of the original thought, nor imagine what the idea might one day become. They'd rather be writing essays in learned journals, I think. Certainly they've failed to grasp the nature of the TV industry as it is today, in which you have to fight hard for attention. They tend to be old and nostalgic for how television used to be, and will surely soon become extinct.

I am trying to distil the essence of the organ-donation film in a line or two – in all likelihood, if the film gets commissioned, the same line or two that you'd read in listings magazines and on the EPG.

I think the reason I'm struggling is that the subject is so complex and emotive; trying to describe it in a few simple words naturally makes you think in clichés, which would make a reader feel like they'd seen the film before.

I'm considering these problems in a lovely comfy armchair in someone's cosy living room. Or rather a set made up to look like someone's living room. The set has a good view of a vast shop floor, full of similar sets for other rooms, and thousands of pieces of furniture. Everywhere there are families. You know the place I mean. And suddenly the sentences I need suddenly start coming to mind.

I came here to buy a fan for my bedroom, because lately the nights have been hot and still. But I'll take any excuse to visit. I love it here. I love the fact that the people shopping here are pretty much all buying things to help manage important transitions in their lives.

There are dozens of pregnant women and their partners, carefully picking out items to turn a spare room into a soft, hushed home for their baby. There are older, shattered-looking mums and dads remodelling those same nurseries into bedrooms and playrooms for their turbo-charged toddlers. There are mums and dads in middle age shopping with grown-up children, about to leave home for work or university. And young couples moving in together, buying cheap crockery and pots and pans, laughing and awkward, playing at being adults.

People often complain about the place, and say that it's full of frustration and anger. But I genuinely find it to be full of love. It always makes me feel happy and optimistic. And today it's dismantled whatever roadblock the donor film had set up in my brain.

Unexpectedly, the words start to come. Prose that's clean and honest. Simple sentences describing what I witnessed – two parents' astonishing act of love, towards children they'd never met, and probably never will. I'm writing them down with a little wooden pencil, on the back of a printed sheet about the features of a bestselling sofa.

June 26

I find it hard to enjoy watching TV these days. It feels like work, so I tend to treat it as such, and watch programmes at my desk. But not tonight. I'm watching a film made by a friend, at home on my sofa, like two or three million other people are doing right at this very moment.

The film is about a drug dealer trying to go straight and it's what all documentaries should be like – vivid, honest and totally engrossing. It doesn't want you to think about what it is or how it's made. It doesn't want you to think at all. It wants you to let go and lose yourself in the story. I'm happy to be doing just that.

Another text comes through from You Know Who.

'Time to end this', it says. 'Time to come clean.'

June 27

Back at the top of the tower tonight, feeling tired and oppressed. The novelty wore off days ago. Now it feels like work and I'd rather be somewhere else. Which is exactly how the other cleaners feel, which is how come they're starting to accept me.

None of the bankers has wanted to talk. At the end of the day, when my shift begins, they rush to the lifts to get to the bars and restaurants on the ground. The late workers keep their heads down. I'm not sure they can even see me.

At break time, in the cramped little room where we keep our things, one of the cleaners offers me a cookie her child has made at school. Another has a flask of tea. For the first time, they invite me to join them.

They're all working two jobs. They all live miles outside London and travel in and out every day. They're all exhausted, all the time. And they've all made the same decision – that their own happiness and well-being don't matter. They've given up everything to make a better life for their kids.

This is interesting and moving and humbling, but hardly revelatory. I'm thinking this might all have been a waste of time.

Then one of them says that he's planning to call in sick tomorrow.

'You should too', he says. 'Because tomorrow is bonus day.'

June 28

I volunteered to cover the guy's shift. Now I'm filming undercover, with a camera disguised as a name badge.

This sort of thing is hugely problematic ordinarily; a broadcaster's lawyers want you to establish clear evidence of wrongdoing before you can rig up to film it. But this is just development.

The bankers are drinking champagne out of bottles and hoovering up lines from their desks. They've been going a couple of hours, and some of them have puked already, then come back for more. Their behaviour is revolting. Two of them are on camera throwing stuff on the floor just to have a cleaner pick it up. Another lights a fat cigar with a burning £50 note, a living cartoon of a cunt. The cleaners just carry on as normal, their backs stiff and their faces like masks, which feels like the worst of it. The baying and stupidity and waste is nothing new. They've seen it all before.

Standing slightly apart from the rest, trying and failing to keep up a smile, is a young man with a delicate face. He has a half-full glass in his hand, but I suspect it's only for show. His eyes are sober and sharp.

As I'm cleaning up the kitchen, he comes over to say that he's sorry, and asks if I'll say so to the others. I tell him I'm new and say that it's come as a shock. He says this is nothing, and tells me stories of his colleagues' arrogance and contempt for ordinary people. He's a decent and likeable man with a weight on his conscience, eager to unburden himself to anyone who'll listen, even a lowly cleaner.

'This is the job I dreamed of', he says. 'I'm not sure I'll do it much longer.'

A good subject for a film, maybe; a whistle-blower in waiting.

June 29

Mills said to me today that if you do things that arseholes do, and go places that arseholes go, and say the sort of things that arseholes say, you're almost certainly an arsehole yourself.

I'm at an industry party, thrown by a channel for a commissioner who's leaving after ten years' service to set up his own company. It's like a fever dream. I'm walking around, saying hi, having conversations with people whose voices I can't really hear above the music. The faces of some of the worst people I know loom out of the darkness, smiling and sneering. Mills declined my invitation, so I'm here on my own, one more arsehole among so many.

I'm trying not to think the thought that always rattles around my head at these things, that maybe everyone in the room – *everyone* – is better at TV than me.

I'm looking for one commissioning editor in particular. She finds me amusing. I find her attractive. I want to tell her about the skyscraper and the bankers. I've brought my cleaner's ID as proof of my investigations.

She's the kind of woman other women don't tend to like – super-confident and vaguely predatory. Tonight she's in a short skirt and boots, purple lipstick and slicked-back hair.

She says that she's much more interested in the victims than the perpetrators of the financial crisis, and thinks that her viewers would be too. Don't we already know that bankers are callow and selfish, and generally awful? What about the hard-working people who've lost their homes? What's that doing to relationships and families?

I show her some of the undercover footage on my phone to try to convince her she's wrong, but I think she's probably not.

More time and money wasted.

'Someone should make a film about you', she says. So I switch from trying to sell her the idea of a film about bankers to the idea of coming to bed with me.

Different goal, same method. Work out what she wants to hear and say it loud and clear.

'You're funny', she says. 'Always selling something.'

But tonight she's buying nothing. At least not from me.

That's okay. Tomorrow is another day, and one good day is all you need.

June 30

Two bad things happened today.

Firstly, the gangster project, complete with finely crafted taster and carefully written treatment, was politely but firmly turned down. The commissioner called me to let me know. When the receptionist patched the call through, I was very confidently expecting a yes. So much so that when he said that he wouldn't be commissioning it, I said, 'Fantastic, thank you', because that's what my brain had prepared me to say.

Beyond the money the channel put up, I reckon we've spent an additional 5 or 6k, ignoring all the time Mills and I have spent on it. When I told him, Charlie just nodded.

The second bad thing was that Rankin himself came into the office. He was passing by, he said, and thought he'd come and see where we keep ourselves. Mills and I took him to the meeting room. We did a bit of small talk. And then he said, 'So what's the news?'

I said, 'The news is good! The film has been commissioned.'

Mills looked at me in an interested way, but otherwise her expression – smiling sociably – never faltered.

Sometimes in life you do things that you know are going to cause problems. Serious problems, perhaps. But you do them anyway. I'm not sure why. Curiosity, maybe. Or boredom. Or to foster creativity, by building a labyrinth you'll need to escape from. I suspect that most people don't know why they act the way they do.

I said, 'We only just heard. I wanted to confirm the details before calling you, but since you're here … '

Rankin said, 'Good boy.'

I said something lame like 'This is going to be fun!'

He said, 'Good for you. Good for you, and good for me', and cheersed me with his coffee.

I don't know what he meant by that. It didn't seem like the moment to ask.

He left happy, with his arm around my shoulders. I caught Charlie's eye as I saw him out the door. His eyebrows were caught between surprise and a frown; he's happy the film got rejected? I tipped my head very slightly towards him, in a way that I hope said 'Yes, I know; people are strange.'

I'm not sure still, seven hours later, exactly what I was thinking in the meeting. If I was thinking at all, it was that Rankin would have walked for sure if I'd dared to tell him the truth. That I needed to buy some time.

Now I'm Scheherazade, in a shadow realm of bollock-talk and evasion, telling tall stories to a dangerous man, postponing my fate while I figure out what to do.

My phone buzzes in my pocket. Another message from You Know Who. The same as last time with one small addition:

'Time to end this. Time to come clean. Time is running out.'

CHAPTER SEVEN: JULY

July 1

Three or so years ago, a pair of well-known MPs were caught selling influence, charging hundreds of thousands to make introductions, facilitate deals, speed things up and slow things down. Some very senior figures in government were implicated. Two cabinet ministers were forced to resign.

I'm reading about it now, at my desk.

Mills appears, in a breezy mood this morning. She hands me a coffee and peers at my computer. 'Since when have you cared about politics?' she says.

I can't think of a plausible fib so I tell her the truth: 'I'm looking into this guy', pointing at a picture of the article's author underneath the headline.

John Donovan. The guy with the manicured fingernails from the Brightwell Estate. The guy behind the texts. His picture makes him look shrewd and challenging.

Mills leans forward and looks more closely at the screen. At Donovan's byline in particular. It says 'John Donovan: Investigative Reporter'. Then she looks back at me, her eyes steady on mine, giving nothing away, saying nothing at all.

'I can't seem to find out much about him', I say, avoiding her gaze, in a way that I hope sounds casual.

Mills' breeziness has gone now. She says she'll see what she can do.

July 3

'There's no right and wrong with this.'

'No right and wrong?'

'No rules, I mean. It doesn't matter what you do or say. So relax, okay?'

'But there's always rules. Someone's always listening.'

Me and a man in his forties are on the top deck of a bus.

He looks much older than he really is.

He's just been given his freedom, after 20 years in prison for a crime he didn't commit.

It has taken me several weeks to win the access, negotiating with the man's lawyer in wood-panelled offices in central London. I've told three commissioners that I'll be meeting him at the prison gates, and spending the next two days with him. All three of them are interested.

Often with this sort of thing, whether or not you win a commission rests on how close the reality of a situation comes to what everyone imagines. The three commissioners are picturing a man who might as well be coming back to earth from space. Since he's been away, the world has changed beyond recognition. So much faster now, so much more connected. So much noisier, more colourful and varied. They're also imagining a man with interesting things to say about innocence and forgiveness. His best years have been taken from him, in a terrible miscarriage of justice. I did nothing to disabuse them of these fantasies. Partly because I'd been seduced by them as well. And partly because at that stage I still hadn't met the guy either.

It was evident within sixty seconds of shaking his hand this morning that somewhere along the line, his mind had broken. Perhaps even before he started his sentence. Now he looks terrified and bewildered. He starts sentences and then his voice fades away. I ask him how he feels, and his eyes looks full of fear and pain. But he has no words to describe the pain. And no words means no commission.

I've been coaxing and filming him all day, more and more half-heartedly. You see things in a different way through the viewfinder of a camera. It's strange how seldom we look long and hard at someone's face His is both childlike and ancient. This poor shipwrecked man. He doesn't even know yet how hard it's going to be. None of the certainties he knew before he went away apply any more. All of his friends and family are lost. A well-taken picture would win awards for photography. But pictures, no matter how striking, don't count for much in documentary film-making. You need people to be themselves and tell you what they're thinking and feeling.

At the end of the day, I take him to the office of his solicitor, with £20 to buy himself a drink. He insists on buying me a pint with the money, and we sit in silence in a dingy pub. He seems perfectly pleased. Happy, even. Soon he'll be another person I once met. I feel depressed.

I ask him, 'Didn't it torment you? Didn't it fill you full of rage?'

The interviews are over now. There's nothing to be gained. I'm asking the question because I want to know the answer.

He looks at me, blankly.

'Didn't it keep you awake at night?'

He slept soundly every night, he says. Because he knew that he was innocent.

He's innocent the way a child is. He never harmed a living soul in the life he used to live – not even a worm or a beetle. And, for more than two decades in the same grey cell, never again had a chance to.

July 4

We've been trying to track down a girl once feted as a child genius. A tabloid newspaper has revealed that she's been working as a prostitute, having turned her back on the life she used to live.

But it looks like the newspaper has her under wraps. They do that sometimes – put people up in fancy hotels with a journalist to babysit them, to keep their exclusive story exclusive. No one else will be able to get to her now, not even her own family.

Shut out of the story, another paper has a piece about other child geniuses, and the sticky ends they usually meet. It includes a brief reference to a very gifted boy in the States, described by one psychologist as 'the most astonishing genius ever to grace the earth'. The interesting thing is that he's missing, and has been for years.

Clever people have an IQ of around 140. For super-clever people, it's around 160. This little boy, at the age of just six, scored well over 300, the highest ever recorded.

I decided to dig a little deeper.

His mother had him whilst still very young, and seemingly raised him alone. After a while, she returned to her education, sometimes taking him along to classes. One day, to keep him amused, she claimed to have handed him a copy of the test the class were taking, expecting him to do nothing more than draw on it with his crayons. Instead, he steadily worked his way through the questions and handed in his paper when the test was over. It came back with a score that put him close to the top of the class. He was just two-and-a-half years old.

It wasn't long before he could read aloud and play multiple musical instruments. Home schooled by his mother, he was playing competitive chess by the age of four. At just five he began taking high-school classes.

His high-school principal would later report that teachers struggled to keep pace with the boy's thirst for knowledge. Everyone agreed he was dazzling.

Then, at the age of six, he began to study at a local university, attending lectures with classmates three times his own age. Now the world began paying attention, newspapers from a dozen countries reporting on the arrival of a prodigy to rival Mozart and Picasso.

But then, suddenly, the hype fell away. The story of the world's cleverest boy began to unravel.

Accompanied by his mother, he had toured the US, standing on an upturned milk crate to lecture audiences of philosophers, teachers and the parents of other gifted children on the unfairness of age discrimination in education. But while his presentations were extraordinary, observers noticed that he didn't seem able to answer any of the questions he was asked. And then the boy started to regress. His photographic memory disappeared, and he began sucking his thumb, throwing tantrums, and playing with toys designed for toddlers. He was almost eight years old now, but seemed to be living out the infancy that he'd skipped the first time round. He was enrolled in a school for gifted children, but refused to study. And then an empty bottle of painkillers was reportedly found on his bedroom floor.

A professional assessment found the boy to be suffering from severe psychological problems. It concluded that he was 'a danger to himself'. A new IQ test revealed his intelligence to be 'approximately average'. But it seemed that he spent much of that test hiding under furniture. He said that the questions were stupid.

He was taken away from his mother, placed into foster care, and sent to an ordinary school. His mother was charged with neglect, and accused of using him to satisfy her own need for attention. His grandparents expressed concerns about their daughter's mental health, and doubts that the boy was ever gifted. A local newspaper began to investigate, and reported that most of the claims about his extraordinary abilities could not be verified.

Some who knew the boy continued to believe in his genius. But then came a startling admission from his mother – she had manipulated and falsified the results of the boy's exams, including his world record-breaking IQ test. It emerged that most of his high-school and university coursework had been completed at home, his dealings with teachers conducted largely by email.

At the same time, she admitted charges of neglect. But she continued to maintain that the boy was a bona fide genius; she only cheated, she said, to open doors for him.

After several years in foster care, the boy was returned to his mother. And then the two of them disappeared. A private investigator hired by the boy's great-aunt and -uncle has failed to locate them.

So is the boy a genius or isn't he?

Was he ever really gifted? Or the victim of someone else's fantasy? Or even of a scam, designed to make money from sponsorship and advertising? What does his story tell us about 'the gifted community'? Have the boy and his gifts simply been misunderstood? What sort of life might he be leading now? What will be his place in the world?

I really want to know the answers to these questions.

I think this is one of the best, most gripping stories I've encountered.

July 6

One of the main broadcasters has tipped off a handful of favoured companies that it wants to commission a series of blue-chip 'access pieces' – series that take you behind the scenes at places of interest.

There are two problems with this sort of thing.

The first problem springs from a fundamental law of television, that the usefulness of any piece of information is inversely proportionate to the number of people who know about it. A 'handful' of companies could mean anything from two to 20. Which could mean 20 people like myself doing the exact same work at the exact same time.

The second problem is that there are only so many blue-chip companies, organizations and institutions in the world that are truly household names, and genuinely of interest to the man in the street. Google and Facebook. The White House and Number 10. The Met and the Louvre. Most of these entities are far too big, successful or important to have any inclination at all to allow in cameras; there's nothing to gain, and lots to lose.

The companies that will countenance filming – mainly because they want the publicity – have become pretty familiar to the TV audience. Places that need to sell themselves in a competitive market, like top-end department stores, 'heritage brands' and airlines. And such places generally want to exercise control over what is filmed and what is broadcast. Of course they do. So would you. When a man called Gerald Ratner was caught on camera describing an item for sale in his jewellery shops as 'total crap', his customers stayed away, and the value of the company fell by half a billion, narrowly avoiding collapse. But the broadcasters don't want puff pieces. They want accidents and mistakes and unguarded moments. Glimpses behind the curtain, of what's really going on. A series about an airport, for example, that unfolds without these glimpses would feel like being stuck in an airport when your flight's been cancelled, killing time with aimless browsing and zombified shuffling about.

Gettable, new to TV and brave enough to embrace all that filming entails is a tough set of criteria. It leaves just a handful of places to target. A theme park, maybe. Or one of the big London hotels. And those places are deluged with bids and pitches. A press officer at the famous jewellery store I called this morning wearily told me I was the 15th person to call that day, all no doubt prompted by the same 'exclusive' broadcaster tip-off.

So what do you do?

It seems to me there are two ways to go.

The first is attempt to spot something that everyone else has missed, to use your ingenuity and cleverness to identify a place or a thing that everyone knows or needs or loves, but no one really thinks about. The kind of company or place that seems entirely obvious once someone mentions it. Series about London's night buses and a chain of cheap and cheerful high-street bakeries were both big successes in recent years.

That's what we spent our time discussing this morning. A researcher suggested a motorway services. Everyone spends time there. But no one wants to; people go for a pee and a coffee and leave as soon as possible, so it's hard to imagine what we'd film.

I suggested a conference hotel, where companies go for their AGMs. Which are boring, of course, but because of that everyone takes off their ties at night and behaves like it's the last days of Rome. That might be an interesting way of looking at the lives of office workers. But wouldn't the boring bits be torturous? Who wants to listen to a regional sales manager talking about quarterly targets?

An AP suggested a national museum, from the angle of the pressure that all great collections are under now to repatriate their treasures and artefacts. What would the British Museum, for example, look like, stripped of all the wondrous things it stripped from other cultures and countries 200 years before? Interesting and timely, for sure, and a good way of telling stories about the history of art. But what's in it for the museum? I can't imagine that we'd find one willing to play ball.

Mills suggested a leisure centre. It's a place we can all relate to. We're taught to swim there as kids. We hang about there as teenagers, drinking cider and flirting with each other. And we go there as adults of all ages to play sport and unwind and meet with friends. There are thousands of leisure centres in the UK, which used to be funded and run by local authorities. Now cutbacks in funding are transforming the sector; each local leisure centre will become a business, that will stand and fall on its ability to attract paying customers.

This seems like a good territory to explore, with a clear, timely reason for doing so. We're sending out dozens of emails, hunting for a manager with charisma, who might see it as an opportunity.

The second possible response to the problem of access is to approach the sort of place that would usually say no with a pitch or approach so smart and fresh (and free of risk) that it will overcome decades of resistance.

Within my team of diverse talents, persuading people to do stuff their better instincts are telling them not to is my particular speciality. Mills and I are compiling a list of places to try.

'You're quiet', Mills says. 'Has something happened?'

I tell her everything's fine.

What if we persuade Britain's most unpopular companies to put their biggest critics in positions of power for a period of time? An energy provider, say, hated for its terrible customer service, putting outraged customers in charge of its call centre. Best-case scenario, the customers have good ideas and things improve, and the company is seen as brave and open-minded. Worst-case scenario, the customers fail and everyone sees the problems the company are up against, most of which aren't the company's fault.

Maybe we could persuade a struggling chocolate-maker to put kids in charge of its product development?

Prisons are fascinating places, but notoriously hard to access. What if we offer them something in return? A big-name business guru willing to help them rethink the whole idea of jobs in prisons. Instead of turning clothes into rags, couldn't the man- and brainpower be put to better use? Perhaps businesses could grow and flourish in prison? Perhaps prisons could one day pay for themselves?

'So it's a secret', Mills says.

'What is?'

'Whatever it is that happened.'

She's as calm and even as ever, with the slightest light of anger in her eyes.

'You're gonna lecture me about secrecy? I hardly know a thing about you!'

'I have things I tend not to talk about. Things I consider to be private', she says. 'You have things you hide.'

'There's a difference?'

'There's a difference you need to learn if you expect me to help you.'

The rewards for nailing high-end access are significant – high-profile series that almost guarantee large audiences.

Charlie would love me to bag something like this. You need imagination and diplomacy to pull it off. But probably more than anything else, you need a measure of good luck: the right person to read your email or answer the phone, at exactly the right time. It feels too much like buying a raffle ticket to me. That's why my heart's not in it.

And Mills is right, of course. My mind's on other things.

July 8

'About your journalist', Mills says.

'John Michael Donovan. 38 years of age. No criminal convictions.

'Said to be driven, tenacious and entirely single-minded. No wife, no family. No partner even. Invests everything in work.'

This is worse than I thought.

'He's a good-looking guy, right? Maybe we could put him on TV? "John Donovan Investigates".

I say this as sweetly and brightly as I can. Mills is ignoring me, her brow low and serious.

'First-class degree in English. Hired straight onto the staff of a major newspaper after a piece in a student paper exposing malpractice at one of the country's oldest universities, whereby rich families were allowed to buy places on competitive courses for their under-qualified kids.

'Went on to uncover some of the biggest stories of recent times. Mainly ones to do with corruption and abuse. Sees himself as some sort of crusader. Obsessed with truth and justice, and doesn't give a fuck about the fallout.

'He was told live on a news programme that the subject of one of his stories had committed suicide and didn't even blink. It was shame made the guy do that, he said, not the story he wrote.

'Said by some to be unscrupulous, though he's been sued ten times and never lost, and twice cleared of bribing bureaucrats for information following official enquiries.

'Hates authority. Impossible to manage, so no-one tries, which makes him his own boss, answerable to no one. But he's never erratic and never makes mistakes. Never picks a fight he thinks he could lose.'

Mills stops and looks up from her notes. The same steady gaze she always uses whenever she's pissed off with me.

The info is all very interesting, but there's nothing of any use. Nothing to deploy as leverage. Nothing I can work with.

Mills is packing up now.

I ask if she'd like a drink.

'Sounds like a worthy opponent', she says, looking at me closely. 'Sounds like you, in fact. A real piece of work.'

'Be careful', she says, collects her coat and leaves.

July 9

Every great documentary idea is actually a great story. And in the case of the very best documentaries – the ones you really remember – there's often a story behind the story, a sort of creation myth that elevates the film and makes it feel divinely ordained. Like the workaday clown documentary that became *Capturing the Friedmans* when one of the clowns told the director about his fucked-up family and extraordinary cache of home movies. Or the way *Hoop Dreams* began as a half-hour documentary, transformed by luck and circumstance into an award-winning, three-hour epic.

A few weeks ago, I spoke to an American skip tracer – a bounty hunter, effectively – who specializes in finding people who have abandoned their lives and gone on the run. They might be criminals, but more and more, in an age of economic turmoil, they are ordinary men and women who have accumulated debts and lost the ability to pay.

He told me about a respectable husband and father who'd built up his business and made a comfortable life for his family, but the credit crunch had crept up on him, and suddenly he found himself going under. He'd simply fled – no goodbyes, no explanation. Just a note that said 'I failed and I'm sorry'. His wife and children were traumatized by the sudden arrival of the bailiffs. His employees, the previous day making plans and looking forward, were confronted by a padlocked door and sickening uncertainty. It was an almighty mess, but not necessarily an irretrievable one, so long as the guy could be persuaded to come back and face the music.

But where was he?

The fugitive had planned carefully. He'd been withdrawing cash for weeks. His credit cards and ID were in his wallet on the table by the bed, where he left them every night. His car was in the garage. He clearly didn't want to be found, and the police had better things to do than look for him. In any case, the guy hadn't really committed any crime. So the wife had called up the skip tracer – find my husband, persuade him to come home and face the music, and you'll get 10% of everything he owes.

Two weeks later, 900 miles away in a cabin in the middle of nowhere, the skip tracer had the guy in a bear hug, telling him everything would all be fine as he sobbed and said he was sorry.

On the phone, he told me how he tracked the guy down. 'You can change your name and your clothes and even your face', he said. 'But you can't change who you are.' Meaning your tastes and preferences. The things that interest you, and the things you enjoy and care about. Combined, these things create a behavioural fingerprint, a set of actions and behaviours unique to you, which someone might use to find you. And it turned out that the guy in question had one great passion in life; he loved to go fishing. Fly fishing, to be specific. All around his study were pictures of him holding fish and smiling, his eyes screwed up against the sun. Salmon, the skip tracer reckoned.

You need a licence to fly-fish for salmon, and in the days since the guy disappeared, 515 licences had been applied for across the United States. 157 had been paid for in cash, 46 of which had been retained for collection at the applicant's wish, rather than being put in the post. 15 of these were made on a single day and related to the same stretch of river. A fishing party, probably. 22 pertained to remote locations in Montana and Alaska. You'd have to trek to reach them, and the guy was out of shape and accustomed to comfort; not the trekking type. Which left just 9 applications. 8 seemed unexceptional. The ninth stood out because of the name on the application: Mr J White. It sounded to the skip tracer like it might be made-up. Black. Grey. Blue. Liars tend to fall back on colours.

Six separate lodges and cabins were available to rent in the area covered by that single licence, and the Skip Tracer called the owners one by one. Was there anything unusual about their current guests? No sir, there was not. Has anyone made any specific requests? No sir, they had not. Except for one guy, who'd asked for a coffee machine. The old-fashioned kind, with filters and a pot. The owner had given him the one from his office, which no one used any more.

'Did your husband like his coffee?' the skip tracer asked. It turned out that he loved it, and the ritual of making it. Always had a pot on the go at home and in the office. Always the same blend. Loose grounds put through a filter machine. The old-fashioned kind, with filters and a pot.

I've been trying to sell the idea of bringing the skip tracer to Britain, to use his skills on businessmen and women who have given up and run away from trouble. I like the idea of transplanting his drawl and his pickup and his ten-gallon hat to the home counties, swapping motels with blinking neon signs for prim B&Bs, arrow-straight interstate highways for the commuter crawl of Sevenoaks and Oxted.

But I've also been applying the secrets of his trade to finding the missing boy genius. And last night I struck lucky.

I read an article about the boy that suggested he had an incredibly rare aural processing problem, which doctors were struggling to understand, let alone treat. His mother was said to be doing all she could to understand it herself, to improve her son's quality of life. So I researched book titles on the subject, and then did a US-wide search for the books on the public library system. These books were very specialist, and only one copy of each existed. Five of them had been specially ordered, by a one-room library serving a small town in Utah.

Bingo.

I called up the library, and asked the librarian to pass on my number to the person who'd borrowed the books. Two hours later, I had a text message from a US cell phone – 'We are away at the moment. You can reach us on this number next week.'

Now this is 100% not true. The bit about the library books, anyway. I do have a number for the boy. But I got it in a much less interesting way, by phoning everyone with his surname in the state where he was born. 58 separate households. Eventually I made contact with his great-aunt and -uncle – sweet-sounding, concerned, talkative people, who run a small convenience store. They had indeed spent all their savings on a private detective to find the boy. They had no idea where he was.

Then, out of the blue, a flurry of long-distance calls. Mother and son had got back in touch. They were running short of money.

The great-aunt and -uncle were happy to pass on the boy's contacts, thinking a documentary might help to bring him back into their lives. In truth, I don't think they felt they had much to lose.

The library thing is a good story, though. Commissioners will love it. It'll make them feel like this is a once-in-a-lifetime story, in the hands of someone super committed to telling it. It'll give the whole thing the feel of a story that's meant to be told.

But as yet, I have no idea what the boy will say.

July 10

I have no plans at all for today, except for maybe a nap. I'll stay in my flat all day if I can. Maybe even in just one room.

I've had the same headache for weeks now. Pills don't seem to help and booze only makes it worse. I'm lying still and trying not to think. In particular about Ray Monroe.

Another chiding message comes through on my phone.

It feels like Donovan can read my mind.

'Last chance', the message says. 'Tell me what you know about Monroe or the story becomes about you.'

July 11

Our researcher has found some fantastic footage of the missing genius's mum, speaking confidently and impressively about her son's magnificent mind. It's hard to believe the accusation that she made the whole thing up.

But TV has always attracted fantasists, because fantasists crave attention and exposure.

A journalist friend once put me in touch with a man who described himself as an expert in the female orgasm. He claimed that he knew so much about it that he could make a woman climax just by talking to her. I thought there might be a film in it – a funny one maybe, about the mysteries of female sexuality – so I gave him a call.

His thoughts seemed jumbled and the language he used was not that of an expert in anything, so I thanked him for his time and wished him well in his endeavours. He phoned the office every day for the following month. The receptionist took pity on him and heard him out eventually. It turned out he was a mini-cab driver who'd been suspended for saying creepy things to customers.

It's an unoriginal thought, yet somehow always shocking whenever it occurs: people aren't always who and what they appear to be.

Another time I spent a week shooting a taster with a charismatic man who described himself as a professional monster hunter. In the past he'd led expeditions in search of vampires and Abominable Snowmen. Now he was planning to look for a gigantic prehistoric swamp lizard that features in the myths and legends of a dangerous part of South America.

I had him pegged as a fantasist from the get-go, of course. Indeed, the film I was proposing was entirely about the pleasures and importance of dreaming and fantasizing, which are things that we generally grow out of doing. I wanted to present the guy and his ragtag team as keeping alive the spirit of gentlemen adventurers of the nineteenth century who set off into uncharted territory in search of Troy or Atlantis, or sea monsters or lost tribes of giants. They generally weren't taken very seriously either, but they often found remarkable things. I think it's a shame that the modern world is such a known quantity, and life is generally so humdrum. Wouldn't all our lives be improved by the occasional fantastical quest?

The monster hunter was a great character: poetic, magnetic and mysterious in just the right sort of way. I never managed to discover where he got all his money from. He took his monster hunting seriously, and never let failure or disappointment get him down. As far as I'm concerned, the guy's an inspiration.

I really wanted to make the film, but no one wanted to commission it. People said that it was too unreal. I said but it's *totally* real. He's a genuine, bona fide fantasist. They said he won't find any monsters. I said you're missing the point.

But perhaps in retrospect the person missing the point was me. What audiences and commissioners want is characters that are extraordinary but also of this world, getting on with life rather than living out strange fantasies.

Much of what Lord and Lady Delamain and their offspring do and say beggars belief. They're fabulously rude and dismissive. They come across as lazy and feckless, and appear to care more about their dogs than they do each other. They're somehow both penniless and rich, and seem to spend all their money on parties and having fun. They're like caricatures of posh people. But they're also entirely authentic. You couldn't make them up, which is why I think they'd be brilliant on TV.

I just need to get them to see things the same way I do.

Put like that, it doesn't sound hard. And in truth I don't think it is.

I've turned around far less promising scenarios. Not through skills I've learned or force of personality. Through the simple expedient of not giving in and never giving up.

July 13

'I know someone who could probably help', Rankin says.

With the Monroe issue, he means. He says it was a journalist like Donovan who brought his empire down. Nosy and persistent. The police read the piece in the paper and showed up the next day with sledgehammers for the doors, dogs, guns and bulletproof vests. He says it cost him millions and five years of his life.

We're in a disused amusement arcade on the seafront where Rankin lives. Around us are machines I recognize from when I was a boy, inert and covered in dust. Rankin owns this place. He uses a room at the back as an office, and the full-width basement for storage. He didn't say what he stores there.

Outside, the windows are boarded up and there's a thicket of scaffolding that's been in place for years, the building frozen in a permanent state of non-improvement, though men in high-vis jackets regularly come and go. There's a sort of cage around the door, secured with a pair of heavy-duty padlocks.

At the back there's a compound with high walls on all sides, that Rankin drove us into, then triple locked the gates. It's a place that makes him feel safe.

We're drinking coffee in pink and white cups from the ice-cream parlour next door.

'He's a very persuasive man', Rankin says. 'Good at getting people to see things from a different point of view.'

I consider it for a moment, and politely decline.

Big mistake.

Not the declining part. Or even telling Rankin about the journalist on my case, though I don't know why I did that. I hate feeling powerless, I suppose. I wanted to know there's some way out, even if it's not one I could ever take. It was a relief and a thrill to consider it. I felt a sort of surge.

It's the pause that was the problem. A fraction too long. Just enough to look weak and needy. Like I'm firmly in Rankin's orbit now, rather than the way it should be, the other way around.

Now we're discussing the phantom film that Rankin thinks we're making, and the business he built buying and selling guns. We came here because he wanted to show me the item that made his name, specially modified in a workshop at the back of the arcade, where penny cascades and pinball machines were once built and repaired.

He opens his briefcase and hands me a machine gun, barely bigger than a pistol. 'Designed for special forces', he says. Purchased from Russia for 8000 roubles – roughly the same as a good night out – and sold in Britain for £10,000.

'This is the prototype', he says, 'used for demonstrations'.

It's been heavily styled, tiny dark crystals on the grip and a gold tattoo on the barrel.

'Like jewellery.'

He looks at me three seconds longer than is comfortable. 'Sure', he says. 'Like jewellery that shifts a thousand rounds a minute.'

The important thing, he explains, was a mechanical change he made, to stop it spraying upwards when you pull the trigger. Made it much more reliable, and very much more deadly.

'Sold hundreds', he says, and grins at me like a shark.

I'm wondering where this will end. I don't think anywhere good.

July 15

The college I went to had three libraries, none of which ever closed. You could find people in them at any time of the day or night, on any day of the year.

I loved the stillness and the air of contentment. There were no laptops or mobiles in those days. All you could hear was the rustle of turning pages and the scratching of pen on paper.

The main library was established in Victorian times, in a large and gloomy old church. This is mainly where the college's undergraduates went to study. I generally sat in a sloping gallery at the back of the library, which would once have housed the choir. The dark wood, heavy carved desk and tiny round windows made it feel like the captain's quarters in a great wooden ship.

The second library was built in the 1700s. It had a blood-red carpet and ladders to reach to the top of the bookshelves. There were just ten oak desks, each with a brass table lamp and a padded leather armchair. This is mainly where academics went to write their books, in little pools of light.

The third library dated from the 1400s. It housed very rare books and manuscripts, and smelled of spices and dust. It creaked and groaned as though alive, and was mainly used by frowning postgrads engaged in original research.

At exam time the atmosphere in the main library became more charged. At the end of the first year, with an essay to write, I went in search of calmer surroundings and settled in the second library, which was entirely empty. It was a cold grey day, a good one to spend at a desk, but I couldn't settle my mind. So, with no one to disturb and no one to tell me not to, I decided to explore.

I had a nosey at the work left on the other desks, and browsed a couple of old books that were chained to the wall. I went up and down the ladders to see if there was anything of interest at the top. And then behind a heavy curtain at the furthest end of the room, in an alcove that housed the library's handwritten catalogue, I found a door that was locked.

It took me four hours to find the key, in the bottom drawer of the librarian's desk, in her cramped little office. But once I'd found the door, there was no way I was going back to my essay.

Behind the door was a tight spiral staircase, heading down to an underground room. I knew the fellows of the college had a wine cellar. Perhaps this was it?

It wasn't. It was a space full of shelves, each tightly stacked with wooden and cardboard boxes.

I went back to get a torch.

The room led on to another, and then another.

There were dozens of rooms, all crammed with boxes, which got older and mustier the further into the labyrinth I ventured.

I was in the library's stacks, in the vaults of the oldest part of the college. The boxes contained the possessions and records of the college, reaching back who knows how far and containing who knows what. It looked as if no one had been down there for years.

I spent the whole night there, opening boxes like it was Christmas. At dawn I put the key back and went to bed.

For the remainder of my time at the college I went back often, with a blanket, spares for the torch, and a rucksack with a few supplies. I'd pick my moment and then step through the secret door and vanish.

I tried to ration my visits, so I wouldn't spend too much time there and neglect my work and friends, but I rarely lasted more than a week. I don't remember much from my studies, but I remember every discovery I made in those thousands of boxes. There were intimate letters and pieces of treasure, trinkets and inventions, notebooks and ledgers, specimens and vials of mysterious liquid. The possibilities felt endless and the excitement was immense. It made me fall in love with finding and uncovering things.

And it taught me a lesson that sounds banal but isn't. If you come across an interesting-looking door, always, *always* go through it. If it's locked, even more so. Or at least knock and see what happens. Life's too short and boring not to.

I've got my hand on the handle of a very interesting door at this very moment.

When I came to leave the college the librarian shook my hand. I didn't get the degree I wanted. 'Never mind', she said. 'Education is not about degrees. Education is about discovery. And you have made, I'm sure, discoveries in your time here. Which makes it time well spent.'

She knew, in other words. Her eyes told me she'd keep the secret, and I felt relieved.

But really I hadn't been doing any harm. I never took anything, and never wanted to. If anyone had caught me, it would have been a ticking off. A withdrawal of privileges at most.

That's certainly not the case right now.

One, two, three.

Turn the handle and step inside.

Quick, before anyone sees.

July 16

It feels good to override a thought sometimes. To go with the impulsive animal bit of your brain, that deals only in the risks and rewards of the here and now. To give in to the pleasures of doing things that are wrong.

But yesterday nearly didn't go well at all. I'm trying to figure out what damage I might have done.

Anyone can go on a tour of Castle Delamain. It's £30, including tea and biscuits. Sometimes Lord Delamain does the tour himself. That's what I was hoping for. But yesterday the guide was a local historian.

It was clear from the tone of the tour that the historian disapproved immensely of Lord Delamain and his family, which is probably why Lord Delamain himself was nowhere to be seen. Every crumbling cornice and cobweb was noted with a grimace and a sad shake of his head. He mentioned that he was from the village, where his family had lived for 400 years. If his great-granny or her granny had been a bit more attractive, it might have been him in the house, opening fetes, judging things and whooshing about in a Bentley. Or maybe they were beautiful and full of life, but insufficiently wary of the charm of roguish toffs? Maybe the historian and Lord Delamain have the same blue blood in their veins?

Several letters to Lord Delamain at home and at his club had met with no response. I thought we might encounter him whilst touring his house, but we didn't.

So what was my plan? I didn't really have one, and the tour felt like it was winding down.

Then we thinned into single file to pass through a narrow corridor in the oldest part of the house. I let a party of old ladies go ahead, which put me at the back of the line.

At the other end of the line, I heard the historian say that the doors we'd be passing are the family's private rooms. '*Private* rooms', was how he said it, full of envy and resentment. '*Strictly* out of bounds.'

All the doors were firmly closed, four of them in total. I recognized the door to the library. The hunting party had taken tea there on the second day of the shoot.

I hung back till the line cleared the corridor and turned the squeaky handle.

'This is okay', I thought. 'I can just say I was looking for the loo. Just putting my head round the door. Just being nosy.'

Closing the door behind me would be harder to explain.

Hiding behind a screen would be harder still. But that's what I did when I heard the shrill voice of Lady Delamain growing louder and louder.

'Go and ask Henry how many are coming', she said, I don't know to whom. He's in his study. *His facking 'staady'*, like studying is the last thing that happens there.

Poor Lord Delamain, attacked from every side.

Then Lady Delamain wafted away, and the room went very still.

I crept out and stood for a moment, listening. Then continued, heading the opposite way to the direction her ladyship had left in.

In some sort of sitting room, a dog looked up and I stopped dead. There was china set up for tea on the table, and a steaming cup.

I shushed the dog, and showed it my hands.

It gave a look that seemed to say 'for fuck's sake', like this happens all the time. He put his head down, breathed in and out deeply, and went instantly back to sleep.

I tiptoed through another two rooms. The floors groaned and creaked.

The next room was full of model soldiers, arranged into scenes from great historical battles.

I started to look at one, and a voice said loudly, 'Are you lost, young man? Or have you found what you were looking for?'

Lord Delamain, sitting in an armchair in the corner, reading the *Daily Mail*.

It was some hours later before I left. The sun had just gone down. The walk to the nearest village was a mile or more.

Twenty strides in, something made me look back. Not a sound or a movement, but something intangible. Some sort of ripple, meaning some sort of danger. I wonder what part of you it is that picks up on such things? A primitive region of the brain, perhaps. The bit that's still part lizard.

In the gloaming, as bats began to flitter, there was Lady Delamain, hovering at a second floor window like a ghost in a Gothic novel, pale and luminous, her eyes furious and fixed on mine.

I considered waving but decided on balance not to.

July 18

The old boy didn't seemed surprised at all to find me creeping around his house. Didn't even ask for an explanation.

At first I thought he might have mistaken me for someone else. But he remembered me well enough from the shoot and that day at his club.

In truth I believe he was bored, banished from his house by a tiresome tour, and steeling himself for a looming confrontation with his formidable wife.

He folded up his paper and poured us both a drink, whistled in the sleepy old dog and pushed the door to. Terrifying as Lady Delamain might be, she wouldn't venture in here.

'Tell me, are all TV producers so persistent?' he said.

I told him a little about the industry and my particular part in it.

I learned that he likes television, and watches lots of it. There's an ancient old set in the corner of his study, with huge push-button switches for the channels (just three of them), and aerials at the back for reception.

'It's an "empathy machine"', he said. 'Empathy is the thing it makes and what it's for. And it's good for people to understand each other.' He wishes people had a better understanding of him and the life he leads.

I wondered if he was talking about the sour-faced historian romping around his home, or maybe his wife or his children. Or if he was referring more generally to men in his position. Or even the class that he's part of.

'Do you feel understood?' he says.

'As much as I want to be, I suppose.'

He nods thoughtfully at this.

It's best to tell people outright and upfront why you're interested in them, if you want to put them on television. But the best characters already know why, even if they've never considered it before. They're already the stars of their own life stories.

Lord Delamain can see himself on TV. He enjoys the idea of the series, and so do his several sons. But his wife very much does not.

I like this kind of talk. The kind of talk that gets to the nub of the problem. It puts you halfway towards getting what you want.

'Is she worried about intrusion?' I wondered. 'Or disruption? Or what her friends might say? Because these are problems we can work around.'

He sipped his drink and shook his head.

'The problem', he said, 'is that she doesn't like people like you'.

Tonight I'm at an awards do, at a hotel in central London.

I know exactly what Lady Delamain means. I don't like people like me either.

A film I made last year was nominated for an award. I didn't expect it to win, and it didn't. The competition was far too stiff. The best film won, as they usually do.

But no matter how low your expectations, in the moment when your category comes up and they read out the nominations, your heart still goes like a train, and you start to believe that this might be your night.

The disappointment feels like a kick in the balls.

Then my rival Nicolas Sanderson, the guy from the pub in Scotland, won for a boring film he made about a children's charity, which felt like the same thing again. Probably, if anything, a little bit worse.

This is why the parties that follow awards dos are such strange and uncomfortable things. 20 or 30 people will be roaring and boasting like Georgian dandies. The rest will be recovering from being kicked in the crotch, sometimes repeatedly.

Some will never recover. Like mountaineers within touching distance of a summit they've dreamed of, only to find the last few feet unscaleable. Knowing what it took just to get so close is enough to put some people off ever really trying again.

Not me, though. All I want now is to get back to work. I want to make something happen.

July 19

Outside it's a warm, quiet evening. The breeze smells floral and sweet.

Inside you're hit by a wet, sour smell and a ferocious roar. 50 semi-pissed hacks in the hour before home time, loading up on each other's expenses.

It's a wine bar, still stuck in the '80s, when wine bars were the thing. There are plastic vines pinned to the walls and candles in empty bottles.

In an alcove at the back, surrounded by colleagues and telling a tale, is John Donovan. He's a big deal in here. A hero, in his element.

I go to the bar and buy two drinks. Proper ones, not wine.

I stand over the group in the alcove, and wait till all of them are looking my way.

'Why don't you talentless parasites fuck off while me and this cunt have a chat?'

Best to get on the front foot good and early in situations like this. Half playing a part, half relishing being off the leash.

The people in the group are looking at each other now. A couple of them are smiling, then they look back at me and stop.

The youngest of them stands, snarling. I open my shoulders towards him.

'It's okay', Donovan says to the boy on his feet. 'Leave us. This won't take long.'

The girl from the party I went to with Monroe complained about the film we made to the organization that regulates the TV industry, just short of three months after the film went to air. One more week and the window for official complaints would have closed. She was old enough to complain by just two days, a brave thing to do without the support of her parents.

She alleged that the film was a whitewash, an unfair and incomplete representation of Monroe in general, and of specific events that happened during filming. She asked that the rushes of the film be scrutinized, in the belief they would support her primary allegation, made to local police, that Monroe had tried to abuse her that night.

An official investigation followed, led by the regulator and lawyers at the channel that broadcast the film. It found that a tape had gone missing as the film transferred to the edit, and that the missing tape was the only one shot during the party at the home of the complainant. As the girl's complaint related specifically to the events of that night, the absence of the tape, as the only independent record of what had taken place, meant that nothing could be proved.

In the absence of hard evidence, and confronted by silence from the other guests at the party, the police reluctantly dropped the case.

The regulator cleared my name, though losing tapes doesn't look good, and their report was careful to note that.

As no adverse findings were made, the report was never made public. It's all there on record, though, if you know where to look.

Donovan takes his drink.

'What is it with you and texting? Like a fucking teenaged girl.'

'Got a very generous package', he says. 'Unlimited free texts to liars. Saves me a fortune.'

He says he's been after Ray Monroe for over three years now. He says Monroe used his fame to hurt and abuse young women and girls. Standing up the case has been hard, though. None of his victims has been willing to go on record.

Since that day in May on the Brightwell Estate, Donovan's been after me as well. I can picture his delight on discovering he could get two for the price of one.

'What's this got to do with me?'

He says he door-stepped Monroe at a recording of some daytime chat show. He fired a question at him about the missing tape, implying that he'd seen it, and got a telling response – a fleeting look of horror, followed by denial that he knew what Donovan was talking about, followed by immediate insistence that the tape in question doesn't exist.

Here was a chink in Monroe's armour, the thing that could finally bring him down.

'The girl was right', he says, his voice even but his features contorted with disgust. 'You knew what was happening, or must have suspected. You filmed something telling and you buried it. You colluded with Ray Monroe, which means you're as bad as he is. Some people might think you're worse.'

'I made a film is all. Shot 50 hours for a 46-minute programme. Can't use everything. Especially footage on tapes that get lost.'

'If it got lost, it was you who lost it.'

'I'm obsessively careful with my rushes. I was more upset than anyone when they told me they couldn't find it.'

'I'm giving you a chance to make amends', he says; 'not everybody gets that'.

He thinks if I go on the record, say what I know about Monroe and what was on the tape, others will be emboldened and come forward. Monroe will get what he deserves. And for Donovan, of course, another sensational story.

I imagine that this is the point where people usually fold, confronted by Donovan's moral certitude and lust for justice, coupled with just that hint of kindness. The suggestion that he can forgive.

I refuse to go on the record, of course. To do any sort of interview at all. I tell him everything I wanted to say about Monroe was there in the film I made.

He says he'll run the story of the missing tape instead – the documentary maker who knew the truth but refused to do what's right.

He says maybe that's a better story? In the sense of a bigger splash. People love TV, but they love to hate the people who make it.

'Think about it', he says, smiling.

I finish my drink and stand up to leave.

'Do they know you're gay?' I ask him, nodding at his cronies at the bar.

His smile falters, but only a little.

'Who told you that?'

'You just did.'

Something about his manner as I watched him from the bar. In full flow, but holding something back. Suppressing something vital. Keeping himself in check.

No one believes in the truth at all costs. Everybody lies.

He says, 'This changes nothing.'

We'll see about that. A crusading bully is a bully nonetheless. And bullies crumble when the tables are turned. I want him off my back.

I tell him I'll see him around, and blow a kiss to the boys at the bar.

July 20

Today we're working on the blue-chip access challenge, writing emails to companies, chatting about brands and places we've been.

What about the Albert Hall? Or Blackpool Tower? Or Notre Dame?

What about Amazon, or Asos? Or Cheltenham Ladies' College? Or the zoo in Central Park?

The windows are open and there's a gentle breeze. We had lunch in the park, and I bought ice creams for everyone mid-afternoon.

The junior researcher and the AP are together, I think. In that golden, weightless period of their first few days as a couple. Still a little hesitant around each other. Still projecting the best of themselves. No doubt thinking they're keeping it a secret, but unable to disguise the signs. I'm pleased for them. They look good together. They're as sunny as the weather, and it's making the rest of us feel good.

I love these people. They'll all move on eventually, to better or bigger jobs. Or they'll get bored of their commute. Or the minor frustrations of the too-small fridge, or the bad-tasting fair-trade coffee in the kitchen. Or they'll lose faith in the things we're working on. Or they'll lose faith in me.

But right now, today, we are content. A happy little band, relaxed in each other's company, making each other smile, working productively.

One hour before home time MacLean, the new guy, comes over. He looks impeccable. Not too smart, not too casual. Better dressed than the young people in the office. Less formal than the owners. Perfectly judged. I can see why everybody likes him. Mills calls him 'Squeaky' MacLean, primarily for my benefit.

He says, 'Truman, I'm sorry to interrupt. Do you have a moment?'

With no trace at all of swagger or pride, he tells me about the commission he landed earlier today. A documentary series about all the weddings that happen on the second Saturday in June, the most popular day of the year to get married. You see the build-up, and then the weddings, and then we follow the couples through their first year of married life, finally joining them for an assessment of what marriage means, what it feels like and what it's for, on their first anniversary the following summer. A really simple, elegant idea, commissioned with minimal fuss.

I'd be lying if I said this didn't come as a blow. The only thing worse than not getting what you want in life is someone else getting it. And now that's happened twice in three days.

MacLean says, 'Charlie told me about all your projects. Very exciting, all of them.'

Then he says he needs some help to get his commission ready to go into production, and Charlie suggested he borrow some people from my team.

July 21

I'm on a National Express coach with Mills, from London to the coast. Might National Express be a company we could negotiate access to? They provide cheap seats from anywhere in Britain to anywhere else.

We went to their ticket office in Victoria, and bought two returns on the next coach out of the station.

There's a happy buzzy atmosphere, from 30 people excited at the prospect of a day by the sea. Hard-working people, I suspect. Treating themselves and their families to a rare day away.

Later we'll start chatting to other people on the bus, and get a sense of how they feel about the service, and whether a documentary series on coaches across the country would be an entertaining thing to watch. For now, we're settling in, enjoying looking at the city slip by. I've lived in London for 15 years now, and I still get the same fizz of excitement from seeing St Pauls and the Houses of Parliament as I did when I first arrived here, a skinny northern boy with everything I owned in a single bag.

I'd left my girlfriend behind, and come south with a one-month contract and a small room in a big house share in Shepherd's Bush. When I turned up, late on Sunday before my first day at work, they told me that they'd let my room to someone else and would return my deposit in due course. I spent the night in a dosshouse; £5 for eight hours. Four other men in a row of single beds in a standard double room, still warm from the last set of occupants. The other four men were homeless. I suppose I was too.

The next day, scared and rumpled, I told a guy I met in the office kitchen what had happened. Without thinking for even a moment, he invited me to stay at his place, just four or five sentences into our relationship. It was an astonishingly kind and generous thing to do, and that night he took me out for dinner. I had a whole month to go before I'd be paid. He picked up the bill.

So many years later, it's still the kindest thing that anyone has ever done for me. I thanked him, of course. But I don't think I ever thanked him enough. The people I met at that time are my best friends still.

The other passengers on the coach, though not all as young as I was then, are at a similar stage in their lives, it seems. Starting out on something new. Trying to get somewhere in life. Vibrating with nerves and hope and expectation. At the beginning of a big adventure. Striving. Trying to make things work. It makes me think that there might be something in the idea we're here to explore. All good documentaries need a strong theme.

We play a game that's become a thing between us. A brainstorming game that we've adopted as our own. You say (or text or email) titles to each other, and try to think of what the programme might be. *The Sperminator. Ten Tonne Wedding. My Fake Baby. Badass Mother. I Love You To Death. Girlfriend in a Coma*, and so on. Good titles are very important. It's probably as good a way of having ideas as any other.

Then as we hit the motorway, everyone on the coach goes quiet for a while.

'Everyone needs to run away sometimes. Everyone needs to escape.'

Mills looks out of the window and starts to speak in a way she never has before, about her life and herself.

Her dad left her mum when she was nine or ten. There were days when her mum just sat and did nothing, and some days when she got drunk. So she looked after her younger brother. Fed and bathed him and put him to bed, and then looked after her mother.

There's something else, I can tell. Something she doesn't want to say. Maybe never has, to anyone, and maybe never will.

She did okay at school, but not as well as she could or should have.

She looks after her mother and brother still. Most of the money she earns she gives to them.

I think she must have felt terribly lonely.

There was a boy earlier this year. They almost got engaged. Did, in fact, for a week. And then she broke it off and split with him for good.

I say that I'm sorry.

'You look after your mum and your brother', I say, 'but who looks after you?'

The muscles flex in her cheeks. She's not going to let herself cry.

She turns away, cross with herself, and I put my arm around her.

She stiffens and shrugs and pulls away. 'Don't do that', she says, very quietly. Then gives in and puts her head on my chest, and stays there, sleeping, all the way to the sea.

July 23

Charlie has come into the office very early, with two coffees and a bag of pastries. This is a bad sign.

No need to go into the meeting room, as it's just the two of us. No one else will be around for another couple of hours. Whatever he's got to say, he wants to keep it casual. But his face looks stern.

He sits at the desk next to mine, and takes a long look at me. And then says that I have to improve. Not work harder. Just do better.

'Your credit-card bills are twice everyone else's', he says. Overalls and buckets. Ammunition for a shotgun. 20 mobile phones (I give them to hectic characters who think that they're presents but are actually just a means of keeping in touch). A large amount of imported specialist pornography (from a doomed attempt to win access to the last 'real' porn shop in Soho, before the internet killed them all off). 'And – God help us – something called "Tissue" which turned out to be a human placenta' (very interesting what happens to those; there's a booming black market I was trying to explore).

'I never ask questions', he says.

'Frankly, I don't want to know. Then there's your team, which is twice as big as anyone else's. And you're more than twice as arrogant. All of which is fine, so long as it's underpinned by commissions. Commissions are the thing that pays for it all, and the thing – the *only* thing – that can possibly justify the way you behave.'

I consider telling him about all the leads and the access ideas and the emails. The bankers and the organ film and all the rest. But there's really no point. Commissions are what matters.

He says, 'You don't think like other people, which has a certain value, though it comes at a certain cost. You have your own way of going about things, and I respect that. But I keep catching you looking over your shoulder. And I think what you're looking for is a grown-up to tell you to stop. You can't see a grown-up, so you carry on, running risks, playing at doing your job. But the grown-up is there. The grown-up is you.'

I say, 'People don't change, Charlie.'

Charlie says, 'They do, because they must.'

July 24

It's a lovely mellow morning. A woman is working little white flowers into a wreath that reads 'Beloved Son'.

The shop she runs is the nicest on a rundown street of bookies and pound-shops, done out with frilly lampshades and dark, heavy furniture from a house-clearance place two doors down. There are buckets of fresh flowers everywhere. Down-to-earth stuff, mainly. Nothing too exotic. The front door is open and a wind chime is tinkling in the breeze.

In the back, Rankin is sniffing a single red rose.

'Roses have glands on the lower petals', he says. 'That's where the smell comes from. They respond to warmth and sunshine. That's why roses never smell as nice when it's cloudy.'

He's been going on like this for a while now. I'm wondering again if this guy's for real.

'It's the smell that makes them stand out', he says. 'So subtle and complex. The only smell the human nose never gets tired of. That's a fact.'

His girlfriend is sitting on an old-lady walnut dresser, sulkily pulling petals off an oversized daisy and kicking her heels against the dresser doors. There's a general air of mutiny and mischief about her and she's making me feel nervous.

'To preserve the fragrance, people used to put the petals on glass smeared with rendered fat, and use light to make the fat absorb the essential oils. They'd replace the petals, over and over, for thousands of hours. In the end, that gives you something called a "pomade". Then the oils would be separated from the fat with pure-grain alcohol. And then they'd evaporate the alcohol away, and what you're left with is an attar that smells like angels. It's called an "absolute of enfleurage"'.

He pauses and looks up from the vase of roses he's been toying with. 'An absolute of enfleurage', he says again, enjoying the words. 'Weighs one six-thousandth of the weight of the petals you started with. Worth way more than gold.'

'You gonna get some flowers for your ladyfriend?' the girl says, looking at me, a faint fuck-you smile at the corners of her mouth. Rankin's been ignoring her, like a dad with a petulant child. I wonder how many times she's sat through this before.

'Exquisite', Rankin says. 'Men will risk all sorts to possess something so special and rare … '

A decent preface for a discussion of almost any kind of criminal enterprise.

'You must have one, good-looking boy like you?' says Rankin's girlfriend. 'Or maybe you're more the kind who takes it where he finds it?'

Rankin lays down his rose, controlling his temper, moving on, his little bit of theatre spoiled for today.

'You're like a private eye', he says, turning to face me. 'Go anywhere you want and ask people questions.'

I'm about to say no, not really, but it's clear this is not a discussion. This is part two of his speech. The bit where we get to the rub.

'And people tell you stuff? Trust you, don't they?'

'Not always. Usually.'

'Because they like you.'

'Because they can tell I'm interested.'

'In the stuff they do.'

'In them.'

'I've got something you'll be interested in', he says.

'I'll be the judge of that.'

He smiles a wide forced smile. Patient. Letting it go.

'Let's call it a favour in return for the one you asked me.'

I say nothing now. Seems more sensible not to.

'There's a pub', Rankin says. 'More of a club. With girls.'

'A brothel?'

He smiles again, the same patient menace on his face. His girlfriend is still and quiet now. Watching, interested.

'Not that. A boozer. For a certain clientele.'

I'm thinking of all the ways in which this could be dangerous. Too many to count.

'There's a guy there who's devised … a new kind of entertainment.'

I raise my eyebrows, but that's all the information I'm going to get.

'Ask for Mr Bixby', he says. 'And ask him how's Vee.'

'Ask him yourself.'

He takes a breath at this.

'I can't', he says. 'We're not on good terms. I'm sure he'll talk to you, though.'

'Why's that?'

'Because you're gonna find him interesting.'

July 25

The missing boy genius is missing no more. I spoke to him at some length this morning, as the cleaners were finishing work and the office was coming to life.

People tend to respond to things the way they think they're expected to. So if you're interested in who a person really is, the best way to interview them is not to. Rather let them speak, and listen out for the things they're omitting, the things that don't ring true.

The boy is still a genius, though. At least he seems to think so.
I'm afraid I'm less convinced.

July 26

We're in a nice suburban house, with a couple in their thirties. The woman is in good spirits, humming to herself as she makes coffee in the kitchen. The man looks like he's suffering some sort of inner apocalypse.

Mills has read a piece in a women's magazine about a 17-year-old girl who suffered a fall on a skiing holiday, and lost all her memories from the age of 10. Her mother had taken her on a sort of road trip, to fill in the seven-year hole in her life. She'd had to remake almost every relationship. Mills met her and said she was hugely likeable – childlike and vulnerable, but a survivor deep down, and determined to get her life back on track. Now she's at the end of the process. If we'd caught her at the beginning of it, it would have been a heart-stoppingly brilliant film.

So we've negotiated access to a charity that helps people with serious head injuries. We're interested particularly in amnesia, and how it impacts on relationships. We want to find someone yet to come to terms with their accident, and then follow them through whatever happens next.

We drink our coffee, and try to keep it light. 'So you're friends of my husband?' the woman says. I explain that we're TV producers. The man explains to her what happened. They were in a car crash. She was badly injured; flown to hospital and put into a coma. Part of her brain was bruised and damaged – the part that makes new memories.

The woman is aghast. She dashes to a mirror, hands on her head, looking for signs of trauma, finding nothing but the faintest of scars.

The man has explained the same thing every morning for the past year and a half.

And then he does something shocking.

'I'm sorry but our marriage is over', he says. 'Now I'm with someone else.'

The woman looks like the ground has dropped away beneath her feet, her stomach lurching, her mouth opening and closing. Mills looks horrified. The man looks entirely broken.

Every day he comes to the house and breaks up with his wife, and nurses her through it as best he can, and then goes to work and tries to live a life of his own. The next day he comes back, hoping that she'll have remembered. And when it's clear she hasn't, the whole thing begins again.

Today I think he wants to us to see how hard it is, so he's being callous. Mills is hugging the woman now. She's sobbing quietly. I'm sitting outside on the step with the man as he smokes a cigarette.

At first, he says, they carried on as before. But nothing ever stuck. No matter what happened in their lives, every day they'd be back at that same place, the morning before the accident. And then he met someone else.

It's an acutely miserable scenario. A man who cares about his wife too much to abandon her, but not enough to stay. And so they're both stuck in limbo, endlessly reliving the same crushing day, unable to break free.

I know what the man wants. He wants us to tell him it's okay to leave her, and this time not come back. He wants to make a film in the hope that it will change things. It might. People might come forward to help.

Afterwards, in my car heading home, we're quiet for a while. Then I say what I've been thinking, that a film about what we just witnessed would be astounding – charged and unique and stranger than fiction. Like a movie. Hard to watch, but completely and utterly gripping.

Mills says that men are cunts.

I laugh at that, but she doesn't.

'The woman doesn't care about all the stuff she's lost', she says. 'All the time and the memories. So much of herself that she'll never get back. She only cares about losing the person she loves.'

We both pause to consider this.

'Men are selfish and stupid', she says.

I say, 'You can't choose who you love. You just do or you don't.'

'When someone loves you that much', Mills says, 'the least you can do is love them back'.

July 27

When you're developing and pitching programmes, you have to believe that they're excellent, or at least have the potential to be. That if they make it onto the screen, people will love them, and tell their friends about them. That they'll provide the highlight of someone's week. Maybe even be the basis for good memories, for children growing up and their parents. We tend to watch TV with the people we love. My happiest memories of my own mum and dad are of them letting me stay up late, and falling asleep between them while they watched their favourite shows.

It's generally understood that the complications of real life and the exigencies of the production process will make a programme less good on

TV than it was on paper. All sides are prepared to accept a finished product, say, 80% as good as everyone hoped. Or, to put it another way, everyone is prepared to live with a disappointment factor of 20%. If you were aiming high enough at the beginning, 80% of the show you wanted to make will still be something worth broadcasting.

You should never pitch ideas that are merely adequate or serviceable. No one wants to buy anything that just does a job, not when there are so many other options to choose from. Whatever the product, we want to believe that we're buying the best we can afford. The principle applies to ketchup and toilet paper, so of course it applies to commissioners shopping for content.

If you say 'I don't have any great ideas, but here's one that's okay', you're on a slippery slope. Commissioners want to shop in boutiques and you're setting yourself up as a discount retailer. Now those commissioners will only come to you when they need something cheap and disposable, for a late-night slot say, or at very short notice when something else has fallen through. More likely, they'll stop coming to you altogether.

I'm in a pitch meeting right now, with Charlie. For as long as I've known him he's been talking about the same idea, which is dated and poor. I've told him that many times, to which he always says that it's no worse than most of what he sees on TV. Which is true. Then I say, 'What sort of a pitch is that? Buy this; it's no worse than the worst of what you've already got.' And generally that's an end to it.

But not today. Today's the day he's decided to finally pitch it.

I understand why. We're short of commissions, and he's starting to lose confidence in me. So he's doing what any boss would do; he's rolling up his sleeves and getting stuck in.

By doing that, though, I think he might well make those commissions even harder to land.

People are always pleased to see Charlie. He's charming and affable. He makes people laugh and feel relaxed. Commissioners remember the hits he had in the past.

I've pitched my idea about commuters on the Westway, and the intimate conversations they have in their cars. We watched the taster tape, a well-crafted piece of work, but the idea was politely declined. Too repetitive and dull to watch for an hour at a time, was the commissioner's view. In any case, she said, the channel is already underway on a series about a breakdown recovery service. As ideas, the two aren't even similar, but commissioners don't think like the rest of us. In her eyes, they've got people in cars well covered.

I looked to Charlie for a word of support, but Charlie looked away.

I've pitched that idea to everyone now. Absolutely no one wants it.

Then I tried an idea about the history of offices, that applies different ways of working through time – the windowless typing pool of the '60s with offices for the bosses, the cubicle farms of the '80s, the open-plan spaces of the 1990s, and the modern-day adult playgrounds of Facebook and Google – to a single ordinary company across a normal working month. Which works best? And which makes for the happiest workers?

Then another about the sales and marketing team at one of the world's biggest tobacco companies. How do they go about selling cigarettes in the face of ever more restrictive legislation? How do they persuade people to do something for fun that will kill them if they do it for long enough?

Interesting but too niche was the verdict on both. I argued otherwise – more than ten million of us work in offices; what's niche about that? But the word has a different meaning in the mouth of a commissioner. When they say something is niche, it often just means they personally think it's uninteresting.

'I'm sorry', she says, kindly but firmly, like a schoolteacher. 'I'd love to watch them both, but they're just not ones for us.'

Then Charlie says he has an idea too. His pet idea – a grand history of the working class.

'Never been done', he says. 'Not really. Not properly, anyway.'

Now he's rich, he wants to be remembered. That difficult issue of legacy again.

It's been several years since he last pitched an idea, and he's rusty, but it comes back to him as he's talking. He's described it well, but that's doing nothing to disguise the fact that it's rather dull and very old-fashioned.

All creatives drift to the centre over time, no matter how brilliant they were at the start. Bob Dylan does Christmas albums now.

You can see the disappointment on the commissioner's face. Awkwardness too. Because now she has to find a way of telling a well-respected TV figure, some 20 years her senior, that the idea he's pitching is barely an idea at all.

Turning down ideas is hard to do well. It needs to be handled with gentleness and grace, because it might be an idea that's very dear to you. But it also needs to be done unflinchingly, so as to leave no room for doubt. No commissioner wishes to get stuck in a long discussion about an idea they know they do not want. Or worse, for you to go away with hope in your heart, spend lots of time on it, then come back and pitch it again. Commissioners are important people, or at least they mostly think they are. Certainly they're very busy, and they hate wasting time.

Charlie persists, and the tone of the conversation changes. No one wins commissions by grinding commissioners down.

'I'm sorry', the commissioner says again, more purposefully this time. 'I'm just not a fan of that kind of programme.'

Meaning the kind of programme that people stopped making 20-something years ago.

'It feels like such a trek', she says. 'Such a very long plod from Dickens to now.'

But that's given me half an idea.

'What if we don't do the long slow trek? What if we go backwards instead?'

The commissioner is leaning forward now. 'That's interesting', she says. 'How would that work?'

These are the moments in pitching that I love the best, when all plans have been discarded and all you can do is react. Who knows where this will lead? I certainly don't. But everyone's looking my way.

I tell them a fact I learned about the mum with the disappearing daughter. Going back five generations, her family were upstanding citizens – hard workers all their lives, members of the temperance movement and owners of their own pew in church. What went wrong? How did the working class become the underclass? Could we take notorious characters, reviled in the red-tops – people with huge families who've never done a day of work, spongers and scroungers and benefits cheats – and do their family tree?

The commissioner scribbles in her notebook.

'This is off the top of my head, but maybe we could help those families? Give them a perspective on their lives and empower them with knowledge.'

I'm thinking of my social mobility idea now.

'Maybe we can do more than just empower them? Maybe we can help them get back to where they were?'

'I love it', the commissioner says, all chilliness thawed and forgotten.

She offers us money to develop the idea.

Charlie smiles at me in the lift like he's remembered why he hired me. He's feeling good about himself. Back in the game.

I'm safe, at least for another few weeks.

July 28

I'm looking at a selfie on my phone. Donovan with an attractive young woman. They're wearing the same expression, eyebrows slightly raised: Hey Truman, what do you make of this?

At first I thought he'd sent the picture by mistake. Then I recognized the woman's face.

She looks very different now to the last time I saw her. Confident and self-possessed. But it's unmistakably the girl from the party. The girl from the missing tape.

It's clear he's not about to drop this thing. Part of me admires that.

No words this time. No need. The picture says it all.

Donovan has nothing on me. At least, nothing he can prove. But he might not let that stop him. It hasn't in the past.

Publish and be dammed, as they say.

But the damned would be me, not him.

July 29

Believing your ideas to be excellent, so that you can pitch them with the passion and conviction you need, involves telling a particular sort of lie.

This kind is worse than lying to your colleagues or employers, though moralists might disagree. Certainly it's more injurious to your health and happiness. Because the person you're lying to is yourself.

All the best salesmen in TV do it, in a way that becomes second nature. You have to ignore the sensible voices in your head that sound like schoolteachers. What's so different about this idea to all the ones you've had in the past, that have failed and fallen away? Is this really as good as you think it is? Will the access really hold up? Are you and your company really the best people to make it? Is it really the sort of thing that people want to watch?

You tell yourself 'this is the one', like a hopeless gambler. One more bet, even though you know full well that the odds are stacked against you. Bet after bet has gone bad. But still you're willing to back yourself. One big win makes everything okay.

To listen to these lies, to shrug off all the rejection and disappointment and keep on developing and pitching ideas, you have to be a certain sort of person. A romantic, really. A dreamer. A believer in happy endings.

I want to believe that the boy genius was and still is exactly that.

I need to believe it, in fact, because the alternative makes the film unmakeable and uncommissionable.

The boy told me his story, and I was utterly spellbound. As he spoke, I pictured a feature-length documentary, constantly shifting the viewer's sympathies back and forth, wrong-footing the audience at every turn. A film that could play in cinemas, even. A film that could win awards.

But he didn't tell the story the way you imagine a genius might, with clarity and precision. He was faltering and fuddled at times, groping for words and using them wrongly.

He said 'Everything is so clear sometimes. Then suddenly it's not.'

It's fine for the film to play with the uncertainty surrounding the boy's giftedness. That only makes the story more enthralling and delicious. But it has to end the way you hope. Otherwise it's just the story of a fucked-up little boy.

July 30

I'm sitting on a bright red seat at a bright blue table, looking around the room at words block-printed on the bright green and yellow walls: create; inspire; celebrate; enquire; inform. It's like the bedroom of a hot-housed toddler.

I know for a fact that nothing hopeful or creative or meaningful has happened in this room. Despite the fact that its purpose and function is to host and facilitate the birth of new ideas and programmes. I'm here to pitch the genius film, and I've been waiting for 20 minutes for the meeting to start.

I'm wondering at what point not leaving would begin to look weak. Maybe that point has passed already. Leaving would be almost entirely self-defeating. The relationship would be, if not ruined, then permanently scarred. The commissioner would never look at me again without thinking either 'There's the guy I made wait for half an hour. So embarrassing. I don't want to think about it' or 'There's the arrogant prick who's so self-important he couldn't bear to wait for half an hour while I attended to something pressing.' So I'm sitting and quietly struggling to suppress my bubbling rage.

When she eventually arrives, red-faced and stressed, neither of us is in much of a mood to conjure into existence a new piece of television. Stuck here in this joyless void, each of us wishing we were somewhere else, this is going to require one hell of a piece of salesmanship.

But as I begin telling the story of the missing genius, including the made-up story of how I found him, a great thing happens. Both of us get drawn in. I find myself more and more animated. By the end, I've made the hair stand up on the back of my own neck. Across the table, I think I've had the same effect on the commissioner. She's giving me buying eyes.

'Imagine how that must feel. A genius in hiding. A genius pretending not to be.'

'Or an ordinary little boy pretending to be a genius', she says.

'Either way it's compelling, isn't it? Like nothing else you've seen.'

I finish speaking, and there's a moment of silence.

And then she says 'So which is it? Is he really a genius?'

'Exactly. Is he or isn't he? It's like a novel or a movie.'

She says, 'You don't understand. I need to know. Specifically that he *is* a genius. I couldn't possibly commission it otherwise.'

I understand all too well.

July 31

It's not long after 9 am. My belly is empty and I've had too much coffee. I can hear it in my ears. The caffeine is battling the booze from last night, and I feel distinctly queasy.

But at least I'm awake. The audience I'm looking at is barely conscious. We're in a soundproof basement and the lights are low. Some have got their eyes shut.

I give lectures and seminars from time to time to help out a friend. Generally I enjoy it. I like the way it forces you to think in different ways. Not much thinking going on today, though.

The subject is ethics and dilemmas in factual film-making – the choices and decisions you have to make on the spot and in the moment. Your career and people's lives can hang on what you say and do. It's a fascinating subject, but I'm bored, because the students are bored. I ask them questions and no one responds. They're bored because they're disengaged. And they're disengaged because students are by nature both idealistic and lazy. They want rules and truths on the one hand, and on the other, shortcuts and things they can use in their coursework. Easy answers, in other words. I'm telling them there aren't any, so they've given up listening.

The morning after I filmed Monroe at the party at his friend's house, and the confession in the car that followed, I woke up excited. I'd filmed something telling and significant, I thought, which doesn't happen often. The question would be how best to use the footage in the film.

But when I watched the footage back a few days later, it was far less conclusive than it felt at the time. The scenes in the house were confusing and messy, the confession in the car slippery and elusive. 'I've done things I'm not proud of', he said, suggestively, slugging his whisky and slurring his words. You could tell he half wanted to unburden himself, to be done with all the lying and deceit. But simultaneously, the other half of his mind was still carefully covering his tracks, a habit ingrained by 40-odd years of practice. When I zoomed in, you could see the strain of the struggle on his face.

'I'm sorry', he said.

I said nothing. Just zoomed in a tiny bit tighter.

'I'm sorry. I'm keeping you up.'

To dispel the torpor in the lecture theatre, I offer it out for discussion, a thought experiment to illustrate the subtleties of film-making. What would you do if you'd filmed an act of wickedness followed by a confession?

There's no discussion or debate. Just a murmured consensus. They'd hand the tape over to the relevant authorities.

But what if what you filmed was ambiguous?

Now the students are shifting in their seats. The ones who've been absent, doodling and daydreaming, are paying attention now.

What if the confession seems less than clear? Or likely to be unprovable?

And what if the person confessing had been drinking? The confession might therefore be a less than fully conscious or deliberate one. It might call the details into doubt, or even make the whole thing unreliable.

In that situation, where do your responsibilities and loyalties lie? With the subject you've built a relationship with? With the people you suspect your subject might have harmed or injured? With the company you work for? The broadcaster that's paying for the film?

Now the students are engaged. A debate is taking shape.

I agonized over these questions, but in the end my position felt clear. I wasn't making an investigative piece. I hadn't witnessed a crime. Nor was I a policeman.

I had a selfish motivation also, of course. I believed I'd shot a good film. An honest and revealing one. It would have been over instantly if I'd reported my suspicions. The broadcaster would have pulled the film. All for what? Nothing at all would have come of it: nothing for the police to go on; nothing for the channel to broadcast; nothing to show for six months of hard work and two hundred thousand pounds.

When the assistant at the editing house reported the missing tape, I expressed bitter disappointment. A touch of outrage, even. The tapes were all there when I sent them across. The edit hand at the production company had laid them all out, 1–70. He even took a photo on his phone, as a record: losing tapes is very bad.

'Where the fuck is the tape?' I said. 'How could you possibly have lost it?'

The editing house turned the place upside down, all to no avail. Completion of four other productions was delayed, at considerable inconvenience and a cost of 25k.

The tape was in a litter bin, on the street outside my flat. I took it from the neatly packaged crate of rushes destined for the editing house, and put it there myself, wrapped up in fish-and-chip paper.

The debate has subsided now. The students are divided.

'So here's a further question for our thought experiment. Let's imagine you chose to ignore the confession and the bad behaviour. You decided instead to press ahead and finish the film. What would you do if subsequent events overtook you? If you finished the film and put it out, and then discovered down the line there was more to it all than you thought? Much more bad behaviour than you witnessed, or even imagined. A pattern of it, going on for years. What would you do then?'

The students are silent.

Then one kid – a lean kid with a sharp face – puts his hand up. He hasn't said a word as yet.

'You should own the story', he says. 'Get ahead of the game. Take charge.' Good idea.

This kid'll go far. The only one of this lot who will.

CHAPTER EIGHT: AUGUST

August 2

The house I'm in is huge, in a way that makes it hard to relax. The furniture feels as though it's adrift. It must have been a beautiful place once: ramshackle, lived-in and full of antiques. Now all character has gone. It should smell of woodsmoke, polish and books. Instead it just smells clean.

There are pictures of the owner everywhere, and pictures of no one else: national treasure and man of the people Ray Monroe.

His wife brings coffee in a cafetière and biscuits in gold foil fanned out neatly on a plate.

She must be 30 years younger than Monroe, and is new since the last time I saw him. There are no kids, and none from his previous marriages. The house feels very still.

Monroe does nothing to acknowledge her. She withdraws without saying a word, blank, and closes the door behind her.

I say, 'They're coming for you, Ray.'

He says 'Yes, I know.'

For me too.

There's no way out – at least, not for Monroe – but I do have a proposition for him: make a follow-up film with me.

Get your response in before the story breaks, I tell him. Take the initiative away from Donovan and the rest of them. Own it. Be brave. Tell everyone the truth.

'The truth?' he says.

'The truth as you see it.'

He makes a noise somewhere between a sigh and a groan. Fear or disgust, I don't know which.

I tell him if he waits, his voice will get lost in all the outrage and the condemnation. Then it'll all be over, and no one will care what he thinks or says. No one will ever listen again.

The era that I wanted to explore through Ray Monroe had some sort of blind spot when it came to celebrities and young women, to the extent that abuse now looks like part of the age. There have been several scandals in the last few years. Several well-known names are now in disgrace. Several are now in prison.

If you made a film about the '70s and early '80s today, ignoring these events would be unthinkable. When I made my film, things looked very different. I focused on racism and homophobia, because they seemed the worst of the age that was passing. I wish I'd had the foresight to include abuse as well. It's so much more telling than outdated attitudes and language. It makes you reassess everything about those times. About the forces that shaped you, growing up. On the surface those years always seemed shiny and innocent. Underneath they were dark and rotten.

I'd love the chance to revisit that era, and Ray Monroe would be the perfect way of doing it.

Monroe shakes his head. 'I can't do that', he says, 'to 50 years of work.'

His name and his legacy will soon be in ruins. He knows the wrecking ball is in place. He just doesn't want to be the one to swing it.

'50 years', he says again.

His wife reappears to clear away the coffee. She seems entirely broken. She glances at me, and quickly looks away.

August 4

No one ever really teaches you to pitch. It's something that you probably just tend to do in all aspects of your life. Which is to say that you to tend to hustle and pester to get what you want. You're drawn to TV, in which everything and everyone is pitched and re-pitched every day. You make a start, and someone notices that pitching is something you're naturally good at. And before long pitching is what you do for a living.

How other people pitch is a bit of a mystery, because pitching tends to be done in private. A good idea is a valuable piece of intellectual property (at least for a while; ideas go sour and stale over time, like milk and eggs), so you need to be careful about when, how and with whom you discuss it. The rooms at the BBC and Channel 4 and HBO in which ideas are pitched and picked apart are like confessionals. It's understood that what's said in the room stays there.

I generally don't care how other people go about selling ideas. What works for someone else probably won't work for me, because pitching, as we know, is a very personal thing. Some people sell hard. Some people are cuter than that, and flirt and tease their way to commissions.

I do think there's a right and wrong way to pitch yourself to institutions that you want to work with, though. Getting this right can be worth a fortune: if you can persuade Disneyland to work with you and give you access, getting a big commission shouldn't be too hard.

When I started working as an exec, I'd write dozens of carefully constructed emails to organizations and companies, and get no response at all. I'd set out my credentials and the company's strengths. I'd write about awards we'd won for similar pieces of television. I'd explain the diligent and respectful way in which we work. All to no avail. Clearly, I was doing something wrong.

What I wanted and needed was to see what a successful, or at least better, pitch for access looks like. But as with ideas pitched to commissioners, access pitches are generally confidential.

So I hatched a plan.

I placed an advert on an online community message board that lots of people in TV look at, because it's a good way of finding stories and subjects.

It said 'Narcissism Support Group. Meets Wednesdays in Shoreditch. Email Jonathan For Details'.

New, surprising, of the moment, comedic and easy to visualize.

I created an email address for Jonathan, and messages flooded in, mostly from TV producers expressing keen interest and asking for access.

The bad ones were all about the companies that sent them, and came across as arrogant and pushy. They felt very easy to ignore.

The persuasive, enticing ones – the ones Jonathan would have replied to – all did the same thing. They explained simply and clearly why making a film might be a good thing for the group and its members. And then explained the company's interest in the group – generally a simple wish to further a reputation for honest, heartfelt, sign-of-the-times programme-making.

In other words, those emails said, our interests align, and we're nothing to be afraid of.

This is the secret of pitching for permission to film. The golden rule of access.

You'll get nowhere without it. But it doesn't guarantee success.

Responses to our access blitz are starting to come back now. Overwhelmingly the answers are no, as they generally are when your approach is scattergun and you're firing blind.

Commissions don't come from writing scores of emails and hoping for good luck, however well-written those emails might be. If you're serious about landing commissions, you have to be smarter than that.

You have to go and find them.

August 7

The woman sitting opposite me says I'm a thoughtless, insensitive prick. She regrets the time she's wasted on me. She very much hopes not to see me again.

And then she says, 'I hope you fail.'

This is worse than being sent packing. It feels like being cursed.

Bad break-ups happen. You have to accept that. It doesn't matter what you look like, or how funny and charming you are. One day you'll get dumped and not see it coming.

One day you'll dump someone else too, and do it badly, no matter how kind and sensitive you try to be.

That's how it goes. Partnering up is a messy business. We blunder about and fuck things up. It's part of the human condition.

Being dumped hurts, and then we move on. But sometimes embarrassment is part of the process, and it's interesting that we embarrass ourselves most when we're most in love. Embarrassing lovelorn messages. Embarrassing tearful phone calls. Embarrassing futile gestures. They all spring from the same sentiment – you don't understand, I really *really* love you. The embarrassment kicks in when you realize that the person not understanding is you. They know you really really love them; the problem is, they don't feel the same.

Most of us know where the limits are with this kind of thing. Our embarrassment is the thing that tells us. When you turn up at a girl's workplace with flowers, and she doesn't want to see you; when her boss has to ask you to leave, and her colleagues are smirking or looking at you with pity; when you're so ashamed you could melt – that's when you know the jig is really up.

But some people don't recognize those limits, or don't feel shame when they should. Or feel love so very deeply they don't care how shaming things get. They just want their lover back.

These people are stalkers.

They're not monsters. They're just like you and me, but further down a road we've all been on. I find it interesting that the worst human behaviour is often produced by the best human emotions.

My idea is to tell the story of a single case of stalking, from both sides, which has never been done before. All previous films on the subject have been heavily on the side of the victim. The stalker comes across as a terrifying, irrational entity that materializes suddenly then vanishes, like a poltergeist. We know them only from blurred and shaky bits of video. We never really see their faces. I want to get to know one, and listen to what they have to say, at the same time as filming with the object of their obsession.

What went wrong? How did something so bad and unwelcome emerge from something so happy and pure?

Wouldn't it be interesting to retrace the steps and see how their perspectives began to diverge? And so very gripping to be both outside a house with someone making a show of their love, and inside with someone feeling trapped and afraid.

How would the story end? It would be like watching a drama.

When something has never been done before, there's usually a good reason. And the reason in this case is that getting in at the start of an incident of stalking is almost impossible. By the time you hear of it, in the press, it's already way of out of hand. The police are probably involved. The story is almost over.

I've had an idea to address this problem. There's a new charity that helps victims of stalking. A victim calls up and perhaps leaves a message. And they call you back with advice on staying safe and dealing with the problem. They've been getting hundreds of calls.

If that charity will put me in touch with the people calling in, and they will put me in touch with the person who is stalking them, there's a chance of making an extraordinary film.

An important film even. Because a change in the law has been proposed, to make it faster and simpler to prosecute stalkers, before their behaviour turns violent. This film could contribute to the debate.

I pitched my idea to the head of the charity well, I think. I was careful to say that we don't want to make a programme that's sensationalist, or that exploits people. Nor a programme that's plodding and dull. Instead, a compelling story, neutrally presented, to make you think and question how you feel. Here's what stalking is and what it's like for both sides to be involved in.

'We all step a fine line', I said, as a final flourish, 'between what's normal and what's not'.

I leaned back in my chair, pleased with myself. I'm waiting for the head of the charity to commend me on the clarity of my vision and the boldness of my idea.

Instead, she's very angry.

'Who cares what stalkers think!' she says. 'They terrorize their victims. Kill them sometimes. And you want to give them a voice?'

'I'm always interested in what people have to say. I generally try not to judge.'

'Make this film', she says, 'and you'll wreck everything we've worked to achieve'.

'I'm going to call everyone I know to advise them that you and your project are toxic.

'Now please leave and don't contact me again.'

It's surprising how you can forget the things you know. When you're pitching for access, your interests must align, or at least appear to, through the power of persuasive words. The golden rule.

But today our interests didn't align. Because the woman I've been pitching to is on a mission – a noble one, to help the victims of stalking. Helping me would do nothing at all to help her help them. Stalkers are stalkers as far as she's concerned. There's nothing else to be said.

'So please leave and don't contact me again.' That's a telling phrase. The sort of thing a victim of stalking might say to a stalker.

I realized as soon as she said it. But there was no way back by then. They were the last words anyone spoke in the meeting. Her mission is personal as well as professional.

I could and should have guessed that might be the case. Certainly I could have checked to find out.

So now I'm in a cab heading back to the office, another good project in ruins.

Today has been a disaster.

This is how not to develop ideas.

August 8

Here's what's on TV this week:

A documentary series about the Tube in London. Another about a big regional hospital. Another about high-street betting shops.

A series that tries to establish the authenticity or otherwise of works of art.

A series in which a well-loved TV personality travels across Russia by train.

A series that follows people living on benefits.

A series about trainee policemen.

And lots and lots of one-off programmes. Something about the history of the Women's Institute. Something about the Beatles' time in India. A film about a teenager who won the lottery. Something about plastic surgery gone wrong. A film about the rise of Islamic State.

These are just the highlights, the sort of programmes that TV guides tend to single out as 'pick of the day'. Dozens of other programmes – a series about the people who maintain our roads, something about Henry VIII, something about sharks, and so on and so on – will come and go without comment.

And these are just shows you might broadly call factual, which is my particular area of interest.

Beyond lies a whole other landscape of softer, semi-factual shows – a long-running thing about people buying antiques; a format about finding your soulmate; a series that watches other people watching TV.

And beyond that, a range of other programmes that you'd be hard pressed to put into any particular category, but which started out as factual ideas, or borrow their grammar, their look or techniques from factual film-making – a soap opera in which all the characters are animals; a semi-real, semi-scripted show about a chaotic lookalike agency; a sort of documentary adventure show, in which people on an island fight for survival.

Then there's current affairs – this week, programmes about pensions, social housing and prison reform. And a range of arts and music programmes, including a profile of a semi-famous actor, a format about amateur bands and a series made behind the scenes at a leading ballet company.

At a rough calculation, 600 hours of new programming will be broadcast this week. 600 hours that I could have made, or thought of, but didn't. Next week will be the same. The world of TV never stops.

Over a year, that adds up to 31,000 hours.

You could probably add another 4000 hours when you factor in TV made by British companies for channels in the US and elsewhere.

Today we finished post-production on the prison visit film, and delivered it to the broadcaster.

Which means that as of now, I'm contributing nothing whatsoever to the GDP of British factual television. Nothing in production. Nothing commissioned. Nothing on the brink of commission. Nothing, save the Delamains, in funded development. Nothing much under discussion. By any standard of reckoning, it's a poor state of affairs.

August 9

I'm at a board meeting, dressed in a suit and tie. Around me are six other men, similarly turned out. We're all looking towards a woman in her forties, at the head of the table. She's expressing her disappointment at our performance over the last quarter. She asks the man next to me to explain himself, and nervously, his dry mouth clacking as he speaks, he begins to offer his excuses.

'I'm … I'm sorry', he says. 'Very sorry. We should have seen it coming. We'll do better this month and next.'

Meanwhile the woman, still standing at the head of the table, has hiked up her skirt. As the man rumbles on, she starts to masturbate. Everyone is looking, of course. But no one says a thing. She comes loudly and quickly, and then tells us all to get the fuck out of her sight.

The man with the clacking mouth offers a final feeble apology on his way out of the room.

It's my belief that if you look for documentary characters in a stereotypical way, you get stereotypical characters. Play is a learning mechanism that we're all born with. Children use it to explore and experiment, to work out the rules and broaden their minds, to learn empathy and what's involved in living alongside others. When we're grown up, we stop playing, and I don't think we should.

It's also my belief that whatever sexual act you can imagine, no matter how exotic and disgusting, someone, somewhere will be enthusiastically engaged in it. Which is odd, when you think about it. The basics of human reproduction are simple. So why all the weirdness and perversion? It's because there's something fundamentally weird and perverted about human beings. Which makes sex an interesting territory to explore.

Prompted by boredom and a vague afternoon horniness, I spent several hours yesterday browsing the casual encounters section of a popular listings website. It's been in the news recently, because it's apparently the website of choice for city traders and hedge fund managers who've lost jobs to the recession and are looking to boost their egos. But what I found there was much more interesting than men who are bored of sitting at home – women being hugely specific and uncompromising about the type of sex they're after. Sounding in fact less like women and more like men.

In place of postings about soulmates and shared interests and cuddling, I found terse four-line ads for men willing to be dressed in heels and a bra and fucked up the arse with a strap-on; for gay men open to the idea of being 'turned' by an older lady; for messy period sex; and men interested in 'kidnap scenarios'. Plus lots and lots of ads crackling with frustration from women with partners disinclined to do the one and only thing that gets them off.

And I found a posting from a businesswoman who wanted to convene an after-hours board meeting. Seven men required. Please send items for the agenda. I will cum. You will not. No sex will be offered.

Six other men – presumably not all television producers, but office workers and middle managers – seemed happy to come along, for yet another meeting at the end of a long day of them.

As we rise from the table, I feel utterly entranced. The rest of the men head for the lifts. The woman is looking out of the window, her back to the room, a titan of industry, glowing.

When I approach her, and explain why I'm here, she's shocked at first. She thinks I've been secretly filming. I reassure her that I haven't, and say that it was a sexy thing she did in the meeting. She says that everything in life is about sex. Except sex. Sex is all about power.

Good characters for TV are larger than life, and entertaining to spend time with. But more importantly, I think, they help you make sense of the world, or a corner of it you're half-familiar with. They teach you something about being human. This woman is a good character. She seems to know the score.

Could I do some filming with you? Not for broadcast. Just to show a commissioner I know. I'm thinking of a documentary called something like 'The Truth About Women and Sex'. And I'm thinking that you could and should be in it. What do you say?

She says she'll consider it, and give me a call. Then nods me towards the lift.

August 10

I very much dislike doing admin and filling in forms, so I very rarely do expenses. The head of accounts came to my desk yesterday with a pink face and said it's been 18 months since I last submitted a claim, which is 17 months too long, and 13 months longer than anyone else in the entire history of the company. I have had 12 cash advances totalling £3300, and have ignored eight polite requests to reconcile them. 'So if you're not too busy, could you please now attend to the matter?'

It sounds like a speech he's been preparing for a while. He just stops short of adding *you arrogant, ignorant fuck* at the end of it.

I reckon they owe me the same and then some, which means I need to process almost £7000 worth of old receipts.

My filing system consists of stuffing them into my bottom drawer and forgetting about them. Not just business receipts, but receipts of any kind. Not hundreds of receipts, but thousands.

I made a start on them at 6 pm. It's just gone ten, and I've run out of steam. I'm sitting on the floor of the boardroom with a bottle of wine, listening to music. There are crumpled and faded bits of paper everywhere you look. They're making me think about how I've spent the last year and a half of my life. The places I've been and things I've done.

There's a big pile of cab receipts, and another made up of bar bills. Lots and lots of cinema tickets and receipts for books and magazines. A few parking tickets. Hundreds of receipts for coffee.

So far it adds up to £4000, which is a lot. But at the same time it doesn't add up to very much at all.

My phone rings. I hope it's Mills. It's not. It's Rankin.

I put the receipts back in my bottom drawer. It's been 18 months. A couple more won't hurt.

August 12

'A key', Rankin said.

We met in a Portakabin in the middle of an industrial estate, way over east. All smouldering mountains of scrap and tyres, wire fences and bleak square buildings with signs that warn you to stay away. I still can't quite tell if he really belongs in these places, or if it's all for my benefit, a part of some sort of elaborate charade. I think he's as much in love with the romance of old-school villainy as I am.

A big man I wasn't introduced to got up when I arrived. A huge man, in fact, reeking of hostility and violence.

'Don't mind him', Rankin told me. 'He's an industrial tool. A jackhammer. Only does one thing. Thinks everything's there to be pounded and smashed.'

The big man went and stood outside. I could see him through the window, smoking sadly and gazing at the moon.

A key. To what? A lock-up maybe? Or a shipping container? There are thousands of those piled high by the docks in Dagenham, used for storage by market traders and importers of cheap things from abroad.

Rankin poured out drinks into dirty, greasy glasses, and we pondered it together.

'Best keep this to ourselves', he said.

When the Nelson brothers finally fell in the '70s, places all over London got raided and shut down. Second-hand car lots and massage parlours, clubs in Mayfair and Chelsea. The police recovered millions in the form of every criminal currency you can think of. But maybe they didn't get it all.

Now I'm in a cab, heading back through central London, window down, enjoying the view, replaying the conversation in my head.

I'm imagining a treasure trove, full of diamonds and gold sovereigns. Or a vault full of valuable information and compromising pictures. Wondrous things, worth turning over a major depository to get your hands on. Worth pissing off a lot of rich and well-connected people to acquire.

Whatever lock the key might fit, it would be a hell of a thing to be there when it was opened. Maybe even be there before the police turned up. That would make news around the world.

Rankin asked me when we'll start filming the doc about him. Soon, I said. Budgets and schedules need preparing. Office stuff. And August is always a slow month in TV.

'Soon', he said back to me. 'Good. It's all going ahead, then? All definitely happening?'

I told him, 'Yes, of course.'

'And you haven't forgotten that favour?' he said. 'Now that I've done yours.'

'These things take time', I told him. 'Like meeting you. Forcing it never works. You've to feel your way in.'

He shook his head a little and said, 'I suggest you feel your way faster.'

August 13

Hope is another part of being human. It keeps us going through life. It's why we have children. It's what makes us stick at our jobs, and put money away, and invest in the future. Everyone needs a taste of hope, every now and then. When you're developing ideas for a living, you absolutely crave it. Without it, you're fucked.

It makes for a poor tactic, though. A bad basis for strategy. But right now it's all we've got. We're chasing every story in the press. Making bids for every piece of access we can think of. Sending every half-decent idea to every possible commissioner. Turning hope into a frenzy.

A youth group has unveiled plans to establish Britain's first gay school, for teenagers who have been bullied. It's very controversial. Critics claim it will be a ghetto for gay children, and will set back attempts to teach tolerance in mainstream schools. We have written to the people behind the plans to ask for a meeting (along with every other TV company in Britain, no doubt).

Local newspapers are closing all over the country as printing costs rise and people turn to the internet for news. I know from personal experience – my first job was on a tiny two-town newspaper – that they're home to wonderful characters, with their roots deep in local communities. Could they be saved with a fresh approach? We have proposed a series, in each episode of which a big name from the media takes over as editor of a local newspaper for one month. What can the newspaper staff learn from their new editor? And what will he or she learn from them?

There was a recent incident in which twitchers from all over the country and indeed the world rushed to see an exceptionally rare bird, which had taken up temporary residence in a quiet suburban garden. They had chartered planes, raced through country lanes (and in two cases, crashed their cars), bribed locals and fought with each other for a glimpse of the unremarkable-looking bird. We've pitched 'Extreme Birdwatching' as a tongue-in-cheek one-off.

The results of a census have revealed a concentration of Satanists in a former mining town in Derbyshire. But what is Satanism? We are proposing to explore it in a TV event: 'Conjure the Devil – Live!'

You might remember the woman in the bright red coat from the ill-fated film about the missing child. She came and knocked on the family's front door. I thought she was probably religious at first, calling to offer spiritual support. She was in fact a 'psychic', claiming to be tormented by visions of the missing child. The mother passed the details on to the police, who politely noted them down and rolled their eyes behind her back; a worthless lead for sure, but one they were duty-bound to look into. I learned that missing persons investigations are magnets for people who purport to have psychic powers, and that one of these people – known to forces all over the country – even calls herself a psychic detective. We have been in touch with her, and are proposing a documentary that will follow her activities (and perhaps expose her as the parasitical charlatan she almost certainly is).

We've got access to a convent that's down to its last three members, now actively recruiting for the first time in its history.

And access to an agency that provides personal assistants to very minor celebs.

Behind my desk is a gigantic pinboard, covered with clippings and headlines and photographs – fragments of dozens of other ideas I've been considering. The board looks like something from the basement of a serial killer in a movie. Or from the study of a maths professor who's lost his mind, struggling to solve a problem that no one else knows exists.

I'm pitching Rankin to anyone who'll listen, trying to convince the commissioner for the genius film to take a leap of faith, and waiting to hear back about the organ-donor project.

'I don't believe this man will ever change', one commissioner said about Rankin.

I said, 'I know he's got it in him.'

The commissioner said, 'What if he hasn't?'

One of these projects must surely come off. Something's got to give. All things in TV are temporary, including barren spells. But that's precisely the problem. Time is running out.

I provide Charlie with a confident account of all this activity. But it's a bad time of year to be doing this. August in TV is a doldrum month. One by one, commissioners at every major broadcaster are heading off for extended holidays with their families. Charlie himself will be away at his villa in Spain, which at least affords me space to breathe. I shake his hand and say, 'This is a great slate of ideas. The best I've ever had. Have a good break and don't worry. We'll celebrate our new commissions when you're back.' Optimism and bullshit are different sides of the same coin.

August 16

I'm in an empty cutting room at work with one of the team, our researcher. She asked for this meeting some time ago. The room is soundproof and private.

She tells me her friends at other companies are doing much better than she is. I tell her they're probably not. Everyone in TV thinks that. It's a feeling that never leaves you.

An email comes through on my phone.

'Re your organ donor idea', it says, 'we admired your treatment very much. But the taster was hard to watch.'

It's been nine months since we had a commission, the researcher says, and she's bored of doing research. She wants to get out there, and make some TV.

Nine months is nothing, really. She'll probably work in TV for another 20 years. But it's half her career so far, so it feels like forever.

'Things'll come good', I tell her. 'They always do. TV goes in fits and starts.'

The taster was indeed hard to watch. Hard to film and hard to put together. I hired a very good editor, but she left two days in. She has a small child of her own, and couldn't stand to watch the rushes.

'Things aren't like they used to be', the researcher says. 'You're never here. And everyone seems distracted. Like you, on your phone right now.'

I finished the editing myself, clumsily, the rawness only making the emotion more intense. It was overwhelming in the end. I should never have submitted it.

Or even shot it in the first place. Mills is always right about these things.

The researcher says she wants to leave. She's handing in her notice.

August 17

The girl in the cutting room yesterday was the first person I hired when I came to work with Charlie. She's funny and cheeky but smart and hard-working also. Everyone loved her from day one.

She played a big part in helping me land a major commission, and the combination of those two things – the commission and the fact that I'd spotted her talent – allowed me to build a team.

I recruited all of them young but paid them well, on long, secure contracts that are rare when you're starting out. I believed in them, backed them and gave them freedom to express themselves, along with genuine responsibility. All in exchange for commitment to the cause of winning commissions and fierce personal loyalty to me.

They were mostly not from London, and moved here together to take up the jobs I offered them. This meant they socialized as well as worked together, and became close and honest in no time at all. A diverse, motivated group of people, all of them interesting and interested in each other.

They didn't know much about TV at first. Or anything else, for that matter, being only in their early twenties. So I taught them how it works, filtered through my own particular values. The importance of exploring, playing and trying things on for size. The value of every experience. The importance of giving yourself time to think, and thinking freely when you do. The importance of curiosity, of being passionate and engaged. The importance of taste and indulging your whims. The importance of talking and listening, and asking people about themselves. The rare and profound pleasure of having a good idea. The importance of going about things with panache and a sense of style.

Above all, I sold them a vision: of TV as an industry that young people can own and remake to suit themselves; of our team as a grand undertaking, a journey to parts unknown, an adventure or even a quest. An idealized vision of what TV could and should be. Something they could invest in.

As an experiment, it worked brilliantly. It was and is the best team I've ever been part of. They went about things with boundless energy, gliding, free of friction and the scar tissue that comes from setbacks and disappointment. They were fearless and unstoppable.

They worked at tremendous pace, especially at the start, but without ever rushing or pushing. With all the time in the world, in fact. They figured things out as they went along and passed the knowledge they acquired on to each other, a self-educating unit. It was clear they felt pride at coming up together, and solving the problems we faced. They were happy and full of belief, convinced that their destiny was in their hands and no one else's.

And I loved working with them, of course, being part of their discoveries, part of new things and new horizons, a sensation that Darwin called a chaos of delight. It's not often in your life that you'll feel that sensation. You should gorge on it when you do. I helped them pick a route through it all, which made me feel okay about getting older. I needed them and they needed me.

Together we hit a rich purple patch. Commissions flowed, big and small. Commissioning editors liked what we were doing. They enjoyed hanging out with us, and wanted to give us work. It all felt easy and natural.

I'm prouder of the team I built than any other thing I've done.

It's in the nature of a starburst, though, that it can't go on forever. Over time it will only dim and fade.

My researcher wanting to leave feels like the beginning of the end. Starting again after something so good would be terribly painful and hard.

But that's not the situation quite yet.

Today I asked her to change her mind.

'Ten more weeks', I said.

She said 'I'll give you four.'

August 18

I haven't told anyone yet about the organ film. It's painful even to think about.

I'm not sure now where my next commission will come from.

I'm not going to panic, though. I've got the little reel of Super 8, in a shoebox under my bed.

The film we'd make from it would be simple and impactful. A moment-by-moment analysis of the seven minutes of footage, with psychologists and sociologists, politicians and commentators, supporters and critics and ex-members of the same elite club, all mining the reel for what it says about class and politics, and the people we are willing to follow.

I don't think it would be hard to get this film commissioned. But I do think that life might become hard for me after it went to air. I'm not an investigative journalist. My career has never been about exposing wrongdoing or skewering wrongdoers. Success in my world comes from people being happy to work with you. And the film in my head might make a lot of people very unhappy. Which is why I still haven't pitched it.

August 19

A new message this morning, from Donovan.

'We're going to run the story', it says. 'In the weekend papers, a month from now. The second week in September.'

I feel myself sway on my feet.

'We believe it is in the public interest to do so.

'You are aware of what is alleged.

'Please consider this message a formal offer of your right of reply.

'No response will be taken to mean you decline to exercise this right.'

At the end, entirely out of keeping with the rest of the message, is a tiny smiling face.

August 20

Two big men on the door of a grand old pub pay no attention as I step between them. Inside an old man sitting at a green baize table wants a £5 'membership fee' and to know my name, which he writes very slowly in a narrow-lined ledger. There are grubby marks by the light fittings on the walls of the hallway behind him, and thick black grime on top of the skirting boards.

Inside the light is fag-stain yellow. No more than half a dozen punters, staring at their beer. No one is talking. Everyone's alone.

I ask a red-faced man in a navy-blue suit if he's here for the entertainment, and he tells me how it works. Local girls. Girls you see around. They dance then take round a pint pot. You put a pound in every time, at least, otherwise you leave.

I tell him I've been to places like this before.

'Not like this', he says, eyes much brighter now, bulging slightly. 'You get to a certain level – £80, then 100, then 200, then 250 – and the girls go that bit further. Take a bit more off. Show you that bit more.'

I'm wondering what the appeal is. A response to all the sex on the internet, maybe? More real. More eye to eye, for men jaded by all the GIFs and videos, and all the furious fucking. Something more cheerful, to brighten up your day, like Page 3 used to be? Something nostalgic. Innocent even. Something to whet the appetite for jaded married types, on their way home at the end of a day? Men like the red-faced man in the navy-blue suit. I'm trying to imagine his wife, God help her.

I ask him, 'Anything else?' He makes his mouth into an O, about to speak, and then goes back to his pint.

A skinny guy with narrow shoulders is standing on my blind side, a fraction too close for comfort. There's a sharpness to his eyes, a slackness elsewhere on his face. Not bright, but not stupid either. Alive to possibilities, but deeply wary also. Someone used to coming off worse. A chancer. Mr Bixby, I presume.

You can tell from a glance that trouble follows him. Trouble that Rankin wants me involved in.

I should go but Rankin was right. Whatever's going on here, whatever game Rankin is playing, it certainly has my interest.

It's hard to put an age on Bixby. Mid-thirties maybe. People who've had tough lives can sometimes be that way. Older on the inside than they are on the out.

I tell him he's an entrepreneur, and now he's smirking, in spite of himself. He's pleased with his innovation. 'Like a video game', he says. 'You want to unlock the next level. See how far you can get. Makes you want to bring your mates.'

'Unlock every level', he says, 'and you get to see the lot. Right between their legs.'

On the other side of me, the red-faced man is nodding emphatically.

'Psychological', says Mr Bixby.

He's turned something humdrum into a game by adding some basic incentives, and thereby transformed it. I can't help admiring that. It's a good, simple idea.

'So what's this about?' he says.

I tell him we're thinking of making a film about men in pubs. Why they go there and what pubs are for, in light of all the headlines about pub closures and the death of a British institution. That sounds plausible enough. I tell him people are talking about his idea, and how it's turned a failing pub around. It's clever and new.

He's smirking again, awkwardly, delighted and firmly on the hook. He's wondering about expanding, he says. There used to be hundreds of pound-in-a-pint-glass strip pubs. Maybe there will be again.

Just before the hour there's a huge surge of customers. Men, of all ages, excited but not speaking, most of them wearing a hungry sort of look.

Then two girls come into the bar and start dancing. Neither is stunning, but both are beautiful in the way that young people are. They're in their late teens or very early twenties. Students, maybe. They strip off to their underwear, slowly, unsteady on their heels.

The men are watching closely, their backs to the bar, eyes flicking, picking out details. Some of them just look sad.

The girls are laughing and talking to each other. They look like they're having much more fun than the men.

Then the music stops and the girls go round the room with pint glasses, smiling and chatting, and the men put in their money.

The girls tell me it's fun. They get to hang out together, and free drinks all night. Plus £50 each, cash in hand. Three nights a week, and all over by ten, which leaves them with time and money in their pockets for a night out of their own.

Bixby is hovering. Watchful and wary again.

The girls like the idea of being on TV. They take me through to their changing room. It's full of half-naked girls, none remotely self-conscious. They're mostly high, on this or that. Gossiping and pouring out shots. Shopping for shoes on their phones.

I know without asking that I've found Vee, the girl Rankin was interested in. The reason why I'm here.

'Just find out how she is', he said. 'Have a look and tell me what's what. Tell me how she *seems*.'

She's the only girl with clothes on, putting make-up on the others. Quiet and sober. Smaller than the rest of them. They're gentler with her than they are with each other. Tactile and protective.

'How she seems?'

'How she looks', Rankin said. 'How she seems to be.'

She has dark blue eyes and cream-coloured skin. Fine, delicate features. And deep black bruises on both sides of her face.

August 21

'Truman, you sweet man. How are things?'

'*Very* well, thank you. *Very* busy. Lots of good things on the go.'

I'm having drinks with a man I used to be friends with.

It was a good friendship. We were close and honest with each other. We talked about difficult things. We enjoyed spending time together.

He is a little older than me, and he's very well-travelled and well-read. He was always in the midst of reading a good and surprising book. His perspective on anything was interesting to hear.

I love learning new things, best of all when the person doing the teaching is someone I have a relationship with. The guy taught me about wine. We'd meet up for an expensive bottle somewhere not too loud, and sip and savour it and talk for hours. Later, as we got to know each other better, he taught me about food. I tend to think about food as fuel, and I don't own an oven or a stove. He was appalled by that, and invited me back to his house for dinner. He cooked with his wife as I sat at the kitchen table, feeling warm and mellow and just the right degree of pissed. He didn't lecture me about cooking, which would have been dull and uncomfortable. He just enthused, and brought over things to taste. I took them out for an elaborate dinner to say thank you, and then elaborate dinners, booked months in advance, became a thing we did.

I taught him to fish, and how to fix things. He was delighted when I showed him how to service his car and mend his broken bike. We spent a happy weekend together building a shed at the bottom of his garden.

I valued our relationship more than any other in my life. It's probably not an exaggeration to say that I loved the guy, in a fraternal sort of way.

And then he became a commissioning editor.

The first thing that happens when your appointment as a commissioner is announced is that dozens of people you vaguely know write or phone to express their delight and enquire whether you might want to get together for a drink. Then as you become more prominent, through appearing on panels or speaking at events, that number is multiplied. Now *everybody* wants to be your friend. And some of the many people inviting you out for lunch or offering you a ticket to the game will be an upgrade on the friends you used to have. They'll be better connected and more influential. They'll be brighter and wittier. But you should beware these new friendships, because they are not real.

Like account men in advertising, senior people in television are good at forming relationships. With so many channels, all with a high turnover of commissioners, they get a lot of practice. Good relationships mean good steers on the kind of ideas a broadcaster wants to commission, which of course is good for business. They'll make you feel cleverer, sharper, more attractive and generally *better* than any friend ever has before. It feels great to spend time with them, not least because their friendship comes free of all the taxing emotional stuff that can weigh genuine friendships down – people complaining about their jobs or crying over break-ups, and so on. The sort of things that friendships exist to help us deal with. Factor in the geekiness of most commissioners, and the fact that they were never that popular at school, and all this new attention can become utterly addictive.

Gradually, I felt my very good friend drifting away. Until one day I emailed him to say, 'It's been a while. Shall we get a drink?' And he emailed back to say, 'Yes, let's. Speak to my assistant and she'll put something in the diary.'

Now we're in a sort of no-man's-land, somewhere between friendship and something professional, tiptoeing around the landmines.

We swap gossip. A senior commissioner whose best days are behind her has had her tits done. Two people we both know who seem a very unlikely pairing were caught *in flagrante* in an empty cutting room. A big series which was supposed to run to eight episodes has gone very badly, and will now be just a two-parter.

There's tension not just because we used to know each other well, but also because we both know that at some point I'm going to mention an idea that he's been sitting on for some time.

I pitched the idea in an email. Just a couple of lines at first. A half-thought on the way into work. Could we make a series of films that unfold in real time, sixty minutes of rushes broadcast exactly as they were shot? Life-changing moments – the verdict of a major trial, a parent meeting a child he never knew he had and so on – presented in unvarnished form, as honest a record as a film can be.

Most TV is over-edited, I think. Too dense and misleading. Too heavily constructed. Not this series, though. These films would feel real, like experience.

You'd see thoughts occurring on people's faces, and live through their best and worst moments with them, exactly as though you were there.

He really wanted it, then everything went quiet.

As we know from the ring shop and other ideas, the way commissioning operates is that commissioners take their best ideas into a meeting with colleagues in the same department, and there's a general discussion. Notionally, everyone is collaborating over the same task, which is to identify the best ideas and work out how best to make them happen. In actuality, it's a very competitive environment. You're battling your colleagues to get your ideas taken forward, because that's how you get on. Conversely, if you're a commissioner who never commissions anything, you don't last long in the job. So all of the commissioners in the meeting are selling to their head of department, just as producers like me have worked hard to sell ideas to them. Later on, all of the heads of department at the channel will get together at another meeting and try to sell their ideas to the channel controller, who finally decides what's made.

As a producer your idea won't get made, no matter how cleverly you developed it and how eloquently you sold it, if the person you sold it to fails to sell it on to his or her colleagues. So you try to pitch only to commissioners who are good salesmen themselves, or you pitch to commissioners you've built a relationship with, in the hope that they'll go the extra mile on your behalf.

What happens at these departmental meetings – especially who says what – generally stays inside the room. If your idea didn't go forward, what you hear back is something like 'I'm sorry, I gave it my very best shot.'

The thing is though that sometimes commissioners don't.

There might be all sorts of reasons for this, but they all come down to the same thing; he or she is unwilling to stick their neck out. Worse than pushing indifferent ideas at the meeting, worse even than having no ideas to push, is pushing an idea which might make the commissioner concerned look bad further down the line.

I bring us another drink, and use the break in the conversation as a way of bringing up the subject of my idea, as if it had just occurred to me while I was at the bar.

'I'm working on it', he says. 'We ran out of time at the last meeting.'

He tells me he didn't want to rush pitching it to his colleagues. He says it deserves a proper discussion.

But I know him well enough to know when he's being evasive.

'As a friend', I say, 'is there a problem with the idea?'

He says that people have been talking about MacLean, the new guy in my office.

He says that people are speculating that him joining might lead to changes at the company.

He says that people are wondering if turbulence may lie ahead.

In other words, he thinks I'm on my way out.

He's worried about commissioning a big, expensive idea, and then discovering that the idea has been orphaned. Programmes need a huge amount of energy and willpower to make them successful. There are always difficulties to negotiate, often serious ones. The people who sell ideas generally go on to supervise them as executive producers, on the assumption that you'll do what's required to see your own project through to completion. If I leave the company, the series might not be as good at it should be, or might even fail to make it to the screen altogether, which would make the guy who commissioned it look very bad indeed, and call his judgment into question.

So he's keeping the idea in his pocket, and waiting to see what happens.

It feels for a moment hard to breathe.

If everyone feels this way, I'm fucked.

August 22

I'm dialling another commissioner I know. Same broadcaster, different department. His own phone, not the one he uses for work.

He's irritated that it's me. He says, 'This is really not a good time.'

I tell him I have something he's definitely going to want.

I can hear him leaving a meeting. Then his voice goes echoey. He's in a stairwell maybe. Somewhere private. He says, 'This better be good.'

He listens quietly and goes away.

I feel sick and pace about. 20 minutes go by.

He calls me back, breathless. He's discussed it with his boss, and they want it. They'll pay top dollar – 350k.

'Come in for a meeting tomorrow', he says. 'And bring the reel with you.'

You're in trouble when the narrative of your career slips out of your control. Whatever else might happen, this will at least change the narrative. No longer a producer on the slippery slope. A producer who makes things happen. A producer with dynamite property to pitch.

But two hours later, the commissioner calls again.

'I'm sorry', he says. 'It's a no. From the top.'

It's a broadcaster that loves controversy, but this is the wrong sort. Controversies surrounding poor people are one thing. Picking a fight with the rich and powerful is something else entirely.

'I'm sorry', he says again. 'I'm sure you'll get it commissioned elsewhere.'

August 23

I was surprised upon waking this morning to find a woman in my bed. It hasn't happened for several years now. I never bring girls home. For a few moments, I wasn't sure who it could be.

I met Selena last night in a basement bar I usually go to alone. She was there in a professional capacity. We spent the night drinking and talking.

I barely recognized her at first. She looked stupendous, listening attentively to a fat-necked man in a houndstooth suit. She was touching his knee very lightly and laughing. Leaning in. Listening and smiling. Making him feel like the sort of man he wishes to be and plainly very much isn't.

When our eyes met, she came over and sat with me at the bar, her demeanour quite different to the show she'd been staging for the guy in the suit. More like herself. Or at least more like the woman I'd come to know.

It's been years now. Several years.

She said, 'What kind of girl are you looking for?' I considered my response. Then she said, 'What kind of girl would you like me to be?' Which made me realize how much we have in common.

We kissed in the cab, all the way.

While I was making coffee, there was a short, loud knock at the door. Because no one knows where I live, I felt safe to ignore it. Then I heard the door open. And soon after I heard it close again. A neighbour, I thought, asking after a parcel. Or someone come to read the meter.

I took the coffee back to bed.

'Who was at the door?' I asked.

Selena said, 'It was a girl with short brown hair. She said she must have the wrong address.'

August 24

Half of my team have been researching upcoming anniversaries, traditionally the last refuge of the creatively bankrupt producer.

There's no fun or pleasure to be had from this. No room for creativity.

It's 20 or 50 or 100 years since all sorts of things, of course. It always is. Moments in space exploration or popular culture, or literature or sport. High points and disasters in the personal lives and careers of politicians, thinkers and entrepreneurs.

Commissioners like this stuff because they believe it will attract attention and make a programme feel bigger than it really is. Something that will stir viewers' memories, or appeal to their sense of history. Something they might watch because it feels like they probably should.

These programmes almost always go to the biggest companies and personal friends of the commissioner concerned. We're hoping to find something that no one else will have spotted. But if no one else has spotted it, it's probably too insignificant to warrant a programme. It's a game you can't really win.

The other half of the team have been discussing ideas for an upcoming season of factual programmes on the uninspiring subject of food.

Someone has suggested a countdown of the most expensive ingredients in the world. This is not a good idea. It's all too familiar and feels wrong in an age of food banks and rising poverty. Then someone suggested we improve that idea by getting a celebrity chef to source all the ingredients on a globe-trotting travelogue, then combine them all into a single three-course meal – a Million Dollar Dinner. This is even worse, pointless as well as vulgar.

Everyone suggested something. A cookery school for divorced dads, to help them care for their kids and themselves. A series about the multibillion-pound British industry in crisps and salty snacks, and the never-ending search for new flavours, new shapes and sensations and a new family favourite. They all did their homework. They all want a commission as badly as I do. But the ideas all felt tired to me. I'm not sure any of them is worth pitching. And the truth is that these seasons often fail to materialize. They're fishing expeditions, used by broadcasters to get a sense of what sort of ideas might be available on any given theme. As likely as not, we've been wasting our time.

A journalist friend has sent me details of a woman she's writing about, who's been making video letters for her children to watch as they grow up. Advice on starting school, comfort for a broken heart and so on. She's ill and won't live to see those moments herself.

My AP is off meeting a 'pet psychologist' making a killing in Kensington.

I feel bored and it's hard to focus.

In France, a plane has vanished. The authorities don't have a clue what happened. Relatives of the disappeared are gathering in Paris. They're planning to somehow find it themselves.

I text Mills. 'How about we go explore this? See if there's a film in it?'

There's no reply. I haven't heard from her in over three days.

August 25

I'm lost. Not like when you're trying to find somewhere in a place you've never been. Lost like a child. I don't know where I'm going. I don't know where I've been. I don't know where I am.

That's okay.

There's a squirt of fear in my stomach every time the path divides. Now there's no path at all. But it doesn't feel bad. It feels like being alive.

For most of this week I've been in meetings.

Last night I drove from the office to the biggest stretch of wild woodland in Britain. Today I'm looking for something that might very well not be here. Might not even exist.

Thirty years ago a convoy of 600 New Age Travellers heading to a festival at Stonehenge ran into a police roadblock. The police were present in huge numbers – around 1300 officers – to enforce a ban on the festival taking place. The confrontation turned violent. Reports suggested that women who were pregnant and holding babies were amongst those beaten by police with their truncheons. 16 travellers were hospitalized, and dozens more injured. All of their vehicles were destroyed and 537 people were arrested, the largest mass arrest since World War Two. The incident became known as the Battle of the Beanfield.

The purpose of the New Age Traveller movement was to create an alternative way of life. But legislation passed after the Battle of the Beanfield made that way of life difficult to sustain.

The movement is now a fraction of the size it once was, and has splintered into tiny groups, sometimes no bigger than a single family. They're dispersed around the country, constantly moving from place to place, living mostly on unauthorized sites in rural areas. They're frequently evicted, and accessing basic services is a problem. They earn money from seasonal or temporary work, or by making things to sell at markets. Their children are mostly home-schooled. They depend on each other to get by.

I want to find these people, and ask them about their lives.

The air was green as I headed out of London, and there were thunderstorms all night. The rain came down so hard it set off car alarms. Today it's warm and bright. The ground smells sweet.

I haven't seen another person in four hours or more. There's no signal on my phone.

This isn't the first day I've spent looking for travellers. I've been given the run-around several times by people I've asked for information – people who run traveller-friendly shops and businesses. I'd trek to a deserted campsite. Or sometimes to a campsite that never was, a sort of middle-of-nowhere fuck-you to nosy journalists. Then I realized I'd been asking the wrong people for help – I needed not friends of travellers, but enemies.

I got to know a half-mad retired army officer who spends his time pointlessly mapping the movements of traveller groups and individual families. He assumed that, like him (or any other right-thinking person), I hate travellers and want to expose their deviancy.

I don't hate travellers. But I think it's interesting that lots of people do.

The series I have in mind is simple. Two directors and two crews, one with the mad old major and one with a bunch of travellers. A game of cat and mouse. Viewers would make up their own minds who they wish to side with.

August 26

It's pitch black, and I come awake with a jolt.

It's the oldest, most terrible human fear there is. Someone or something out there, unseen.

I can hear it breathing.

Last night I walked and walked, and then it started to get dark. I thought, how can it be possible to be this lost, just 70-odd miles out of London?

Eventually, I had to stop. I was very tired and very hungry. I found a place where the ground dipped into a natural hollow underneath a fallen tree. It felt safe, and I cleared away sticks and stones to make a sort of bed. I took off my coat and put it over me like a blanket. I thought about Mills. She'd like this. I imagined us here together, like children in a fairy tale. But if she was here, we wouldn't be. She'd have led us out of the woods.

I was cold. I imagined the warmth of her body. I imagined my arm around her, like that day on the bus. I imagined the vast city of London, far away. And then I was asleep.

The thing is getting closer. A second or two more, it'll be upon me.

Is this a dream?

It's not.

I like to think that I'm a practical sort of man. Good in a tight spot. Self-sufficient and resourceful. But I don't know what to do right now. There aren't any choices. I can't see. I don't know where I am. I don't know what I'm dealing with.

I lurch forward, and fall, and the thing is in my face.

Then there's a light, and a man shouting.

I can taste blood.

'Who the fuck are you?' he says. 'Who the fuck are you?'

When I wake up again, I'm in a child's bed, under a brightly coloured knitted blanket. It's sunny and I can smell coffee. Three blond children with dirty faces are running around outside. The dog that found me is sitting bolt upright in the room, looking at me.

A very beautiful woman hands me a mug. The man says, 'What were you doing in the woods last night?'

I say, 'Looking for you.'

August 27

I'm well-rested, well-fed and happy, and about to say goodbye.

The family were wary at first. The authorities have been after them for keeping their kids out of school. The owner of the woodland wants them arrested for trespassing and ejected. The tax man wants to take them to court.

Hiding away and never staying anywhere for more than a couple of days seemed to me a high price for freedom. But by the time we were having dinner last night, cooked in a pot over an open fire, I understood the point of it all. They were close in a way I'd never seen in a family before, and totally at ease in one another's company. The man touched the faces of his wife and children all the time, and was in the moment with them every moment of every day. He was totally in love.

As we found wood for the fire today and prepared another meal, I told them that I wanted to make a series about them, and families like them that they know. The series wouldn't judge or pass comment. We'd be with the family looking out at the world, rather than standing outside looking in. Hopefully viewers would come to it as a sort of celebration of all the things that family life should be but often isn't, because of the crazy way we live now, giving the least amount of time to the things that are most important.

Neither of the couple was sure. I started directing my comments to the woman.

I told them a little about myself, leaning forward and speaking softly. I told them why family is a theme that matters to me. The woman came over and hugged me.

We say farewell, and promise to speak again soon. The woman hugs me again, followed by the kids. The man shakes my hand, and then pulls me into a hug as well.

I set off down the path they point out to me, with bread and cheese in my pockets and a can of beer. It will be a four-hour walk back to the nearest village. I can get a lift back to my car, on the other side of the wood, from there.

I've been going five minutes when the man comes running up behind me.

'My wife wants to do this', he says. 'You persuaded her. She likes you. If it happens, she wants us to be in it.'

I tell him thank you, I'm delighted. They'll light up the screen. Everyone will love them.

'I don't want to talk her out of it', he says. 'I won't be able to, anyway.'

I say, 'You want me to drop it.'

He nods. 'Because it'll ruin what we have. And no bit of telly's worth that. Right?'

August 29

Some time ago, I had an idea for a series about a city council, a conventional obs doc, filmed over a year, telling stories of the council's employees and the people who use its services, which is pretty much everyone who lives in the city. What I hoped might set it apart was a focus on the cost of everything, and the way the council spends its budget.

Councils have been much in the news for the last year or so, because of a crisis in funding. Council budgets have been cut across the country – very drastically in some places – at the same time as councils are facing unprecedented demand for frontline services and social care. Councils are overspending by tens, even hundreds, of millions a year, and some of them are said to heading for insolvency. Supporters say more funding should be raised through higher taxes, whilst critics accuse council leaders of deep-rooted inefficiency and wastefulness.

What is the truth of the matter?

The series I'm imagining would attempt to present the facts in the simplest way possible, telling gripping and emotional human stories but also keeping track of the money being spent. This is how much it costs to put a child into foster care. This is how much it costs to help someone addicted to drugs or alcohol. Or people who find themselves homeless. Or the victims of domestic abuse. This is how much it costs to empty the bins, investigate complaints about antisocial behaviour or care for trees on the streets and in parks. And this is how much it costs every time someone sues. There isn't enough money to go around, so what should be the priorities of the people in charge?

In their position, what choices would you make?

Mills found a council willing to entertain the idea, and we put a meeting in the diary.

Today is the day of the meeting.

I arrived not expecting to see Mills, but she was there in the waiting room outside the chief executive's office, looking smart and professional. But also shiny-skinned and drained of colour, as though she hadn't slept. There was no expression on her face at all.

I'm often in the doghouse about one thing or another, so I just sat down and started talking, my voice conspiratorial and low. What do we know about the CEO? What will his reservations be?

I'm thinking aloud about what we should say and what we shouldn't.

'Where *the fuck* have you been?' Mills says, loudly.

The CEO's assistant, a prim and pinched lady half hidden behind an old-fashioned beige computer, looks up and then away.

'I could ask you the same', I say.

She doesn't respond, so I tell her about getting lost in the woods, and the family and how much they love one another.

I tell her I convinced them to be on screen, hoping for a smile and word of praise. Praise from Mills is precious.

Mills says, 'That's the problem with you. You can convince anyone of anything. I have no idea when you're telling the truth.'

August 30

My phone buzzes. Number withheld. I apologize and ignore it.

The lady from the boardroom and I are having a drink.

She's always found the tension and boredom of meetings sexy, she says. She likes the way men look at her in the meetings she arranges. It's a fantasy made real.

Which makes it the opposite of online dating, she says, a world of reality made fantasy, full of serial liars. Full of dishonesty and deceit. Everyone knows where they stand at one of her meetings, she says. She gets off and then she goes home.

'What about boyfriends?' I ask her. 'What about proper sex?'

My phone buzzes again. I step away to take it.

The man's voice is smooth and precise. I bet he knows every nicety in the book, but right now he's using none of them.

He says, 'I understand you have in your possession a little reel of film. I would like to acquire it.'

'Why?'

'As a gift', he says.

'The going rate is 50, but I paid more.'

He says, 'How much do you want?'

'Let's say a hundred.'

He says, 'Yes, I see. A nominal sum. Very decent of you.'

'K.'

He says, 'What?'

'K. Meaning thousand.'

He says that some things are more important than a grubby little programme.

I say 'Here's how this works. Every time you say something I don't like – even a tiny bit – the price doubles. So now, if you want it, it's going to cost 200.'

'Extortion', he says.

'No, business. You called me, remember?'

He grunts down the phone.

'And by the way, I really don't like the word "extortion". So the price just went up again. You see? Next time's really going to cost you.'

There's a pause. Even over the phone, I can tell his face has gone clenched-knuckle white with rage.

'400?' he says.

A longer pause.

'Thank you', he says. 'We have an arrangement. I'll wire the money to you.'

'You'll put it in a bag. 20 pound notes and 10s, all used.'

I have no idea how practical this is. That's just how they do it in films. I'm starting to enjoy myself.

'I'll be in touch', he says. And then the line goes dead.

The woman is posting a new advert. Dozens of responses appear within seconds.

She wriggles happily in her seat.

'Such a turn-on', she says.

'Why don't we get a bottle? Drinks are on me tonight.'

August 31

I'm at a party, in a snooker hall which I think was once a cinema. There are pools of light above the tables, and everywhere else is dark. The place is packed with singular-looking people, most of them male. It's a long time since I was a boy, but I feel like one in the presence of these men.

The event is a party, thrown by Rankin, to celebrate the commissioning of the film.

I am, to say the least, finding it hard to relax.

I invited Mills to come with me. Asked if she would, in fact. For me. I feel stronger and better when she's around.

She said, 'I like you like this, desperate and scared.'

I was pleased to be teased by her, but still she declined to come.

There are all sorts of drinks on offer, but mostly people are drinking whisky, neat. All evening people have been introducing themselves, and asking if they can be in the film. They'd be amazing on camera. I've been talking persuasively about the film all night. I keep having to remind myself that it doesn't actually exist.

Rankin wants us to sit down and make a plan.

Soon, I tell him. Just a few more bits of paperwork and we're good to go.

He growls at that, but seems happy enough.

We need to talk about Vee. But this is not the time or the place. I'm assuming the bruises were Rankin's own doing. I'm assuming that's why he can't see her himself. I'm assuming the mission he gave me was to compile a damage report, an assessment of the injuries he caused. I'm choosing to assume he's wracked with remorse. I'm asking myself what the fuck I'm doing.

He wants me to meet someone, a wiry man ensconced at a table in the corner, surrounded by girls in short skirts and men in dark suits. Someone important, at the centre of his own private party.

The wiry man looks me up and down, and then looks at Rankin, saying nothing.

'It's okay', Rankin says. 'This guy's one of us.'

CHAPTER NINE: SEPTEMBER

September 1

The summer is over. Commissioners are back at their desks. A storm surge of rejection is up on me, an entire cliff face of effort collapsing and crashing, reduced to rubble and gone for good.

Rejection comes hand in hand with developing ideas. 99 in 100 are brushed aside, and every time it bruises. Some people become cynical as a form of self-protection. You can't allow rejection to do that to you. The trick is to take something from it, and come back stronger and wiser. To distil it into rocket fuel and use it to power you onwards.

Rejection is failure, of course, but you don't have to treat it as such. There's no need to feel wounded or judged. You learn to do it in style, in a way that bosses respect. Bad luck and never mind. Chin up. You're smart for having had the idea. They're stupid for turning it down.

But there's nothing stylish about my failure today. This sort of failure is abject and complete. Rejections for ideas that mostly deserved it. Too badly thought-through. Too expensive. Too derivative. Too flimsy. Too hard to make real.

Nothing at all to take pride in. Nothing at all to learn from.

I feel like a gambler at first light, the day after a ruinous spree. Pockets empty. Hangover booming. Dazed and stumbling. Full of swagger and belief the night before, with chips thrown down all over the place and the ball still spinning, everything still in play. A wreck of a man this morning, lonely and broke.

September 2

I left a message for Rankin at teatime. Not many words. Just that I have some news.

It was late and I'd just got home when he called back. Or rather someone called on his behalf. 'Mr Rankin would be pleased to see you at the Bombay Sapper.' No discussion. Just that sentence, then whoever it was rang off.

It took me an hour and a half to get there, in crawling traffic, and then some time to find. A tired-looking restaurant with a pink neon sign, in a side street off Brick Lane.

It's dim inside, flock wallpaper the colour of dried blood, and empty save for three guys too pissed to speak, moving in slow motion, like puppets clumsily worked. They're barely able to find their own mouths with their forks, but drinking doggedly still. Tinny sitar music gives me an instant headache.

Rankin is downstairs, eating alone at a table for four. He glances up and says nothing, but gestures at the food.

I tell him I'm not hungry.

He pours me a glass of dog-rough red. It's been a long time since anyone ordered wine in here, I think.

'Vee's face is badly bruised', I tell him. 'Her eyes are black. I'd say she's scared. But the girls are looking after her.'

Rankin grunts and nods.

'You already knew that, didn't you?'

No response.

'Tell me it wasn't you. She's just a girl. She's half your size. Less than half. She's tiny.'

He shrugs. 'It wasn't me.'

Silence as we look at each other.

'So?'

'So what?'

'You said I'd be interested and now I am.'

'She's a lovely girl', says Rankin. 'A really *lovely* girl. Just going through a phase, is all. Rebellious.'

'Which leaves us where?'

I can feel the anger surging. Teeth clenched, chin down. I want to show him how it feels. I can't abide a bully.

Two men come into the room.

'Ding ding, sunshine', Rankin says. 'This is your stop.'

The first man is an Asian guy. Mixed race maybe. He's fastidiously turned-out and distinguished-looking, tall with black hair greying at the temples and a close-cropped salt-and-pepper beard. He seems disgusted at the surroundings. Interpreting them – correctly, I imagine – as some sort of slur.

The second man, two paces behind, is well-dressed too, in a dark grey suit. He's not big, but lean and lithe. Calm but alert. Highly tuned. Trained maybe, like a soldier.

'Dr Baloch', Rankin says to the first guy, ignoring the second.

Behind Rankin, in the shadows at the back of the restaurant, two shadows detach themselves and lumber forward. I hadn't seen them till now. They'd been completely still and silent. Shut down, conserving energy. This is their moment, though, straightening and wincing, muscle-bound and heavy, taking up position behind their boss, staggered slightly, according to rank. A ceremonial show of strength.

A waiter comes and clears the table. Head down, wishing he was somewhere else.

Rankin gets to his feet, wiping his mouth with a napkin, his mouth still full of food. He nods my way – off you go – then looks the tall man in the eye, a look settling on his face that makes the room feel colder.

All within the space of 30 seconds. I want to see what happens next.

I pause for a moment, adrenaline draining, then turn around and leave.

Rankin shouts my name as I reach the door.

He says, 'Vanessa's my little girl.'

September 3

I'm in a casino with Mills. It's only two in the afternoon but there are no windows and it feels like night, so I order myself a drink.

Mills says 'Not for me.'

We're notionally here to research the lives of professional gamblers, and maybe find someone to make a film about. A film about luck, perhaps. Or compulsion. Or the drive that some people have to self-destruct. As a producer looking for ideas, you want to put yourself where things are happening, and emotions are raw. Gamblers are always on the edge of something. The edge of triumph, the edge of despair.

We're actually here because I want to be somewhere that speaks to the hollowed-out way I feel. In the cheerful surroundings of the office yesterday, I felt like an alien, painfully out of place. Today I want to be amongst people who feel the same way I do. My own kind.

Some of the people around us look like they're still at it from yesterday. Their eyes are red, and their suits look crumpled. The croupiers keep smiling, but it seems to me their eyes are imploring the highest rollers to stop. Two stick-thin wives or mistresses are sitting at the bar, still from tiredness and resigned to boredom. They've long since run out of things to say. Amidst the perfume and aftershave, the sweet smell of polish on the panelling and a faint suggestion of cigars coming up from the heavy carpet, there's a definite tang of tension in the air.

Here we are, at the start of something once again. Who knows what will happen next? Is it possible that I'm addicted to this sensation? My mind is free of fog. I feel calm and happy and ready for adventure.

I'm thinking about throwing some dice. I've got £200 burning a hole in my pocket.

I say to Mills, 'This is promising.'

Mills says to me, 'I'm pregnant.'

I know that there's a perfect combination of words to use right now. A beautiful sentence that will make everything okay. But for the life of me I can't think what it is.

We got together in the summer, the day we took the coach to the seaside. It was getting late when we headed home, tired and tipsy on sunshine and fresh air. The coach was quiet and we talked in whispers, our faces close and intimate. I don't recall what we spoke about; we were both half-asleep. And then we were kissing. London felt immense and cold. We went to Mills' flat.

In movies and TV dramas, in situations like this, the man suddenly knows that he loves the girl, and he smiles, and she smiles, and the music swells. You know at that moment that the film you've been watching is just about to end. They're going to be together, and you know as a viewer that they should be.

Well there's no smiling happening here, and no ballad rising on the soundtrack. Just the throb of my pulse in my ears.

I always know what to say, more or less. Which is generally to tell people what they want to hear. But right now I can't think of a single word that doesn't seem clumsy and stupid.

What does Mills want to hear? How does she feel? Her face, as ever, is giving nothing away.

I say, 'Congratulations.'

Mills says, 'Truman, you'd be a terrible dad.'

September 5

Mills has left the company. I don't think people know why, exactly. But they know it's something to do with me.

One of the older production managers gives me a tight-lipped smile, like a disappointed parent. Half 'I'm sorry, I know you were close.' Half 'You'll get no sympathy from me; you brought this upon yourself.' People liked Mills, much more than they like me. She was funny and kind. In so far as some people in the office ever liked me at all, Mills was the thing about me they liked.

A new girl is taking on Mills' workload, transferred over from a different part of the company. She looks like she enjoys healthy things, like netball and muesli. She expects to do well in life, and I'm sure she will. By fitting in and doing what's expected, which she's temperamentally much inclined to do.

I tell her about the ideas that have survived the cull. The genius boy and the travellers. She says that neither of them sound like the sort of ideas that Charlie wants us to work on. Which of course is entirely true.

She has ideas of her own. One that tells the story of a single hospital bed over the course of a month or two. One about a dealer in second-hand Rolls-Royces. And a series about quirky competitions – Britain's Best Public Loo, Caravanner of the Year and so on.

'Are you impressed?' she says.

I tell her they've all got potential, and her big proud smile collapses.

None of these are bad ideas. And I don't doubt that she discovered them or thought them up herself, and felt excited to have done so. But they're very familiar to anyone who works in development, the sort of thing that gets pitched all the time. Eventually, they'll all get commissioned and made. But generally the response from a commissioner is disappointment, and a well-rehearsed explanation of why it's not going to fly. Ideas need a freshness about them. They need to get people excited. A bad new idea has a much better chance than one that's good but old.

The reason these ideas make me feel depressed – and the reason they're so ubiquitous in television – is that they're the product of off-the-shelf thinking. They're the sort of ideas you have if you went to a good school and a good university, and got good marks by doing exactly what your teachers asked of you.

She's a nice person. But I'm not sure how well we're going to get along.

September 6

A final message from Donovan. It says, 'Seven days to go. When the story appears you're going to feel angry. You're going to want your voice to be heard. Don't be tempted to go elsewhere. That will only make it worse. You have my number. Call me.'

It would be professional suicide to admit to deliberately binning a tape and burying information, so collaborating, now or later, is completely out of the question.

But what are my other options?

I've got nothing to fight back with. Nothing on Donovan, and nothing from Monroe.

The best I can hope for is to ride out the story. Deny everything and dismiss the story.

I could attack Donovan for shoddy journalism, but that would align me with Ray Monroe, and the truth about him will emerge sooner or later.

Maybe I could use the piece when it appears as a way of landing a commission? 'Monroe and Me', or something like that. A follow-up with or without Monroe's participation.

That would be a good response. A way of denying wrongdoing whilst putting myself on the side of the angels, asking questions about Monroe.

It's a hard sell to a commissioner, though, if the thrust of Donovan's story is that I'm not to be trusted, however strongly I might deny it.

I can't see any other way ahead, except for Rankin's 'persuasive' friend.

It's like standing on some railway tracks, waiting to be hit by a train.

September 8

Around me are ten astonishingly beautiful girls and boys, with their prim and anxious mothers. We're in the reception area of a modelling agency, in an upmarket part of London. The floors are wonky planks of antique oak. The walls are whitewashed bricks. The roof is held up by ornate wrought-iron supports. I wonder what the people who worked in this space when it was built – luggers of heavy bags of flour or wool, or seamstresses in rows – would make of what's happening here today, a casting call for a new range of children's clothes.

I have an idea about physical beauty, and I want to ask an expert for some help.

I'm not good-looking myself. Not gross, but not pretty either. Unexceptional. Most of the people I grew up with looked the same. When I came to London and started work in television, I was astounded by how many beautiful people I encountered. I met young women with beauty and brains, who should have had all the confidence in the world, but could never get past the idea that every good thing that happened – every job they landed, every promotion they won – was about their physical attractiveness, and the desire of some middle-aged man to possess it. And handsome young men – tall and rangy, with perfectly defined features and winning smiles – with the opposite problem; happy to coast through life, exploiting the strange assumption that a square jaw and sharp cheekbones somehow signify talent, forever disappointing people with their laziness and vapidity. And older women, beautiful once, now elegant and perfectly groomed, and well-paid and powerful, but consumed with resentment at the effortless attractiveness of the younger women around them. I was fascinated. Here, seemingly, was a set of considerations that might dictate the shape of someone's life, none of which I'd ever been aware of before.

My theory is that your face shapes who you are and who you become, through the responses and feedback you get from other people. Maybe more than the things you think and the things you say. My idea is to follow a diverse set of beautiful children over several years, from childhood into adulthood, to test this theory. Every year, we'd catch up with the kids in an hour-long film. We'd be asking questions about the human face and human interactions, and about the values and priorities of our society.

I'm thinking of the faces of people I know. Charlie's matinee-idol good looks, which make strangers want to know him. Squeaky MacLean's Harley Street blandness, all sincerity and reassurance, always so pleased, with himself most of all. The big-eyed innocence of my want-away researcher, and her heartbreaking expressions of shock and betrayal at the wicked ways of the world. Selena's elegant smile, classy but suggestive and worn like make-up for the benefit of others. And her face without that make-up, full of understanding, warm, kind and calm. Motherly even. Very beautiful, always.

But above all I'm thinking of Mills, her face boyish and defiant, and the look she used to get thinking through a new idea, her eyes lit up like a child. Another look, of profound contentment, after I'd taken her to dinner when she'd been working too hard and forgotten to eat. I suppose the look of someone who's being cared for. And a look, fleetingly glimpsed, that she'd sometimes get in meetings or pitches, as I was describing a good idea we'd had or an interesting discovery we'd made. Smiling just faintly, thinking thoughts of her own. A hard look to define, but one that made me feel ten-feet tall.

And finally the look she had the day she cleared her desk. Grown-up and proud. Determined to get through it without drama or fuss.

I helped her to pack up her personal belongings into an empty tape box – mostly souvenirs from the places we've been together. We didn't speak.

She hugged people goodbye, promising to keep in touch. All the producers and assistant producers and production managers. And then me, for just a fraction longer than everyone else. Long enough to whisper a very short sentence. And then she was gone.

'It's okay', she said. 'I don't love you either.'

Everyone went back to their desks, the producers to the treatments or scripts they were writing, the researchers to their phone calls.

The agent I've come to meet is beautiful herself. She's listening intently but doesn't really get what I'm talking about.

'So it's about modelling?' she says.

I tell her no, not really.

I want her to pass on my contact details, but only to the parents of kids who are interesting as well as beautiful. Bright or driven, or awkward and shy. Poor, maybe. Or possessed of the sort of beauty that seems to come from nowhere, the offspring of ordinary or even odd-looking parents. I want to see how their beauty plays out, and the difference it makes to their lives.

'How their beauty plays out?' she says.

She thinks that beauty is only ever good. A pure and simple thing. A sort of gift from God. As far as she's concerned, there's not much more to be said. I'm seeing complexity and difficulty where there is none.

'What if you're beautiful and you'd rather not be? What if it gets in the way?'

She smiles at me, sympathetically. Poor ugly man, she's thinking. He really has no idea.

Or is her smile a put-down? Typical ugly man. Trying to turn beauty into something bad. Trying to make it a problem.

I'm struggling to make myself understood.

Mills would have sorted the problem. We were good together in meetings like this. Good at connecting. We talked to each other and made ourselves laugh. Drew people in and got them onside. There was a chemistry, I think; something that people liked being around and wanted to be part of.

I feel lost without her.

September 9

The film I'm watching is terrible. It's loud and very violent. Exactly what I'm in the mood for.

The cinema by the ring road is empty and cold, and smells very strongly of damp.

I've never heard of the movies on offer. They're cheaper than mainstream films, I suppose. Trash destined for DVD. Maybe not even that.

I couldn't face other people today. Or even lying about where I am. I turned my phone off this morning, and headed straight out here.

You can learn a lot about telling stories from watching films this bad. I saw hundreds as a boy, from the video shop at the end of our road. My cousin worked there in the afternoons, and let me have films for free – whatever I wanted to see, a dozen a day in the holidays when my parents were out at work.

How do we tell the story of Rankin? In such a way that someone might want to commission it?

Backwards maybe? Or in flashbacks? Or from the point of view of the policeman who put him away?

Or that of his mum, or a boy he took under his wing?

Or maybe we go arty? Film him directing an actor playing himself in a film of his life?

Or give it an on-screen author, to cross swords with Rankin and challenge him to tell us the truth?

He's a flawed but charismatic man, from a fascinating world, with a remarkable story to tell. And he sees the world very clearly, a quality I've always found attractive.

I like him. I want to know him better.

I told him we need to figure out what form the film will take. 'Beginning a production without that sorted doesn't feel good', I said.

He said, 'Trust me Truman, there are things that feel much worse.'

I know there's a way to crack this. I just can't seem to figure it out.

September 11

I'm with the new girl, at a 9/11 reunion being held in central London.

On the way here, she described 9/11 – as she tends to do with anything troubling and unfamiliar – as 'weird'. The day is just beginning, but I'm already feeling annoyed with her.

I made a film about 9/11 once, for the first anniversary of the attack, about a bunch of strangers who came together in a stairwell and helped each other escape, battling peril every step of the way.

I have an idea for a short series that's a sort of psychological history of 9/11 and the years since. You'd see survivors full-frame, looking straight down the lens of the camera, talking to a psychotherapist about their memories and the ways in which the tragedy has affected their lives. You never see the psychotherapist except in little linking passages, when he or she explains things you need to know, like what shock is. Or survivor guilt. Or PTSD.

Most 9/11 films – like the one I made – avoid this sort of stuff in favour of a straight retelling of events, or a story of personal heroism or survival, told in a linear and factual way. This happened, and then this and then this. This is what I did. This is what I was thinking.

These stories are remarkable, and deserve to be told. But they seem to me to miss the point, which is the *impact* of those events on the people concerned. Perhaps this is because the impact of events on the people concerned is just too troubling for a TV audience to consider.

The organizer is introducing us to people. Not everyone thinks it's a good idea to have invited people from the media. The new girl looks very ill-at-ease. There's no rule book for encounters like this one. You have to feel your way.

One of the men seems somehow separate from everyone else. He looks like a human version of the structures the army uses to contain the blast from a bomb.

The organizer of the event tells me this man's story. He was an ordinary guy who rescued dozens of people and became a national hero, lionized by the president, celebrated in the media. In many ways 9/11 was the best day of his life. Real life after that seemed dull. His relationships crumbled. He's a good man, who's lost his way. He doesn't know how to be.

Which makes him perfect for the series I'm imagining.

I go over and we start to chat. He's reserved and watchful, weighing me up. The conversation goes nowhere. He's a proud and dignified man, and I think he might be happier speaking to a woman. So I ask the new girl to go with him the next time he steps outside for a cigarette.

The new girls says no.

Which is her right, of course. But very annoying. It's a privilege to speak to these people. And if you can't engage with a subject and a situation as fascinating as this one, what the fuck are you doing in factual television?

I send her away with £20 for a cab. Her eyes are burning. When we arrived here, it was merely awkward between us. Now I've made her into an enemy.

September 13

The newsagent near my flat is quiet. Just a couple of dog walkers and a shift worker coming off nights. It's very early still.

My heart is beating fast.

The papers have just arrived. The guy behind the counter is putting them in piles.

I find the one I'm after.

I'm looking through it now, in the queue.

There's nothing at all about me, and nothing about Monroe.

September 14

Same shop, but not so early. The place is full of kids, killing time on their way to school.

One of the newsagents is standing over them, arms crossed and scowling, on the lookout for pilferers.

I'm scanning another edition of Donovan's paper for a lurid headline and a photo of me. Maybe the one his snapper took, that day on the Brightwell Estate? Looking surly and defensive, no doubt, as people generally do when they find that they've been ambushed.

Now I'm combing through slowly. Page by page. Cover to cover.

Nothing at all, once again.

I type out a text to Donovan, then delete it.

I don't know what this means.

September 16

Chalk figures are giant representations of beasts and men, carved into steep hillsides across southern England. They're beautiful and mysterious, created in the ancient past for purposes unknown. Scholars believe that they were made by whole communities coming together and walking around and around markings on the ground in a sort of ritual procession, etching the design into the chalky rock beneath the grass and soil. Every year the same thing would happen, and the design would be re-inscribed, until it became a permanent feature of the landscape.

I've had an idea that involves designing and making a new chalk figure, in a part of the country that is depressed and riven with tension because of immigration. I'm imagining people coming together to forge a new shared identity. It would be a film about the history of Britain and the present and the future.

I'm in Wiltshire to look at a chalk figure up close, and to meet with a local expert.

It's cold and it's started to rain.

The history man is a no-show. When I first started in TV, people would drop everything for a meeting. Producers were held in high regard. Now that respect has gone. Too much TV around, I suppose. Too much for which too little respect is due.

I have no reception on my phone. My car is a 40-minute trek away, across a field full of cows and cowshit. Ten paces away, a distance that says *fuck you*, stands the damp and unhappy new girl. She thinks the idea is stupid, and has said so. I am trying to contain my irritation. I am irritated partly because she's probably right.

But irritation will get us nowhere. She's not Mills, and that's not her fault.

I say, 'Help me figure something out. We have £150,000 to make a pilot with the Delamains, who are the best, funniest, most brilliant set of characters I've ever met. But as things stand, no access to the family whatsoever. What do we do?'

She's wearing the look of a deputy-head prefect offered a toke on a joint, but at least she's engaged.

'Is that usual?' she says.

'The best thing about TV is that nothing is, really. Not if you're doing it properly.'

That was true once, but it's not any more, and both of us are aware of it. Sadly in my case. Cheerfully in hers.

As we trudge back to the car we talk the problem over.

September 18

'We're not open yet', says the barmaid, not looking up, wiping down the bar without cleaning it.

There's no natural light save for a long thin sheet of sunshine through a chink in the curtains, pulled tight but hanging badly on their runners, specks of dust orbiting slowly.

Her clothes look like the ones she sleeps in, a baggy T-shirt and shapeless shorts.

I tell her, 'I'm here to see Vee.'

She looks up and weighs what she sees.

'Vee's not here. Haven't seen her for two or three weeks now.'

'What about Mr Bixby?'

'What about him, love?' she says, a little too fast. She sounds hurt more than defensive, though. Maybe she had a thing for him?

'Could I speak to him instead?'

'You're the TV man?'

'We talked about making a film. He told me his plans for expansion.'

The barmaid huffs. 'Disappeared', she says.

He stopped coming, then the girls stopped coming. Then everyone stopped. She sounds as though she prefers it that way.

'No one's been able to reach him', she says.

His leather jacket is on the coat stand, newish and stiff. I remember him wearing it on the night I came to meet him, looking hot and uncomfortable. 'Isn't that his?'

'It is. His bag's in the back, as well. And that's his car outside.'

I ask, 'Are you expecting him?'

She says, 'I don't expect anything, love.'

There could be all sorts of reasons a man like that might disappear. All sorts of toes he might have stepped on. All sorts of people he might have upset.

I go outside and try Bixby on his mobile.

Showing Vee Rankin the back of his hand is probably one of a dozen mistakes he's made this summer alone. It's easy to picture how it might have happened. Bixby eager to keep the girls in check, because without them he has nothing. Vee cheeky and defiant, doing it for fun and to annoy her father, feeling untouchable because of her father's name. In her world, no one would ever think of hurting Rankin's little girl. Maybe Bixby didn't know.

I can hear muffled trilling coming from a dirty white BMW by the pub's front door. In the passenger footwell is Bixby's phone, lit up, the glass cracked, vibrating and rotating slowly.

On the screen it says 'TV Wanker'.

Then the light goes out.

'This is Bix. I'm tied up just now. Leave a message, I'll come back soon.'

I wonder if you will, Mr Bixby?

September 19

Good things come of good things.

That was the maxim of a brilliant boss I had for a while, and it made him a fortune. His policy was to hire creative people, and encourage them to express themselves. He was running a TV company, but all the people I worked with had fingers in other pies. One guy was a stand-up comedian in the evenings. Another was writing a novel. A girl with red hair was lead singer in a band, and the woman who sat next to her designed clothes. It was an exciting, buzzy place to work. Commissioners used to like coming to visit. The ideas we had and the programmes we made were always interesting and unusual.

And good things always came of them. Small commissions would lead to larger ones. And there's no better form of development than being in production; instead of speaking to a commissioner once a month, you're suddenly doing it twice a day, which makes you closer and gives you more chances to pitch.

The more good TV we made, the more other channels paid attention. It wasn't long before they were coming to us, and asking for our best ideas. Our opportunities multiplied, but we never pitched anything we didn't really want to make. That way even flawed ideas were part of the positive vibe. Good things even came of our biggest disappointments; good ideas that fall at the final hurdle tend to make commissioners even keener to work with you next time around. We won awards and the good things snowballed.

Good things do indeed come of good things. But the opposite is also true.

Some programmes don't rate well for reasons that are elusive. So long as the programme was basically well-made, you're generally allowed a ticket to go around again. And some bad programmes do rate well, which of course is also fine. A bad programme that rates badly can see you blackballed by a broadcaster. Two on the trot will certainly see that happen. No one will ever say so, but you and your ideas will stop being welcome.

The same thing happens if you pitch too many bad ideas, and commissioners start to think you're wasting their time. Or if you get a reputation for overselling, which is making a commissioner believe that an ordinary idea is better than it really is, which is setting yourself up for a fall. Or if too many of your pieces of access fall down.

Or if someone catches you lying.

Today the commissioner who offered me money for the Delamain pilot finally got tired of waiting for news and six months of broken promises. She called the family direct, to ask them how the pilot was progressing. It was Lady Delamain who picked up.

Immediately afterwards, she wrote me a formal email, copying in her boss and his as well – the Director of Broadcasting, the channel's most senior exec.

'You have no access and never did', it says, correctly.

'The next time you have a big idea, please don't think of us.'

September 21

Often, in the moments before sleep at the end of a long or lonely day, I go to a particular place in my mind.

It's a farmhouse kitchen, with a flagstone floor and a warped wooden table that generations must have gathered at. There's a pantry full of food, and a rumbly old Aga, painted blue. There are pots of herbs, and candles on saucers, and battered copper saucepans hung from the ceiling.

I spent a week there once with the girl I told you about. The one I used to be with, who was also with someone else. We were working together at the time. At night she'd cook dinner, then we'd sit and talk till late. We were sitting there when I realized with shock and total clarity that I loved her and couldn't be without her.

When I go there now, I pull a chair up to the Aga and pour myself a drink and settle in to wait for her, awake in my dream and watching the door, fast asleep in real life.

After we said goodbye, I used to see her everywhere. Or rather I imagined so. Same shape. Same clothes. Same hair. Same laugh.

And then today I saw her for real.

I was in a restaurant waiting to meet a journalist. He phoned to say sorry: he was off chasing the story I'd hoped he might let me in on. I drank my coffee and paid my bill.

I got up to leave and saw her, reflected in the mirrors behind the bar, laughing and luminous, surrounded by people all looking her way. Sitting beside her was a little girl, a pint-sized carbon copy, in her best dress, beaming.

I was almost through the door when I heard my name. It sounds so much better when she says it.

I said, 'So nice to see you and don't you look well?' She touched my arm and said that I looked thin. I wished with all my might like a child at Christmas to go back to the start and meet her again.

We said polite things – I forget exactly what – and then we said goodbye.

The vision of her in the mirror is what happiness looks like. I've been trying to imagine myself alongside her, but I can't. I'm not a happy-ever-after sort of guy.

I don't think I'll go to the farmhouse again.

September 24

Pitching again today, more in hope than expectation.

I have an idea about cat ladies, and one about compulsive liars. Plus access to a new support clinic for people with anger-management issues, and a family-run company of extreme cleaners.

These are new projects, but they already feel tired and old. Regurgitated. Bus-stop puke-puddles of ideas.

This is not a broadcaster I've worked for before, mostly because I've never wanted to. Its reputation is dire, for trashy and exploitative programmes. But it's also known for fast and decisive commissioning, which is very much what I need.

I don't know the commissioner. They come and go very quickly here.

He says that none of my ideas is right – they're far too tame and polite. What he wants is ideas that will outrage and appall his viewers. Programmes about fat kids, scroungers and immigrants have rated through the roof.

He glances at my notebook, closed on the table in front of me, like he's expecting me to write this down. I never take notes; it only looks weak, and you'll remember anything that's interesting or useful. His thoughts so far have been neither.

The other idea I brought with me is the family in the woods. His viewers would love to hate them. They'd find the family's values offensive. They'd light up Twitter with scorn and abuse.

The commissioner likes the sound of them. The sound of the major even more.

'He'd strike a chord with our viewers', he says. 'A hero standing up for what's right.'

I say that I don't think so. The family knows what's important in life. The major has no idea.

It's clear that this guy doesn't like me very much. I can see it in his eyes. He thinks I'm too intellectual to get what his channel's about. He thinks I regard it as beneath me.

He's absolutely right; I do.

Watching this guy's channel is like being stuck in the back of a taxi while a fat, racist driver lists his hates and frustrations. I'd rather fucking walk.

I can't let my salvation be the family's ruin. So the meeting is over, with half an hour still to go.

September 25

A text comes through as I'm falling asleep. It's not from a number I know.

It says, 'You'd better deliver.'

Deliver what?

I start to write back, then decide it may be wiser not to.

I assume it's from Donovan. His own phone this time, perhaps?

Something has changed, but what?

September 26

I'm not close to my own father. I don't miss him, as such. But a man should have an older man in his life, to show him how things are done.

The bosses for whom I've done my best work in television have all been father figures. People who either recognized the need for a father in me, or had their own parallel need for someone to pass on their wisdom to. A son and heir, even if only for a couple of years.

There was Bill, of course. And the good-things-come-of-good-things guy. But three or four others as well.

A bright-eyed, playful man called Patrick, who saw opportunity everywhere he looked. He treated TV like a stage. When you're meeting important people, he said, act like you know things no one else does, like Bogart playing Marlowe. And when you're speaking to those people or pitching them ideas, say stuff like you know it to be true, like something you've known all your life.

A thin, professorial man called Marcus, who taught me it's okay to be flawed. That flawed is good, even. It makes you real and relatable. No one wants to deal with a man made out of plastic.

Marcus looked permanently dismayed, like his mind was tormented by a terrible, unsayable secret. But he had a gift for changing the mood of others, for inspiring them and winning them round.

And Barney, gruff and weathered, the boss who knew and liked me best, who taught me the importance of the ends of the things, of seeing things through, no matter what. Any smart guy can start something off, he used to say, when I brought him a new idea. Starting things off feels good. But will you be able to finish it? Finishing takes sand. It's where the big tests lie. It's how you prove your mettle.

Between them they taught me how to survive then thrive in television. Lessons for life, not just for TV.

I still see them from time to time, at screenings and festivals, and feel huge affection for each of them. We swap news and talk about the things we've been working on. As much now as when they supervised my work, I want them to feel proud of me.

Sitting opposite me in his office, Charlie looks sad.

'A lot has happened', he says.

'Do you remember what I said would happen if you ever lied to me again?'

I feel like a small boy.

He knows about Lord and Lady Delamain. The access that never was. The pilot we never filmed, or even started work on.

The new girl, that day on the hillside in the rain.

'Sometimes', he says, 'a person's character flaws turn out not to be flaws at all, but that person's actual character.'

He says that cleverness and energy and other such qualities aren't enough in themselves. You need a certain maturity to succeed in TV.

He says, 'If you live a life without meaning, you'll have ideas without meaning.'

'Things matter', he says. 'More than you seem to understand.'

And then he says, 'I'm sorry but I want you to leave.'

September 30

Saying goodbye is part of life in television. Projects get completed. Contracts expire. Cards are passed around, and signed with messages of thanks and good luck.

Senior people get poached into better jobs, or sometimes worse jobs with better salaries, and announce that they'll be leaving. Junior staff slip them CVs, in the hope of being taken along. There's cake in reception, and maybe drinks after work. Bosses contemplate the time and expense that finding a replacement will require, but wear a brave face and say thank you for all you've done.

The sands are constantly shifting.

There are snake-oil salesmen that I can think of, who somehow get good jobs, but never stay in them long. Just long enough for the boss of a company to realize that all the talk is just that and nothing else. They always get fired eventually, but not many other people do.

Which is why no one really knows what to say to me today. I'm embarrassed, and so are they.

I'll hand my projects on to MacLean, who is being sickeningly decent and supportive.

'You'll come up smelling of roses', he says. 'Good people always do.'

He smiles sincerely and shakes my hand. I guess that's what maturity looks like.

As I'm leaving Charlie hands me a leather-bound notebook. On the first of 200 pristine pages he's written 'What we think, we become.' And underneath that 'I hope that you'll fill this book with new thoughts and new ideas.'

The page is marked with a ticket to ride, a go-anywhere pass for the Underground, valid for a year. An invitation to go exploring.

I leave my keys at reception and step outside, with nothing to do and nowhere I need to be.

CHAPTER TEN:
OCTOBER

October 2

I had a great idea once, in a state of complete exhaustion. I'd been working long, grinding days on a difficult film, and moonlighting writing a treatment for a friend, for £1000 in cash. I'd drunk a bottle and a half of wine at my desk at home to shush my worries with the film and relax me enough to write. I got into a lovely, fuzzy state of flow, and the next time I looked at my watch, five hours had passed. It was maybe two or three in the morning, but I was both too wired and too tired to sleep.

The treatment was almost done. Maybe just an opening paragraph shy of a pretty persuasive document. I decided that I'd finish it after a breath of air on the fire escape.

I loved sitting on the fire escape, especially at night in the summer. It was a top-floor flat, with a great view of London rooftops and the city beyond. My head felt clear. I thought that maybe my film would turn out okay.

I went back inside, and took my laptop to the sofa to write the final paragraph. I closed my eyes to get back into the headspace of the treatment and think of a killer first line. Something surprising and arresting. A thought about the subject matter that was both original and true. And in that moment, a perfect, fully formed, extraordinary idea for a programme appeared to me like a vision.

I opened my eyes again. It felt like a blink. But now the room was bright with sunshine, and my flatmate was stomping around, getting ready for work.

I remembered my brilliant idea immediately. Or rather I remembered that I'd had it. I just couldn't remember what it was.

I couldn't remember for the rest of the day. I can't remember it still.

Since then I write down every idea, no matter how insignificant. I have notebooks full of them. And boxes full of napkins and Tube tickets with ideas scribbled on the back. And lists on my phone and my laptop. I write ideas on the back of my hand in the cinema, and type them up when I get home. I keep a pen and paper by the bed.

I'm looking through those lists now, lost in a blizzard of bad and indifferent ideas, hoping for one that shines like a beacon.

October 4

DC Lockwood has brought the coffees this time. The weather's turning cold. She's warming her hands on her cup.

It was her idea to meet here, a church the size of a cathedral, not far from where she works. The interior is vast and gloomy, pitch-black alcoves and oratories opening off the central space, neat rows of candles blinking in the distance. There's a trippy smell of incense and, from a woman five rows in front of us, a low, sad murmur of prayer.

Lockwood says it's a good place to think. We talk about that for a while, whispering. I'm going to add this place to my list.

She looks different in casual clothes. Older and more worldly, somehow.

'Are you religious?'

'I used to be.'

'What happened?'

She shrugs, with half a smile. A something and nothing gesture. Something bad, maybe. A crisis of some sort. Or maybe nothing much. Gradual erosion. Too much life experience to believe in easy answers.

'You wish you were still?' Half-question, half-statement. There's a restlessness and a sadness to her, like she's searching for something. Somewhere to belong.

She tilts her head. Maybe.

'Two more people dead', she says.

It's not clear how they fit into the bigger picture, but it's strongly assumed that they do. Both men died the same way as the guy in the warehouse flat: a single shot to the stomach, which Lockwood assures me is a bad way to go. Very slow and very painful. All three men bled to death while some sort of search was conducted.

The object of all this activity must be hugely valuable or important, she says. First, a complex and risky robbery. Now three men have been murdered. People are going to extraordinary lengths to obtain something or other.

The first of the two new victims was a cousin of the Nelsons. The second was some guy in a farmhouse. It looked like more than one person had been living in the farmhouse. It looked like they were expecting to be holed up there some time.

No sign of struggle or forced entry in either case.

Lockwood looks away into space, frowning but not unhappy, enjoying the challenge of puzzling it out.

I think I understand where she's coming from. She feels frustrated and ignored by more senior colleagues. Made to run errands and tidy up mess. She's not getting the satisfaction she wanted from her job. Now she's hoping to find it elsewhere.

I tell her she'd be good at TV. A good producer or director. She's curious and persistent, and knows a good story when she sees one. And she's moral and wants to make a difference, which would give her drive and a point of view.

She shines a big smile back at me. It's the first time I've seen her look anything other than grave, and the effect in the gloom is dazzling. Good at TV is what she wanted to hear.

'I think I'd like to work with you', she says.

On this case, she's attended the crime scenes whenever she can, and when that hasn't been possible, has studied photos and reports at night when the rest of her team has gone home.

In every case, she says, the victim's keys are missing. So the murderer could come back, her boss concluded. But Lockwood has other ideas: maybe what the villains are after *is* a key, but they don't know what it looks like?

She's thoughtful and clever and notices things. Like I said, she'd be good at TV.

'What would you need', she says, 'to make a film?'

I tell her how it works. 'We'd need an angle. A property. A way into the story. Something I can sell.'

But it's almost impossible on something like this. Newspapers and news programmes will cover the basic facts, of the robbery and the killings. A documentary would need to go further and deeper, for which you need access. But access to what? There's no chance of following the investigation. Police access takes months to arrange, sometimes even years. Still less chance of filming with the other side, the people in possession of the missing item. Even if you knew the characters involved, it would be morally and legally impossible, and of course way too dangerous in light of recent events. Which leaves us with precious few options.

Despite Lockwood's tip-off back in April, and the thrill of visiting the scene of a real-life murder, I haven't given the story much thought, to be honest, beyond the occasional reverie. It's intriguing more than anything else. I can see no way to progress it, and no way of accessing the thing that first drew me into all this, the hundreds of enticing little secrets hidden away inside the depository, suddenly – perhaps – set free. By lunchtime, all the pale and anxious faces had melted away, never to return.

Lockwood's gone back to looking grave.

'Maybe when it's all over a film could tell the story behind the story?'

She brightens a little at this. Maybe a drama doc, if you knew all the ins and outs. Information from the inside, that no one else has access to. That information could be your property, a tangible thing you could sell.

She nods.

'What would I do on it?' she says.

'Assistant producer. Or producer, maybe. You'd have to quit your job, though. And TV is a tough and precarious business. It's hard to get a career up and running.'

She considers this.

A woman is singing quietly to herself, arranging flowers in front of a statue of the Virgin and Child.

'If it was a good film, would that be enough to launch a career?'

I tell her that it might be.

'And would it be a good film?' she asks. 'Would it be good enough?'

'Maybe', I tell her. It's hard to say. All the ingredients are there, so far. The heist. The deaths. The missing item. The connections to notorious criminals.

It really depends on what happens next. It depends how the story ends.

October 6

I've always loved to daydream. I used to get in trouble for it at school. I looked forward to the boring lessons the most, for a chance to slip away, unnoticed, to fantasy places far away from the surly grey town I grew up in.

I'm on a Tube train, in the calm that follows the morning rush, letting my mind wander.

I'm on my way to nowhere in particular, the first place I arrive at that I've never been before, to have a look around. I have no routine to keep to now, and no one I need to check in with.

I'm thinking of Lockwood and the key, and all the other projects and ideas I've worked on this year. I can feel them settling, like the flakes in a snow globe.

I should be learning lessons, I know.

I wonder if I've so filled up my head over the years with ideas and the beginnings of things that there's no space left for the things I love. Or if ideas and the beginnings of things are what I love the most.

On the seat across the aisle is a copy of the free newspaper Mills used to read on her way to work. In the two years we worked together, she spotted dozens of leads and potential stories in the classifieds of that paper: a get-rich-quick seminar led by a man who'd made millions (and then lost the lot); a £400 all-in package wedding deal at a hotel on the M25; a woman offering thousands for a kidney to save her daughter's life.

For the last few days, I've been running an ad in that paper myself: 'Adventure planned. Accomplice sought. Call Truman. Please.'

I haven't seen Mills since the day she left. Or even spoken to her. Her number is dead. Her flatmate said she'd paid up her rent and moved away. I don't know enough about her life to do very much more.

I miss daydreaming with her.

October 7

Three missed calls from Rankin.

No messages. Just his wish to speak, hanging, inert, creaking in the wind.

There's a knot in my stomach. Sooner or later, I'm going to have to let him down.

Not today, though. Today I've got my hands full.

A well-groomed man in a double-breasted blue blazer is being shown across to my table. He's very early for our meeting, hoping to settle and maybe gain some sort of advantage. He's surprised to see me, looking calm and in charge, in the way he imagined looking when *I* arrived. But I got here three hours ago.

It's a grand European-style cafe, full of clatter and conversation. People come and go all the time. Others camp out here all day. No one really pays much attention, in that European way.

I shake the man's hand and offer him some coffee.

The canvas bag on his shoulder looks a little incongruous. He doesn't look like the sort who frequents a gym. It will look fine on me, though. And he'll leave with another exactly the same, just a tenner from a high-street sports shop, stuffed with an old pair of trainers, a sweaty vest and some shorts.

And a single roll of Super 8 film, in its little yellow box, wrapped up in a still-damp towel.

He wants to leave but I press him to stay. There's no need to rush, and rushing in here would only seem strange. So I ask him what he does for a living, and he says he's currently researching an article for a journal. I.e. for a living, does nothing at all. But it turns out he's an ex-military man, and the article is about the wars that we fought in the nineteenth century that you've probably never heard of. Everyone knows the Crimean and Boer Wars, of course, but there were dozens more, against the Chinese, the Ashanti, the Maoris and many others. Before long we're chatting like friends. It's interesting stuff. There might even be a programme in it.

'It's been a pleasure', he says, and almost means it.

We shake hands again, and he leaves.

I'm £400,000 richer now, with nothing at all to spend it on. I'd swap it in a heartbeat for a nice big commission, but they're not the sort of thing that money can buy. That's what makes them so precious.

October 8

I've spoken to the runaway genius half a dozen times now, partly out of personal interest and partly a determination to give the commissioner what she asked for – evidence of a truly exceptional mind.

'What would it take?' I asked her. And she said, 'I want to hear him say something amazing.'

So for hours at a time we Skyped each other, the boy always interesting but never astounding, me prompting and coaxing and recording what was said.

I asked, 'How do other people seem to you?'

He said, 'Slower but also speeded up. Brightly coloured but also fuzzy, like footage from the '60s and '70s. Familiar but also strange.'

I asked, 'What do you want to be?'

He said, in a small voice, 'Happy.'

He spoke of all the years of strain and controversy. It seemed heroic that he was still standing; doing okay in fact, with a girlfriend and plans for the future. And that he seemed to bear no grudges. He worries about his mum and what will become of her. He's a good and thoughtful person trying to find his way out of a difficult childhood. I like him a lot.

'Everybody struggles', he said, 'to be the person they wish to be, or even the person they already are'.

I still don't know if he is or was a genius.

In the end, I cut together a few highlights of our conversations and sent it off to the commissioner for her to make her own mind up.

Today I need to let the boy know that I've left the company I was working at. The film is in the hands of someone else now, with their own personal projects and preoccupations. With no one invested in it and determined to get it commissioned, it's likely to wither and die.

Then I need to make similar calls to the people I met for the 9/11 series, and the woman at the beauty agency, the boardroom sex lady and the family in the woods. Orphaned projects now, all of them; unwanted and unloved.

I'd keep them all if I could, but it doesn't work that way.

Maybe I could keep Rankin, though? As far as everyone else is concerned, the project is dead already. If I can just figure out how to get a commission, everything would be fine.

So I'll hold off calling him for now. Another week or two can't do any harm.

October 11

People from my past are filing in front of me. My mum and dad, looking old and slightly sunken now. Getting used to this sort of thing. My sister and her family, her son almost as tall as she is. A few others I used to call auntie and uncle. My grandfather at the front of the line, shoulder-high in a casket.

I can see them but they can't see me. I arrived on time, properly dressed, and found I couldn't face it. I feel pressed into the seat of my car, unable to move, like those dreams you wake up in the middle of.

Probably better this way.

The buildings are low and fearful. A row of dark trees are bristling in the wind.

The column is moving off, stiffly, to the chapel at the end of the street.

A thief I met for a film taught me how to break into houses without making a mess. I'm breaking into my grandad's house now. Easy with such a cheap and flimsy lock.

Inside, the place is spartan, exactly as I remember it. No trinkets or ornaments. Nothing soft or colourful. Not much to show for a lifetime, I suppose. No photos even, except for one of my grandad as a youngish man, his wife by his side and me on his lap, no more than a month or two old. She died soon after, but he loved her intensely the rest of his life.

He wasn't tall or especially broad, but he loved a fight and never lost. He was always looking to take on the world. He knew a lot of people, and how to get things done. He despised bullying and unfairness. Some kind of rage propelled him.

Others thought him a tyrant, but he was always patient and kind to me. We'd go walking on a Saturday morning, and he'd tell me stories. He'd notice things, and talk about the power that comes from knowing stuff, and the magical importance of words. He'd try to answer all the questions I had that no one else had time for, talking patiently about his experiences, offering them to me as ways of making sense of things. He'd take me to the cinema, and then to the graveyard to visit his wife. He'd give her the flowers we'd picked and tell her about the film, and other things she'd missed.

'You need someone like her', he said. 'Because you're someone like me.'

He almost never left the village he was born in, but travelled far and wide in his mind. He taught himself to read as a boy, and read a book every week for the rest of his life, borrowed from the tiny local library. He especially liked books about cowboys. I think he thought he was one.

'Don't wait for things to happen', he told me, more than once. 'Don't be mediocre. Don't settle. Don't let time slip away.'

I take down the photograph in its dusty frame and wrap it in a tablecloth. Good old lad. You can come and live with me now.

October 13

I'm in a household full of women. It's loud and noisy and full of love.

A few weeks ago, one of the girls – the youngest, still a teenager – started to get headaches and went for an eye test. The optician referred her to a specialist. The specialist told her that she had a rare condition, and was in the process of going blind.

And then the specialist asked if the girl had any siblings. The girl said, 'Yes, two sisters.' The next day they both came in for the same series of tests. Both were told that they had the same condition as their little sister. Like her, both would lose their sight.

A journalist I know phoned me yesterday and asked if I might be interested in the story. I paid £150 for their phone number, and caught a train to visit them first thing this morning.

It's unclear how long they'll have before their vision leaves them. Not long at all, perhaps. The condition affects young people in particular. In Britain, hundreds of children, teenagers and people in their early twenties have gone blind because of it.

The two older girls are both pregnant. The eldest already has a little boy.

I start to ask questions, and it's clear that they haven't yet got to grips with what their diagnosis means. 'What will you miss looking at the most? What if you lose your sight before your baby is born?'

I'm upsetting them, so I stop. They're positive, down-to-earth people, and so far they've been purely concerned with the practical problems they'll face. It's not my business to make them confront the rest of it. But the unexplored emotional dimension means that following them, as they start to consider for themselves the things they're about to lose, will be hugely moving. It will make viewers, at home on their sofas – their noisy, messy kids just off to sleep, tired and worn down by problems at work and problems at home – count their blessings and be thankful for what they've got. Which is generally an awful lot. So a sad film for sure, but an uplifting one as well.

Such films are hard to make, though. It's hard to be always present when you should be, at moments of drama and realization. A commissioner will think 'this could all take years to unfold. I've got specific slots in the schedule to fill. And all the money I have to spend is there to fill those slots.' In the merry-go-round of modern TV, that commissioner might not even be in the same job when the film is finished, so he or she sees no benefit in committing to long-term projects. And orphaned films are often never shown, no matter how powerful or moving.

Then their mother says that she's planning a trip.

She works on the railways now. But in her youth she'd been a magnificent free spirit. She'd travelled the world, falling in and out of love. She'd seen the sun set in the Sahara. She'd lived on a beach in Thailand. She'd trekked through the rainforest in Brazil.

'Such a big old world', she says, eyes glossy and far-away. 'So many things to see.'

People are full of surprises.

Her daughters have never roamed far beyond the town they grew up in. Their mother wants them to see extraordinary and beautiful things while they still can, perhaps even as their sight is failing, to help them come to terms with their fate.

They discuss it, animatedly. One of the girls wants to see a vast virgin snowscape, and be the first to make footprints in it. Another has a vision of thousands of brilliant blue butterflies that she has sent into the air, in the deep green backdrop of a jungle somewhere. The third girl, the quietest one, shyly says she wants to see great art, the best of what people are capable of.

What a wonderful thing to film. What a perfect, genuine, beautiful idea.

October 14

Another family home today. Very different to the noise and chaos of the sisters and their mum.

The motion of a small brass carriage clock seems inordinately loud. There are tiny shoes in the hallway and tiny coats on the back of the living room door. There are toys on the living-room floor, neatly stacked in a tidy corner. But none of the sounds that go with these things. Just the sound of the clock and the sound of my voice, hushed, thick and clumsy.

The little girl who lives here is staying with her auntie. I watched the little boy die, and filmed a team of surgeons removing the organs from his body.

The sadness in the room is making it hard to breathe.

I have to tell them that no one wanted to commission the film. I've tried everywhere I can think of and failed.

I didn't want to do it over the phone, of course. I suggested we meet for a coffee. They invited me round.

They take the news acceptingly. They've had to endure so much.

I'm reminded that they lent me all their home videos – dozens of little tapes, of birthdays and holidays and mornings in the park. I never even looked at them. I made the taster only from what I shot that night.

I tell them I'll bike the videos round to them, and they nod numbly.

Then they ask when they can see the taster.

I tell them sorry, that won't be possible.

I've come to believe that no one should see it, least of all the people in this room.

The woman starts to cry, softly.

The man says, 'It would mean a lot.'

He looks me in the eye and says, 'Please.'

October 17

When I bought my flat, it came with a garage in the building opposite.

My car isn't worth the effort of putting it to bed every night, so I use the garage purely to stash stuff – old treatments and tapes and bits of research;

the files you accumulate on every film and project, too precious to discard when the project is finished, too dull to ever return to.

But tonight I'm going through them, half hoping to rediscover something good, half bored of sitting alone at home.

The treatments and casting tapes are a long, sad record of people wooed and seduced then set aside, judged not quite interesting enough to put on TV. Not dozens of people but hundreds. They're all around me now on the concrete floor of the garage, piled up in drifts like leaves.

Maybe I should call some of them up, see what's happening now in their lives?

But that's almost certainly a bad idea. If they didn't make the grade then, they probably won't do again. Better to start afresh.

Tomorrow I'll throw most of this stuff away. Maybe even all of it.

There's a freezing mist on the street, but inside the garage smells rotten and fetid, like something lived and died in here, so I've kept the door ajar.

There's a guy outside my building, looking up to the top floor where my flat is.

He presses the buzzer and steps back and looks up again, perfectly still.

I can't see his face in the mist and darkness, and his outline is blurry and vague, but he seems somehow familiar.

Then he turns up the street and is gone.

October 21

Selena's flat is cosy and furnished with beautiful things.

It was already late when I knocked on her door, and she let me in with no comment or questions asked, as she's done many times before. When I got myself into a fight, with scrapes and cuts and a couple of broken bones, she patched me up and put me to bed on her couch. When I landed the biggest commission of my career, after months of head-down determination, looked around and realized I had not a single friend left to celebrate with, she took me in and made me something to eat.

Talking to Selena is easy. She tells me about her plans. To go back to university. To travel to places that are warm and fragrant. To sit in cafes with nowhere else to be, watching people and wondering about their lives.

'It doesn't have to be like this', she says.

'What doesn't?'

She thinks for a moment. 'Anything.'

A teacher in his thirties has run away with one of his pupils, a 15-year-old girl. In emails and texts made public, they talk about being in love.

They were last seen boarding a ferry in Folkestone. Police across Europe are trying to find them.

I tell Selena the story and we wonder what they'd look like to a casual observer, at a pavement cafe in the south of France. Guilty and furtive? Knowing that what they were doing was wrong? Or slow-motion bouncing in the bubble they've blown around themselves, in love and happy to show it? Everything made so much more intense by the knowledge that one day soon a reckoning will come, and everything will fall apart.

'People never fall for the right person', Selena says. 'It's never as neat and tidy as everyone seems to want it to be.'

I've been considering taking off to try and find them. And maybe film with them while they're still on the run. But I feel like I've lost my licence to practise.

I'm scared that there is no way back to the life I love, and say so. Like life comes in two acts, the story of a rise and the story of a fall, and now the first act is over. I worry that I'll never again feel anything new.

I tell Selena how desperately I miss the thrill of standing on the threshold of something, of taking those first few steps into a new adventure.

'Is it the adventures that made you feel like that?' Selena says. 'Or is it the girl you've been having them with?'

Then she adds, 'The girl at the door, right?'

She puts her hand on my face.

'You take vacations in other people's lives', she says. 'Which is fine and fun. But maybe you should start living a life of your own.'

October 22

I spent ten months in a hospital once. I wasn't ill. Or at least I wasn't at the start of it.

I was working on a film about a spate of stabbings, in which the victims and perpetrators were almost exclusively young and black. It was front-page news, particularly when one boy was attacked at school. Racist groups tried to make political capital out of the stabbings. The phone-in shows on the radio were full of fear and anger, and badly informed but strongly held points of view.

I pitched a simple idea on the subject, that I hoped would serve to tell the truth about the stabbings, educate the public, and perhaps give a focus to national debate.

The plan was to take up residence at a major London hospital in the heart of the area most affected by the stabbings, then wait for a stab victim to be brought into A&E. I'd film whatever happened next – the drama of the fight to save the boy's life; the boy's mother and father, out of their minds with worry; the detectives trying to figure out what happened; the perpetrators brought to justice, or not, as is very often the case.

Around the observational action, I'd try to piece together details of the boy's life from interviews with his friends and teachers. Who was he, and how did he come to be lying in a doorway or a ditch in south London, terribly alone and bleeding to death?

At first I spent only evenings at the hospital, because that's when I was told most of the stabbings happen. Then I missed a stabbing that came into the hospital in the early hours, and started spending all night there, drinking coffee and trying to stay awake. Then I missed one that happened in broad daylight, whilst I was at home sleeping. Before long I was spending *all* of my time there, napping in empty beds and eating in the staff canteen. I got to know everyone who worked there – fantastic, dedicated, funny, insightful people, all of them, from the surgeons to the porters. But mostly I lived in a sort of trance, patiently biding my time.

After six weeks, as I was considering abandoning the project, a boy arrived in an ambulance in a very bad way indeed. Surgeons battled to save his life. I got to know his family, and liked them. The boy had got himself involved in a gang, but had been trying to extricate himself. The family had been about to move away, to give the boy a better chance. There was CCTV footage of the incident, and the police seemed hopeful of catching the people who stabbed him. And then, suddenly, he died.

Another time the police were happy to cooperate with me on a good unfolding story, and then suddenly weren't. I never found out why. And another time again everyone else – even, as it turned out, the perpetrator of the stabbing – was happy to take part in the film, but not the boy at the centre of it, who withdrew the consent his parents had given as soon as he regained consciousness. And so it continued, as the seasons came and went.

I got the story I needed in the end, and the film was a good one, though it missed the peak of the public's interest in stabbings and gang violence by months.

Not very long afterwards, I saw an advertisement for a major documentary series, set in exactly the same A&E I'd spent all those days and nights in, featuring all of the people I had got to know so well. The series was a huge success, and ran to several series more, picking up several awards as it went along. People loved its warmth and the honesty and sincerity of the hospital staff. Despite the fact that having ideas for programmes was my job – making the film was a sort of working holiday, like the film about the missing child – and despite the fact that I was sitting around doing fuck all for weeks and weeks on end, making a series in that A&E department never even occurred to me.

Some years later, I spent time in a fishing community in the States. It was a quiet Catholic town, that suddenly found itself at the centre of a global media storm. Schoolgirl pregnancies were still rare and considered shameful locally, even as nationally rates of schoolgirl pregnancy were at an all-time high. Then, suddenly, it was revealed that 14 girls at the same school had all got pregnant at the same time. The head teacher of the school appeared to suggest that this was due to some sort of 'pact'.

What sort of pact? Why would they do such a thing? How would they have gone about it?

I went there with a commission to tell the story. I spent several weeks hanging out there, getting to know people, trying to find out what really happened, and trying to make contact with the girls involved.

In the evenings, I went to bars to pass the time, and spoke to local fishermen. Once or twice, I gave myself half a day off and went out fishing for tuna with them. They were great characters – brave and charismatic, with an uncomplicated, uplifting approach to life. They were people you'd want to spend time with.

The film got finished and was broadcast. Like most single documentaries, however well-made, it had little impact and was quickly forgotten. I went back to my day job of trying to have ideas, racking my brains for interesting themes and precincts to film in, searching high and low for compelling characters to build good programmes around.

The first time I considered whether the fisherman of that extraordinary town might be good on TV was a year or so later, when I read about the launch of a major observational series about them on a leading channel in the States. It ran to three series in the end, and more than 40 episodes, and made the name of the man behind it.

These films and these failures have been much on my mind today. The lesson of them, I suppose, is that no matter how observant and sharp you might consider yourself, it's entirely possible to miss things that are right in front of your nose.

Selena isn't just a girl I know. I think she's the girl I love.

October 23

In the grim, grey pub at the bottom of the boarded-up flats, everything is as it was, in a state of inertia and limbo. A dull game of football is playing out on the TV, the sound turned all the way down. No one is paying attention.

I'm thinking of all the sportsmen I've watched who were capable of excellence – brilliance even – but in the main were neither.

I'm trying to remember all the times, in what is now quite a long career in TV, when I've been as sharp and impressive as I know I can be.

There was a time when I was pitching for some access, and taking a verbal beating from a very aggressive MD. 'You don't know anything about this business', he said. 'I asked you to impress me, but you are not impressive.' I discovered previous untapped reserves of eloquence and persuasion to win him round. I remember a glorious sense of certainty and strength as I hit my stride, and the look of shock and admiration on the face of the producer who came with me to the meeting. The words and the tone were spot-on. I don't remember thinking about what I was saying. It was totally unfiltered. I surprised even myself.

Another time, making a film that was shaping up to be not bad but boring and tame, I had an idea I thought might save it. I should have talked it through with my exec, because it involved doing something dangerous and reckless, which could easily have fucked up both our careers and the lives of several others. He would have said no, of course, so I did it anyway, disappearing for four whole days, three and a half of them travelling, plus two hours of thrilling, breathless filming. Just me and a camera. Moving without thinking. Totally focussed and totally alive.

Aside from one or two brainstorms when my thoughts were unusually clear and clever connections came quickly to mind, that's pretty much it. Say four or five occasions, in the best part of 15 years. Glimpses are all you get.

This has nothing to do with a lack of application or ambition. I'd give anything to feel so supercharged and in command again. It's just that truly being on top of your game in TV is a very hard thing to achieve.

This is partly because TV is such a tough and complex business.

To be even okay at TV, you need to be good at abstract thinking, be good at planning and interested in detail and be both persuasive and good at listening, which is a very diverse skill set. And you need to be likeable and work well with lots of different people. To produce your very best work, you also need to be at the right company at the right time, which means that you need a lot of luck. And you need to hit upon an idea or a project that speaks to the age you live in and the things that people are into. Finally, as if that wasn't enough, you need to be adaptable enough to deal with the unpredictability of real people in real-life situations.

At any one time, one or more of these elements is likely to be misfiring. Which means your performance will be some considerable way beneath your best.

But that's not all. Even if you acquire all the skills you need, and you have good people around you and resources and luck, it'll still be a struggle to perform at your peak, because you have to factor in you yourself, as a person, and how you happen to feel.

I have a very creative friend who is obsessed with creativity. He has a great imagination and a gift for visualizing things, but fundamentally he thinks like a scientist. He believes that things can be quantified and controlled, and that includes the process of having ideas.

He's forever reading books on creativity and going on courses, and doing things like deliberately getting lost on his way to work and writing stream-of-consciousness letters to people who've inspired him or somehow held him back. He reads and ponders all the articles that people put on Facebook about the habits of successful people. The aim is to unlock an additional layer of creativity that he's sure is there in his mind. Once he's managed to do that, there'll be no holding him back.

I admire him for doing all this, or at least the impulse that lies behind it. He has the same frustration I do at how seldom he's really excelling, despite all his hard work and best intentions. But I have no time for the tips he gives me. I've come to accept that being at my best is just something that comes and goes.

For me, it has something to do with feeling free. Paradoxically perhaps, also something to do with feeling central to a larger enterprise. And something to do with feeling looked-after. Feeling self-confident is part of it also, which in turn has something to do with feeling that someone I like and respect believes in what I'm doing.

All of these are fugitive feelings, and there's not a great deal of control you can exercise over them. Corralling them is almost impossible. Certainly that's how it feels to me.

So generally I try to do my best and wait for the odd day when everything seems to click into place. The one odd day in a thousand.

I feel that way right now. That one odd day is at hand.

I told Selena about the sisters. 'It's the best idea you've had', she said. 'It's everything you stand for. It's what you think TV should be.'

'So no more moping about. Go and get the film commissioned.'

She kissed me on my forehead in a matter-of-fact sort of way, and went back to what she was doing. I felt both startled and utterly calm, everything suddenly clear and obvious.

I finish my pint and leave. It'll be my last in here, I think. Not long now before this place gets razed to the ground.

October 24

The sky is dark. A storm is coming. The air feels thick with voltage. But right now, it's bright and clear. The setting sun has dipped below the grey and black clouds, and everything is vibrant and vivid. Dreamlike almost.

I'm pitching the blindness film. But not pitching, in fact. Walking in the park with a commissioner I think might like it. Talking with passion and conviction, about the girls and their lives and the trip they're planning. Talking about how it makes me feel. Comforted somehow, like everything makes sense.

'Because you're witnessing love and courage', she says.

She's enjoying being out of the office, I think. Offices make you think and behave in ways that often aren't helpful.

I'm thinking about Mills and the day we spent in the park together. All the quiet dramas. Important things said and not said.

The commissioner wants to know if I'd like some development money, to make a taster. That's a good thing, ordinarily. It represents buy-in. But this time I say no. Development money comes with deliverables and conditions to be met. I just want to see where this one goes.

October 26

I'm looking for a bottle of wine, at the shop at the end of my street.

The lights are way too bright, and they're hurting my eyes and making me squint. I need to get the bottles down to read the labels.

There's a dark shape on the edge of my vision in the harsh white light, which makes me look up from the bottle in my hand.

The shape has gone, but I see it in the mirror set up high at the end of the aisle, so the owner can watch out for thieves.

The same shape from outside my flat that night, horribly clear now, stark and close. Very tall and impossibly broad. Stooping slightly. Immensely heavy. Like something from Victorian times loose in the present day.

Rankin's man. The jackhammer.

On my street for the second time in a week.

Do I brazen this out, whatever the fuck this is? Walk up and say hello? Or go outside and wait for him? Or sneak out of the shop, if I can?

He's talking to the shopkeeper.

I can't hear everything they're saying. But I do hear my name, more than once.

My heart is banging. It's hard to stay still.

This can't be a matter of seek and destroy. That wouldn't be done so publicly. But it can't be anything good.

Best to buy time and think.

I shrink back slowly, towards the stockroom and in through the curtain of ribbons, not taking my eyes off the mirror.

There's a small boy inside, sitting on a box, playing a game on a mobile phone.

I put my finger to my lips.

Shhh.

His eyes are wide.

'Have you been bad?' he says, quietly.

Yes, young man, I'm afraid I have.

CHAPTER ELEVEN: NOVEMBER

November 1

I've tried calling Rankin half a dozen times now. At first my calls rang out. Now they don't ring at all. Just a flat, dead tone, the number no longer in service.

I've driven out to the industrial estate where we met, past the great piles of scrap and shipping containers. The PortaKabin was dark and locked up tight.

I've asked around, at the snooker hall and the dingy cafe with the plates on the walls. No one's been able to help me.

Maybe he's in trouble?

One of us is, for sure.

November 2

It's a perfect autumn morning, bright blue and golden-brown.

The people around us are happy. Couples with kids on the riverbank. Teenagers splashing about in boats.

The woman I'm with is concentrating hard, hunched slightly, her head bowed, like she's trying to block the happiness out.

Her name is Carole, the fourth wife of Ray Monroe. She has the same blankness about her eyes and mouth as on the day we met in Monroe's sprawling mansion.

She's quiet for a moment then tells me she liked the film I made, the one about her husband. Affectionate, she says. Funny. I say, 'Yes, I liked him. I still do, despite what people say.'

She nods and hands me a battered box. There's a faded floral pattern on the lid. It might have held a present, once. Then keepsakes and mementoes. Now it contains something else. A small heap of letters and photos. A list of names and places. A lock of blonde hair in an envelope. And three small items of underwear.

'So you'll do it gently?' she says.

Then, 'I didn't know', and starts to cry in a small, restrained way. For the thousandth time, perhaps.

No one knew. But this week, after Carole called me, I ordered up archive of Ray Monroe's old shows. Years and years of them. Outtakes as well as finished programmes. Anything I could lay my hands on. And the signs were certainly there. Monroe was a monster hiding in plain sight.

Hosting teeny pop shows and teatime quizzes, surrounded by giggling girls, there's a kind of wolfish glee about him. His charisma draws your eye, but look away from the centre of the screen, to the girls arranged around him, and the discomfort of some is obvious. Discomfort that looks like something other than the natural awkwardness of teenagers in the spotlight; something deeper and more troubling. The further into his career you go, the more evident it becomes; as Monroe grows portlier and older than the girls' own dads, the disconnect gets worse and worse.

Monroe's fans and the people who grew up with him as a fixture on TV will feel angry and betrayed. Taken in but somehow also party to his activities. Disgusted that we allowed him to be part of our lives. Imagine, then, how his wife must feel. She really did share her life with him. Imagine her growing suspicions. Imagine the moment when she knew for sure.

I tell her what she wants (and needs) to hear. 'None of this is your fault.'

I put my arms around her and she sinks into me, sobbing. Starved of affection, appalled, trapped and desperate to change things, whatever the fallout may be.

November 4

I'm on my way home from seeing the sisters.

We talked for several hours. Made lunch and walked their dog. Played games with the little boy.

We like each other. They trust me. We haven't discussed filming yet. There's no pressure and no rush.

It feels comfortable and simple.

Selena was exactly right. This is how TV should be.

November 7

In general, it's a good idea to offer broadcasters the kind of shows they want, rather than the kind you'd like to make. It's their money that pays for it all. They know their audience better than you.

But they're not always right.

Sometimes you have to listen to ideas and let them tell you what they want to be. Especially the ones with potential to be good.

I made a film once about people selling their stories of personal misfortune to a new kind of magazine.

Overnight, these magazines had become wildly popular. They published the stories people sent in under ludicrous or funny, often-punning headlines. *My Brush With Death*, about a man who'd fallen off a lorry and got a broom handle impaled up his backside. *Aliens Keep Taking My Babies. Crushed By My Monster Boobs.*

The commissioner was a roly-poly, rosy-cheeked chap in his fifties, who loved to make people laugh. He wanted the film to be a romp, and so did I. But the funny stuff was only half the story. Behind every jolly headline was a sad scenario. A setback someone had never recovered from. A terrible disappointment. A public humiliation. The end of something good. The brush man almost died, developed agoraphobia and erectile dysfunction, and lost both his job and his wife. I wanted to include all of this. The commissioner, however, did not.

I took the commission but I shouldn't have. Making the film was agony, and I hated the end result.

Today I had a call from the commissioner I pitched the blindness film to. She asked could we broaden it out to a series instead of a film? A format even? With different young people featured each week, all facing up to the loss of something. Sight in episode one, maybe. Then hearing or mobility, and so on.

As nicely as I possibly could, I told her no. Absolutely not.

November 11

Lady Delamain doesn't like people like you, Lord Delamain told me in his study that day. 'And that, I'm afraid, is that', he said.

He was right. I should have left it there.

It's not easy to remember now why I didn't. I believed the idea to be full of potential. But you learn to let go of ideas, even your best. I think it came down to that particular set of words: 'Lady Delamain doesn't like people like you.'

Maybe I could show her that I'm more like her than she knows, I thought. Or more like her than she wants to believe.

But I'm obviously not like her. Not in the slightest.

Then I had a second thought. Maybe I could tackle the problem differently. Maybe I could show her that *she* is like *me*.

This seemed more promising. I'd just need the tiniest patch of common ground. An angle I could work. Something over which we could reach an understanding.

So I set about my research. I spoke to people in the village around the Delamain estate, and people she went to school with. I looked her up in the society pages of newspapers that no longer exist. I discovered nothing of potential use or value.

Her mother was a proper blue-blood. Her father's family was merely rich. In her youth she'd had several affairs with married men. But in those days – the '70s and '80s – glamorous young women of her class were almost expected to. She went to university to study English and dropped out after less than a year. She has fallen out and feuded with the wives of a former Home Secretary, a famous artist and the owner of a fancy nightclub. And she has twice campaigned unsuccessfully for the chairmanship of the local branch of the Women's Institute.

Nothing there to build a relationship on, or even to kick off a conversation. It seemed that Lady Delamain was and is entirely what she appears to be.

Then I discovered a secret. In her youth, in that period before marriage when aristocratic girls work as nannies and assistants to their father's friends, she had taken a different path. She had been a trainee producer at the BBC.

She had a different name then. A friend of mine pulled her file for me, typed on brown paper and stored away in a vast archive with the details of thousands of others. What struck the interviewer – the thing that got her the job – was a single striking comment she made about not wanting to be the person she was born as. She wanted to make her own way in the world, and see where that might take her.

Lord Delamain is walking towards me. He looks pale and his mouth is pursed.

He's wearing a worn black suit and heavy black coat that must have done decades of service. His eyes look terribly sad.

No preamble or pleasantries.

'I wanted to let you know', he says, 'before you find out from anyone else'.

He hands me a hip flask. I'm wondering how bad this is going to be.

'The series is going ahead', he says.

We walk a little way amongst ancient cedar trees and toppled tombstones, and statues of weeping angels.

He's carrying a small bunch of flowers to lay at the grave of his father. Today would have been his father's birthday. He died when Lord Delamain was still in his teens. That must have been very hard.

It's started to rain. We take shelter in the gothic gloom of the Delamain family vault. One day quite soon Lord Delamain will be laid to rest here too.

'It's funny how things work out', he says. Whether to me or his father is unclear.

Lady Delamain did a short stint in current affairs, and worked on a film about birth control. She was developing a series about the wider royal family – the minor members, and the listless lives they lead – when she underwent a sudden change of heart. She left the BBC. The project was boxed up and shelved.

I tracked down the boxes. They'd started collecting interviews, and amongst the rolls of tape was one labelled with Lady Delamain's own name. She would not be proud now of the things she said.

I phoned Lady Delamain for one last roll of the dice. We could revisit your idea together, I said. Rework it, you and me. You'd be finishing what you started all those years ago, a series about what it's really like to belong to the aristocracy. We could go back and re-interview the people you found. Make it all about how things have changed.

She said, 'Are you trying to blackmail me?' And I said, 'No, of course not. You were interested in TV once. Perhaps you could be again?'

She paused and I thought I might have won her round. She said, 'I asked you to leave us alone, and you ignored me. Now I'll make very sure of it.' Then the phone went dead.

Looking back, Lady Delamain was never less than reasonable and dignified in our various dealings. All that final phone call did was prove that she was right. Poking around in other people's private lives. Never taking no for an answer. All to be expected from people like me. Her formal complaints made clear her distaste.

But it seems I did persuade her of one thing – there must be value in an idea I'd pursued so doggedly, and was so reluctant to relinquish. She called an old friend, still at the BBC – a producer like me, but not like me at all. Like her. And within the hour a deal was done. The family would get £80,000. The series would be ten parts long.

'I'm sorry', Lord Delamain says.

Every year on this date, the flowers laid and news of the estate and the family duly delivered, he goes for lunch at the restaurant his father used to take him to. I've been there myself, a sober, formal place with dark walls covered in pictures and red crushed-velvet banquettes. His father took him there as a child to tell him he'd be sent away for his schooling, and again as a young man to tell him that the estate would soon be his.

'It's a good place for bad news', he says. 'Come with me. Let's drink some wine.'

I tell him I'd be honoured.

'I would have liked working with you', he says. 'I hope we can still be friends.'

November 13

My friend Dan is a master film-maker, brilliant at the things that no one can really teach you. Pacing and tone, and how to tell a story so it draws you in, makes you think and stays with you. His films are not so much things you watch as things that happen to you, and leave you slightly changed.

We're in a room above a pub in Primrose Hill, for a screening of a film he's just finished.

He's a popular guy, the central figure of a gang I used to be part of. Not so much a gang these days as a kind of TV family; firm friends who've grown up in each other's lives, completely relaxed in one another's company and happy for a reason to gather. I haven't seen most of them in years.

Dan and I were best friends once, as young men starting out. If you're good in TV, you move up fast, and by the age of 25 we were fully-fledged directors, well-paid, in-demand and free of all ties and obligations.

One Friday night, we were celebrating. We'd each just finished a film, set free from our cramped, sweaty cutting rooms like sailors on shore leave, and Dan had just been told he'd won an award. We'd met and liked but failed to charm two pretty girls in a bar. This doesn't have to be so hard, Dan said. So we went to a posh hotel. He thought we might find hookers in the hotel bar.

It was in fact *full* of hookers. Fifteen or twenty impossibly elegant women, a few fat Russians in shiny suits and us, in jeans and sneakers.

Neither of us knew how to play it, so we went and stood at the bar. Letting our eyes adjust to the darkness. Surveying the room for clues.

People were arranged in tight groups of three and four, their heads close together, knees touching under the table. The Russian guys were telling stories loudly, the girls nodding and laughing, looking delighted, working hard. All except for one girl, with black hair and smokey eyes, sitting at a table but looking straight back at me, almost like she knew me.

She smiled, in a wide and natural way. Not the smile of a working girl. Or the smile of one person attracted to another. A smile that said 'I'm pleased see you.' A smile of recognition, identified at a glance by a creature of similar stripe.

She headed over, slowly but with purpose, hips swaying, smiling still. And before our drinks arrived, we were deep in conversation, like we'd been talking for hours already. She smelled transportingly of roses and fresh air.

She told me her name was Selena, but I could call her Lenny if I liked.

I paid for her company that night, but never did again.

I invited her tonight, as I've done to dozens of dos in the ten years since I've known her. She always says no, but I think she's pleased to be asked.

Selena's not her real name. I'm still not sure what that is. It's the name she wants me to know her by, and that's okay with me.

Most of the people at the party are married now. Settled and quietly productive. The women all want to know when I'll do the same. I really don't know that I ever will.

I wish Selena was here, though.

November 14

I'm back in the hushed house with the carriage clock, sitting on the sofa with a cup of tea.

The couple's faces look sunken and pale. They're tired and worn. But something else. They almost seem excited.

The man says they've been looking forward to this. They want to see their son again, as he was the day he left them.

We put the disc in the machine, and sit back to watch it together.

It's not the taster I made, though. It's a new one, that I finished last night.

The best editor I know cut it for me, out of all their bits of home video. The little boy as a baby. Then walking and talking, then running around. Growing up right in front of you, adored by his family, happy and secure.

Then he's climbing up a rope ladder at a playground, fearless with strong little limbs. Then asleep in the arms of his mother, tired out from exploring.

And then, at the end, the little boy is in bed, with his mum and dad on either side. As peaceful as you can imagine. No tears or debate. Just a moment of perfect stillness.

Then a short series of cards:

'Jayden died on the 20th of June, at the age of five years and four months.

'Because of the bravery and generosity of his parents, his death transformed the lives of eight other children and their families.

'A six-year-old girl can see again.

'A four-year-old can play with his brothers for the first time in his life.

'The lives of seven-year-old twins were saved.'

It's a celebration of the little boy's life. It's what the family lost, and what they gave back to eight other families.

They're laughing and crying now, and watching it again. It's the taster I should have made in the first place.

Back in my car, I'm feeling okay. Calm and clear-headed. This is what doing the right thing feels like. So much easier outside of TV.

November 16

Damaged people are often really good at something. I suppose it's a response to the damage. But damage is hard to hide. Sooner or later, it shows.

There was a time when my friend Natasha was considered a rising star of the TV industry. She was a hugely successful series producer, on top of every detail, always delivering on time and under budget. We used to work in the same office. No one beneath her ever wanted to work with her again, but those higher up the food chain were in awe of her effectiveness.

She landed a good job at an indie – head of something or other – but left after less than a year. She quickly joined another leading company, in another high-profile and well-paid job, and left again just a few months later.

The next company wasn't such a good one. They probably felt pleased to get her. But the pattern worked out just the same.

'Controlling and brittle' is what people said. Full of ideas for how things should be, bad at dealing with how they are.

Now she's out of TV. Happily, she says. I don't believe her. People struggle to get into TV. Leaving TV can be a struggle as well. People can lose their sense of self. No longer cool or relevant. No longer in demand.

She called me up last night and suggested we meet for coffee.

She's sitting opposite me now, looking good. We almost got together once.

'I heard you got sacked', she says.

'Yes.'

She's trying not to look pleased. I think she could try much harder.

'TV is so low-rent', she says. 'So sordid and chaotic. Smart ideas just don't stand a chance. Wouldn't you say so, Truman? Don't you think?'

Thousands of able people leave the industry every year. Many will have made a start, burned brightly and then faded.

'There are better ways of earning a living', she says. 'More dignified ones, less subject to flux.'

She's doing a course in interior design.

'What about you?' she says.

Whatever club it is she thinks she belongs to, it's clear she wants me for a member.

'You had a decent run', she says. 'Don't take this the wrong way, but I never really thought you were cut out for TV.'

November 17

Today I had a new idea.

Last night it started snowing, and it still hasn't stopped.

I went for a walk by the river, everything muffled and strange. I could hear myself breathing.

Nothing at all was moving. No traffic on the roads. No boats on the water. London is never like this. Everything was shut.

Not a pub by Putney Bridge, though. The windows were orange with light. I was cold and tired.

It was the happiest place I've been in years. Full of warmth and laughter. A fire in the grate. Dozy dogs and kids. Grown-ups giddy with fresh air and freedom, and a couple of pre-lunch pints. The smell of smoke and home-cooked food – soup, fresh bread and nothing else, because the chef hadn't made it in.

It made me think of coaching inns, and taverns in frontier fortresses. Arriving exhausted and lonely, to find comfort and company. Feeling safe and secure, troubles and challenges on hold till tomorrow.

I wondered if there might be a place like this in Siberia or Alaska, for hunters or explorers. Or Antarctica, maybe. A bar at the end of the world.

I looked, and there it was. A bar for boffins and adventurers in the most remote and southerly settlement on earth. If you're there in the autumn, you're there till the spring. Five months with no one coming or going. Just five and a half million square miles of featureless snow and ice.

What sort of conversations might people have there? What sort of relationships might develop?

Anyone can relate to the pleasures of a pub. We know them and long for them. They're part of our ancestral memory.

But this is a pub like no other.

And it's advertising for a barman. Maybe I'll apply.

November 18

I've said before that the best and most memorable characters in documentaries appear to be playing themselves in the movie of their life, even as their story unfolds. They're the hero of the story. Indisputably the central character.

I've always felt something like this about my own life, but with one major difference. Which is that through luck and design, I've been mostly able to write the story myself.

I'm sitting in the chair from the dump, writing a treatment about the three sisters. I'm trying to write honestly about the way they make me feel, and what I've learned from spending time with them. Without recourse to the language of selling ideas, it's slow going, but I'm pleased with what I've got so far. It's like a modern-day fairy tale. Tragic but also beautiful, and full of lessons for life.

There's a knock at the door

My stomach turns over. Maybe it's Mills?

It's not. It's Rankin.

There's a gun in his hand.

He says, 'You don't even work at that company any more. And they don't know anything at all about a film about me.'

I tell him limply that I'm glad he's come round. That I've been wanting to explain.

'I like you', he says. 'But I can't let you make me look like a cunt. Which is very much what you've done.'

Another important lesson for life, unfolding right now on my doorstep. People will forgive and forget the things you say and do. But never the way you make them feel.

The last thing I remember thinking was 'You can't hurt me. I made you up.'

November 23

I'm tucked very tightly into a hard and narrow bed. There's a man groaning next to me, but no one seems very concerned. My head hurts and my throat feels very dry.

Opposite is a man in his fifties, maybe, staring into space. And a pale young man, the blankets on his bed perfectly smooth, his thin arms lying on top of them, all sinew, gristle and bone. He must be asleep, but looks very much like he's dead.

When I think of my career in television, what I remember is not all the paperwork and the meetings, and the fretting and planning, but brightly lit scenes, full of tension and drama, and moments of joy and inspiration. I feel like I've been lost in a world of those scenes, all joined together. Happy but exhausted, and confused and also scared.

The nurse says it's been five days. She says I'm a lucky man.

I tell her I don't feel it.

'An inch higher or this way or that and you be gone', she says.

She holds up her thumb and forefinger. This much space between life and death.

'Doubly lucky', she says, smiling now. 'Being read to and talked to that way. And her sleeping here, in that hard chair! On the edge of the bed sometimes! Right there next to you! Good job she's so slim.'

When I look confused, she says, 'Your girlfriend. She was here every day.'

'Tall with olive skin?'

She frowns and shakes her head at this.

'Small with bright green eyes.'

November 24

I've been in scrapes before.

I made a film about Britain's borders, which became a film about a group of illegal immigrants forced into a kind of modern-day slavery to pay for their passage to Britain. Which became a film about a tragedy. Their gangmaster sent them out to pick cockles on a vast and treacherous beach in midwinter. They were caught and cut off by a fast-rising tide and every one of them drowned.

I went out early one morning with another group of migrants doing the same sort of work. On the way back, two of the wheels fell off the Land

Rover we were riding in. The bolts on the wheels had been loosened. The car fell on its side in the sand, two miles from the shore with the tide rising an inch a minute and no reception on any of our phones.

Another time, filming the doings of a cult-like church, I went to a night-time prayer rally which turned into a midnight trek to the middle of nowhere, which is a reckless thing to do in a lawless bit of Africa. We were kidnapped by men with machetes. It was two days before they released us.

Both times I just carried on filming. Not just calm, but pleased as punch. Most TV is pretty vanilla. When producers talk about jeopardy, they really mean whatever's at stake, which is usually nothing much. Both my films were much improved by moments of genuine peril. Both times I made it look worse than it really was.

Nor am I new to pissing people off. It's part of the job of making films, especially ones about difficult individuals. Comfort the afflicted and afflict the comfortable. It's as good a rule as any for makers of documentaries. A bit of rough and tumble keeps things interesting. Most lives are better for some drama now and then.

The situation I'm in now is rather different, however.

There's a policeman outside the ward. He's been here as long as I have.

November 25

We treat boredom like it's a terrible thing, and avoid it at all costs. We surround ourselves with stuff to watch and do. But it's good to be bored from time to time. It makes your mind wander. It makes you think in interesting ways.

You have to cross a threshold to get there, though. You can't be slightly bored. You have to be bored like a child left alone too long, by which I mean bored of *everything*. Bored to tears, with nothing you want to do, nowhere at all to go, and no one to amuse you. That's when your brain starts amusing itself. It's why children have such brilliant thoughts and ask such brilliant questions.

I've been wondering what it's like to be Rankin. What I would do if I were him? What I would do next about me?

I've been enjoying myself, walking a mile in Rankin's shoes. But not any more. Now I'm bored of the boredom. I feel trapped, pinned down and supervised. I need a change of scene.

It hurts very much to stand. Blood oozes into the dressing on my wound. I feel like I've forgotten how to walk.

Even so, it feels good to be out of bed.

There's a kitchen and some lockers at the end of the ward, most of them still open, personal stuff inside. Whatever this ward is I'm on, they weren't expecting patients to be up and about.

I borrow some scrubs, a white coat, a chart, and the pale young man, still fast asleep, and head out into the corridor, pushing the young man's bed. The policeman outside nods as I go by, so bored himself he can barely see.

It's satisfying when a plan works out. I'm not sure what to do next, though. I wasn't expecting to get this far.

I park the pale guy by a vending machine, get myself a coffee, and push through a door to a stairwell. No one uses the stairs in these places. Hospitals are all about lifts. Which makes the stairwells a sort of nowhere world. A good place for a private phone call.

Hey Rankin, you cunt, I'm still alive.

There's a girl on the landing, smoking. She looks very ill indeed.

Beautiful, though, with delicate cheekbones and purple-blue eyes.

'Have you come for me?' she says.

And then, straight after, 'You're not a doctor, are you?'

It's curiosity rather than worry in her voice. I think she's beyond worrying about anything.

I tell her I'm a fellow fugitive.

'Cancer', she says, offering me her cigarette.

'Gunshot', I tell her, sitting down beside her.

She raises her eyebrows at this. Impressed more than perturbed, I think.

'9 mm', I tell her, 'point-blank range', and pass the cigarette back to her.

'The man who cheated death!' she says.

'Now you've got a second life. So what you gonna do with it?'

November 26

A detective wants to know what I remember of the night I was shot.

He's angry but keeping a lid on it. The doctors told him I was far too weak for questions. And then I did a runner. Got everyone all worked up and anxious, and wasted everyone's time. All for the sake of a crafty fag.

'Do you appreciate the seriousness of the situation?' he said. I assured him that I do.

He's sitting by my bed now, looking at me like policemen do.

I remember preparing to speak, and never getting the words out.

I remember a sort of fizz, then a deafening absence of sound.

I remember lurching back into consciousness, my brain rebooting like a crashed computer, retrieving information, whirring and flashing up files. Rankin. The stairway. The gun. A taste in my nose and mouth that I knew but struggled to place. Like the smell of a workshop or tool shed, or a handful of copper coins. Metallic, but sweet as well. The taste of lots of blood.

I remember feeling like the floor was plummeting, my stomach in my mouth, cold like the air was rushing past me.

I remember sending a message to my arms and legs to move, and getting no response. No movement at all. Total inertia, like turning the key on a car whose battery is flat.

The brain is the last thing to go. The body protects it at all costs.

I remember thinking 'That's me, then. Dead all the way up to my neck. Only thoughts left now. And only a few of those. This is the end of Truman Locke. This is how I die.'

The detective says that in cases like this – of attempted murder, of a murder that someone fucked up – the murderer always comes back to finish the job. Sooner or later. And the copper outside can't stay there forever.

'You must remember something?' he says.

I shake my head on my pillow.

'I'm sorry, no.'

I tell him nothing at all.

November 30

Don't do what they're expecting. That was the police's advice.

So instead of hiding, I went straight back home to my flat.

My downstairs neighbour opened her door wide enough to steal a peek then closed it again as I opened mine, her face simultaneously bright red and white. She called 999 when a bloodstain started spreading like a Rorschach test across her bedroom ceiling. I probably wouldn't have made it without her.

A very good bottle of wine stood on the doorstep. No card. I took it in and opened it.

The flat didn't feel like mine any more. Not a place to disappear. Just a big, cold, empty space.

So I put my stuff in a bag, put a rug on the bloodstained floorboards, and put the flat up for rent.

Now I'm living somewhere new.

I met a guy several years ago, making a film about a posh hotel. He was my favourite character – the concierge, who got the guests stuff they wanted. He lost his job for supplying them with more than dinner reservations and tickets for the theatre.

We stayed in touch when the film was finished. I helped him find work as a fixer for foreign shoots in London, in exchange for the occasional favour. He's a worldly, practical man, and very well-connected.

I asked him to help me find new digs. Somewhere I'd feel at home.

He took me to a messy part of town, to a hotel run by a friend of his. Once, way back, it had been quite grand, a stately place to stay next to London's oldest station. Then, in the 1980s, the station closed, and the flow of rich guests suddenly stopped. Now it's dirty and forlorn, scraping by as a place to crash for salesmen and backpackers, cheaper even than the low-cost chains. Most of the time half the rooms are empty.

The top floor always is. There used to be two large rooms there, knocked into one in the '70s as a penthouse suite for honeymooners and celebrities. Subsequent makeovers, always fast and cheap, left it alone, sealed off and forgotten.

When the manager let me in, it felt like raiding a long-lost tomb, totally still and airless. A gust blew in past us, sighing, equalizing the pressure. Deep carpets and thick curtains ate up all the sound.

The bed was huge and covered in orange fabric. Two monumental cream leather sofas facing each other across a low glass table on a sheepskin rug. A dark wood desk by the window. Mirrors and garish prints on the walls.

I loved it, and it's home now. An unofficial place, with no address. A private elevator down to the ground, and a fire escape at the back. Perfect.

I feel older now. A fraction less tall. A tiny bit less eternal. Refreshed, though, and free. Ready for whatever comes next.

There's a message on my phone: 'I was moved by what you said in the park and we want to commission your blindness film. Make it however you want to. We'll back you and support you. No need to rush. No date for delivery. Let's just see what happens. Let's just make it good.'

CHAPTER TWELVE: DECEMBER

December 1

'Don't disappear', the detective said.

I said, 'No, of course not.'

I once spent a week at an office in London, where people go to change their name. No one does that without wanting to change their life as well. Dozens of people came every day, their forms neatly filled out, all sick of struggling with their own thoughts and personalities, and the way these things would drag their lives off course, like a shopping trolley with a broken wheel. All eager to escape themselves and become someone else.

It's a fantasy everyone has, at some time in their life. To stop, step off, walk away and start over. To live life more freely, with greater fulfilment, and wake up with the feeling that something new is just beginning. The rest of your life. Perhaps even the best part.

I could go pretty much anywhere. Be anyone I want to be.

I've done it before, several times. Every time I made a film, in fact. It would be a very small step to do it again, in a bigger, more permanent way.

The police don't believe my story, of strangers with guns and a temporary bout of amnesia. Mistaken identity, is what I said. They said, 'We don't think so.'

'Can't have people running around shooting each other, can we?' the detective said.

'So we'll be keeping an eye on you. We'd like to know your plans.'

Me too, officer. Me too.

December 2

Something happened to my parents – I don't know what – that made their outlook fearful and defensive. And once they'd started living that way, they never found a way to stop, treading water year after year, kicking hard beneath the surface just to stay still but slowly drifting backwards with the tide.

I've never been afraid of change and reinvention. We are all different people as we go through life. Everyone evolves. I like the idea of beginning again. But in truth I don't know what I'd do if I wasn't in TV.

When I started out, television felt like a fine way to spend a couple of years. All other careers felt available still. The more so, in fact, with every film I made, because of all the new experiences, and the wide range of people you meet.

I seriously considered chucking everything in to work in a steel mill in Poland, because I fell in love with the life and the people I met there. Another time, I was all set to join the staff of a tiny newspaper in an old-fashioned town in the States, where I happened to be filming, because I fell in love with the life and the people there as well. With a girl who worked there, to be precise, who wrote about council meetings and the wedding anniversaries of local people, but dreamed of being a novelist. The editor offered me a job on the news desk – $20,000 a year for 2000 words a week. He'd been a big-shot editor in New York once, and gave it up for the sake of another local girl, now his wife and the mother of his children.

'Just because you set off down a certain road in life doesn't mean you have to keep to it', he said. 'Do it. It'll make you happy.'

It hurt very much to leave, and aches still when I think of it. Finding that place and those people, and meeting that wonderful girl, was a miraculous thing. Being happy is a choice, the editor said. But I didn't feel ready to choose.

There were too many other paths to explore, and all of them felt open to me. But now those options have dwindled. Now I feel enmeshed.

Maybe I could teach TV? Or be some sort of salesman? Or drift from job to job till something good turns up?

These feel not like alternative lives and careers, but like fallbacks and admissions of defeat. Not new adventures but a retreat from adventure. Like failure, in other words, which I don't think I could live with.

And now, at long last, I have a commission! A pretty good one, as well. A commission any exec would be proud of.

So I'm stuck with television, and television's stuck with me.

December 4

Big TV companies see development as a problem. It's expensive and time-consuming, and there's no guarantee that you'll get any sort of return on your investment. But development is necessary. No development means no commissions. No commissions means no programmes. And no programmes means no income from programme production. (Typically companies aim to keep between 10 and 20% of a programme's budget, in the form of fees and charges for overheads like desks and phone lines. If a programme is of interest internationally, it can be sold to the global marketplace, sometimes for amounts in excess of the entire initial budget.)

So what big companies try to do is refine the process of development so that it's super-targeted at the most profitable kinds of TV – entertaining but easy-to-produce formats, which do an important job for broadcasters; they underpin the schedules, and keep viewers coming back week after week. These shows are ordered in large volume, which means that they're profitable to make. And they're often about common problems and relationships – particularly at work and at home – which means that audiences around the world can relate to them, so they sell well abroad.

The development staff of large companies are asked to think almost exclusively about this sort of TV. Ideas for other kinds of TV are strongly discouraged and never taken forward, no matter how good or clever they might be. The senior staff at these companies, meanwhile, spend their time cosying up to commissioners – and the commissioners' bosses, and channel controllers – in the hope that they'll be told simply 'This is what we want. Can you supply it?' If you can get a broadcaster into the habit of *coming to you* with ideas for shows, you can dispense with your development department entirely.

In reality, over-focus on one particular type of television tends to produce copycat ideas. People willing to work 9-to-5 under factory-like conditions tend not to be the most imaginative types. And broadcasters often don't know what they want until they see it. They know roughly the *sort* of show they want. But what they really want is a spark of originality and a freshness that will capture the imagination of viewers, who are generally jaded and want to be surprised. All the schmoozing on the part of senior staff only gets you so far. At the end of the day, someone still needs to have a good idea.

And so those big companies are constantly hunting for creative people. A person who sees the world slightly differently to everyone else, and doesn't think in straight lines. A person capable of a moment of genuine creativity, that the rest of the development team can seize upon and shape into a format, which the senior staff can then go out and sell.

The shareholders and investors of big companies regard such people mainly with irritation and disdain. It's easy for them to understand what a Head of Programme Sales does, or a Head of Production, who is responsible for managing budgets and makes sure that production staff don't overspend. It's much harder to quantify the value of creative staff, because they don't really make or do anything very tangible, and they spend so much time drinking coffee and talking.

And of course if drinking coffee and talking are frowned up, disappearing for days on end, experimenting with booze and drugs in the office and pretending to be a cleaner are completely beyond the pale.

And so here I am, being interviewed for a job at a very big company. The company has produced some enormous hits in the past. But now its formats are looking tired, and reaching the end of their natural span. They want a documentary specialist to help them devise new ones.

The man I'm meeting – I can't remember his name or job title – is a senior person in the organization. He is not involved in devising or making programmes, and never has been in the past. He takes a page out of his notebook, carefully folds it in two and pushes it across the table towards me. He wants me to write a number in it, representing the amount, in millions, I might expect to generate per year in revenue for the company. I open up the folded paper, write a number – 3, based on absolutely nothing – fold it up again and push it back. He opens it up, crosses out my number, writes another number – 6 – next to it, and pushes it back.

There is no one else in the room.

It's clear he doesn't especially like me. And it's clear that the meeting isn't going especially well.

So I do what I always do when I need to pull someone round: I read his mind, and tell him what he's thinking, and what he's worrying about. Then tell him exactly what he wants to hear.

December 6

Smaller companies with ambitions to get big have a slightly different set of problems and priorities to the major players. Generally, television companies are set up by creative people, who want freedom. They enjoy that freedom for a while, and then get tired of the constant struggle: have an idea for a programme; get a commission for the programme; make the programme; repeat until overcome with exhaustion. Maybe their lives change too, so that freedom is no longer quite so important. They get wives and kids, and start thinking about the future and things like financial security.

A successful independent production company that is acquired by investors or a larger company can sell for £20 or £25 million, maybe half of which you get up front. You get tied in to that company for maybe two or three years, and you're given targets to meet. If you meet the targets, you get the other half of the money. And then you're free. Properly free. Free and also rich. At the game of TV, you've won.

But turning a small, fun, creative company into a successful one that's attractive to buyers is a hard thing to do. It needs to grow quickly. Projections for the next few years need to look very healthy. The development and production slates need to be diverse, so that the company doesn't look vulnerable to changes in taste, or particular commissioners leaving their jobs (or indeed entire channels closing down).

The bosses of these companies draw up strategies and business plans. No more hard-to-make films or passion projects. No more wild-goose chases. Some staff will need to be let go, including perhaps people who were there from the start. Tea and cake in reception will be accompanied by tears. But there's little room for sentiment. The company is changing. Becoming leaner and more professional.

I was at such a company at such a time once. Suddenly expenses forms were being picked over. The boss stopped wearing jeans and sneakers and started wearing suits. He stopped coming to the pub after work, and moved his desk away from the rest of us. And then workmen came in one weekend and built him a separate office in the corner. A ditsy but lovely office manager departed. A stiff-backed executive assistant arrived, and then a narrow-eyed MD, forever tutting and shaking her head. The development department started to shrink. The delicate ecosystem that had made the company a joy to work at was broken. One by one, the free spirits flittered away.

As the old guard leaves, new people are hired in. These people generally arrive on heavily incentivized deals, and are put under enormous pressure from day one. Now the atmosphere is competitive and febrile. Succeed and we'll give you equity. Fail and you're on your way. Plenty more where you came from.

And so here I am, being interviewed for a job recently vacated by a friend I'd watched slowly unravel. For all I know, my friend is at this very second sitting opposite Charlie, being interviewed for the job recently vacated by myself.

I'm doing exactly the same thing I did yesterday – telling the guy what he wants to hear, and trying hard to make it look like the thoughts are just this second forming in my head, to make them seem genuine. Yesterday the speech was about being disillusioned with working at boutique companies in tiny teams, and wanting to be a key cog in a much bigger machine that thrums with productivity, turning out TV for the masses. A sort of Stalinist industrialization of my own creative thinking, pitiless and relentless. Today the speech is about being done with adventure and playing games, and wanting to have bigger, more impactful ideas, and wanting those ideas to make me rich. A stirring tale of an overgrown boy becoming a man, feeling the strength in his arms, ready now to do what needs to be done. When I finished speaking, I had genuinely moved myself. I half expected a round of applause.

But this guy is much smarter than the guy at the other company. He's a former film-maker. A guy who notices things. Emotionally, he wants in. He feels lonely and misunderstood in life. His wife probably preferred the previous version of himself, who was more playful and easy-going. Everyone at work used to love that guy too. But now he's the boss, with his eyes on the prize. Some company would feel good. Someone else who feels what he feels.

But in the back of his mind, he knows it doesn't quite add up.

'People say you're very clever', he says, not meaning it as a compliment.

'You mean, can you trust me?'

He says, 'Yes.'

I say, 'Absolutely.'

December 7

I've been in the library all day, reading up on blindness and the rare condition that will rob the three sisters of their sight. I want to know how blindness will come upon them, and how it will progress. I want to understand what they'll see and feel as the world around them grows dim.

I was about to pack up for the day when DC Lockwood sent me a message, asking to meet at a pub in East London.

It's a big old boozer that's gentrified now. Noisy at the front with men in ties, but quieter at the back, the space divided into parlours and snugs with etched glass and nut-brown wood. A good place not to be noticed.

When I arrived Lockwood was sitting alone, looking pale and stern. Rattled, like she'd been in an accident. Rattled but tough. Dealing with it, whatever it is that's happened.

'Thank you for coming', she says, and means it. 'I didn't know who else to call.'

Two days ago she was sent to the farmhouse where the third murder took place on a simple errand, to collect a file forensics thought they might have mislaid there. She hates being treated like that. When she arrived, the place was deserted, so she had a look around.

There were no keys at all in the farmhouse. None in the odds-and-sods kitchen drawer, where people keep their spares and keys they no longer use. None in the outbuildings, including the workshop, amidst the jam jars full of old screws and things that might one day come in handy. None in the barn that doubled as a garage, despite the rusting hulks of half a dozen agricultural vehicles.

Today she told her superior what she'd found. He's a Detective Sergeant and probably always will be. A good guy, though, she thought. She likes him and he likes her. He took her to the car park at the back of the station where he goes to smoke cigarettes. He lit one up, took a drag and told her to forget what she'd just told him, and drop the matter altogether. To keep her head down and do her job. 'For your own sake', he said. Not as a threat, but in a way that suggested he knew the men involved.

'Dangerous men', he said. 'Best not get mixed up in it.'

The murders will probably go down as unresolved, he told her. A turf war, over drugs, perhaps. Likely to simply blow over. And as for the robbery, wasn't that just what it looked like?

Then he stubbed out his cigarette and went back inside the station.

DC Lockwood finished her shift and came straight to the pub.

Now she doesn't know who to trust. She's reeling at what this seems to mean. No more good guys and bad guys. Everything murky and compromised. No one she can rely on.

She's tapping her middle finger on the tabletop, fretfully, like she's sending a message in Morse code. I put my hand on hers. It's cold and clammy. She starts to pull away then changes her mind. I tell her it's okay.

I buy us bourbon and we start to make a plan.

She'll do as the DS said: keep her head down and collect information – the sort a producer might want. Names of witnesses. Contacts. A detailed timeline. Together we'll make a case to present to a broadcaster. I'll put some subtle feelers out. If it gets commissioned, we'll work on it together.

She was happy with that. She definitely wants out. But she wants to know how the story ends. She's scared but defiant, and very much dislikes being told what to do. This way she might get everything. An exciting new life, and her old one rounded off nicely. An opportunity to tell the truth, perhaps, and say fuck you to the cowardly and possibly crooked DS.

'Patronizing motherfucker', she says. '"*Best not get mixed up in it, sweetheart.*" Best not get mixed up with me!'

She laughs at this, in spite of herself. Anger in her belly, still, but starting to relax now.

Everyone loves a true-crime story. But this is the longest of long shots. The case might never be resolved, as the DS said. Not in a way that pulls all the strands together. Not if the police don't want it to be.

December 8

I'm having breakfast with DC Lockwood. Coffee and pastries, sitting on a wall, watching the comings and goings at one of London's all-night markets. I can feel the food putting energy back into my body. Traders are winding down now, noisy and boisterous, cheerful at the prospect of a pint and some dinner after ten hours on their feet. Unsold meat is being auctioned off. Blood on the cobbles hosed into drains.

Last night we talked till late. About the case initially, then other stuff.

The pub had rooms. I paid for two. We used only one.

She seems distant now. Preoccupied.

I'm preparing to say something gallant and funny, but Lockwood speaks first.

'There's something else', she says. Something she didn't tell her DS. Or mention to me last night.

At the farmhouse, the misplaced forensics file was on the kitchen counter, by the door, overlooked in the rush to get home, no doubt. Everything was the same as the day the police packed up and left. Everything except for one detail: there was now a pile of envelopes by the front door. Junkmail, mostly. But also a letter addressed to a Mr J Nelson.

'As in John Nelson, of the Nelson brothers', she says.

She's still for a moment, then slowly takes it from the inside pocket of her jacket.

Dear Mr Nelson. Kings Cross is changing. As part of the redevelopment, all personal lockers will be relocated to the new concourse. As a valued long-term customer, we are happy to do the move for you. You can rely on the same high levels of service and security we have always tried to provide. If you would prefer to move your items over yourself, just present your key at the desk with your 5-digit passcode.

At the top of the page it says 'Your ref: 21218'.

Is that what the key is for? Could it really be that simple?

December 9

I've been offered the job at the smaller indie, and asked back to the larger one to see if the teeth of my particular cog will knit with those of everyone else.

A successful couple of days, then. But I could tell that both men were desperate, in their own different ways. Neither wanted a discussion about strategy, or to hear a detailed plan. They just wanted to feel a bit of comfort and reassurance. A bit of hope. There's no need to talk an employer through your CV, or even explain why you really just left a job that you seemed a perfect fit for. Just look them in the eye and say 'I'm the solution to your problems. I'm the man you need.'

In truth, I don't want either of these jobs. I don't want to be the solution to someone else's problem. Though I suppose that's what a job is.

And in truth I don't need one. I'm in the process of paying £400,000 into my account (slowly, to avoid attracting attention). I bought my flat before flats began to cost the same as large houses. I never really spend any money, and there's nothing I'm responsible for.

Then there's a stab of fear and my stomach lurches. It's a feeling I've been having for the last two months now, every time I remember that I *do* have responsibilities.

At least I think I do.

I don't know where Mills is or how she's feeling. About the baby or anything else.

December 10

Ordinarily, commissioned ideas get rushed into production. This is because broadcasters only start to release a programme's budget when it's properly up and running, and most independent production companies are chronically short of cash. There's not much time to think. You're stuck in a boat on the rapids, trying to steer clear of the rocks.

For the first time in my career, that pressure doesn't exist. For the moment, the blindness film is pristine still, more a thought than a thing, a plexus of possibilities and potential.

Today I'm enjoying that fact, thinking of the film and nothing else. Imagining it.

Trouble will come soon enough. In my career at least, it always does.

December 13

Today is my first day back at work. It feels good.

I should have done something more worthwhile with my time off. Travelled or learned a new skill or something. But I'm trying not to think about that.

And trying not to wince when I stand or sit down, because first impressions count. People would ask why, and I don't want to have to explain; I annoyed a contributor so much he shot me.

I took the job at the up-and-coming indie in the end. We agreed that I'd make my blindness film through his company, which will take four months or so, and work up a few other ideas. Then we'll pause and think about the future. If all goes well, we'll turn the contract into a permanent one, and I'll become part of the company.

The boss has given me a desk right outside his office, to keep an eye on me, next to a stout production manager who looks like she's been drinking curdled milk. This is clearly not going to be fun.

December 16

The company has exposed brick walls, bare wooden floors and shiny white furniture, which sounds nice, but is a clichéd, off-the-peg look for TV production companies. There's no sense of soul here.

The atmosphere is quiet and studious, like something bad has happened and people are keeping their heads down.

This week I'm crewing up the film, which is to say that I'm looking for a director to make it, and an AP or researcher to help. I'll be execing, to give me time to develop and pitch other projects.

The PM has given me a list of directors the company likes to work with. They're all talented people, but somewhat safe. None of them has made a bad film. But none of them has made an outstanding one, either. And they've all been at it long enough now that I doubt they ever will.

The sensible thing when you're at a new company is to fit in and do what's expected. A list of directors 'the company likes to work with' is a very heavy hint, but I've chosen to ignore it. I'm about to hire a director with no experience whatsoever of directing.

She's green, but charismatic. The family will love her. And she'll put her heart and soul into the project. It'll matter to her more than anything, and she'll live it, like I used to do. She'll make mistakes for sure, but I have a feeling they'll be interesting ones, that might make the film better and more real. She's a great choice. I think she'll go on to be a first-class director.

I'm sitting in the boss's office. We're chatting about this and that. Then he says that he thinks my director isn't up to the job.

'Just a feeling', he says. 'Nothing personal.'

The problem we've got is that we want very different things from this film. His preoccupation is growing the company. He wants an unproblematic production that stays on budget and finishes when it should.

That should be my preoccupation as well. Help achieve it, and a share in the company is on offer. I've already walked away from one such opportunity in my career, and just fucked up another. There won't be many more. This could be the last.

But I genuinely think the film could be special. Wonderful, even. I'd rather risk a swing and a miss in pursuit of that than settle for something ordinary.

I want to live up to the speech I gave in the interview, about becoming a TV grown-up. I really do want to feel those things, but I don't.

I don't want to stop having adventures. And I don't like it here enough to spend my time tiptoeing around and playing it safe. Sooner or later, this will become apparent. It might as well be sooner.

I should swallow this feeling down. Do the smart thing, and take a long-term view.

That's what a professional would do. It's the grown-up, sensible choice.

My boss says, 'Will you reconsider?'

I say, 'I'm sorry, I've made up my mind.'

December 17

Last night, a commission Squeaky MacLean got at my old company back in July made it to air. It was good. The best thing on last night. I'm texting him to say so. Also to ask him how the ratings were, because I already know they were very disappointing. The working-class/underclass history idea that Charlie and I pitched together has also been commissioned now, and the workshop pilot has gone to series. The company are doing fine.

My new employer is based in an up-and-coming part of London. There are dozens of coffee shops here, all made up to look old and worn, and all so new you can smell the paint. The place I'm in right now is not like that at all. Its front is boarded up, like the place is derelict, and there's no sign above the door. It's a shabby, hard-working bakery with a stone floor and a tin roof. The guys who own it start work at four in the morning and are always closed by nine. You can go in and buy bread off the street, though most of what they do is for cafes and restaurants. There's a warped wooden table and some mismatched chairs, where the restaurant guys sit and wait for their orders. They make big pots of strong Polish coffee, mostly for themselves. But if they recognize your face, they'll pour you a cup as well.

I've been taking fresh croissants to the office now and then, which is going down well. But I'm not here for the sake of my colleagues. A bag of croissants is the price of entry. I come here just for me.

The first time I came here, I was on my way to work and it was dark and raining miserably. Suddenly the rain came down like nails, so hard it hurt my head. A door opened right in front of me and a guy stepped out in a blast of warm air that smelled like cinnamon and toast. He held the door open for me, and I ducked in without thinking. Being anywhere would be better than being in the street. But I was staggered by what was inside, a place that felt exactly like the bit of my brain that I go to when I'm on the verge of sleep. As the rain hammered down on the flimsy roof I felt delirious, like I was imagining being there. They gave me coffee and let me stay and watch them work till the rain went back to normal.

Somehow it's easy to think in here. It seems clear what matters and what does not. It's easy to see connections and possibilities. No need to force it. Just sit still and wait for ideas to come.

Today I've brought the director of the blindness film, back from her trip to meet the family. Her head is full of thoughts and ideas for things to film. She wants to tell me all about them, but barely knows where to start.

She's excited but also scared. She said so on the phone last night. Scared because she's not sure yet how to make the film. Scared because she thinks she might not do it justice.

She needs some comfort and clear thinking, and I want to help. I'm hoping this place might do for her the same as it does for me.

It's a clear, sunny day outside, so it's very cold, but the bread ovens make it warm in here, and the air is thick and sweet. There are three younger guys buzzing around an older man with a grimace on his face that looks like a smile. It's effort, I think, the kind that feels good. He's working hard to shape the bread into loaves.

She says, 'Everything's in motion. I can't make sense of it all.'

I tell her, 'Sure you can.'

We talk about the family and their relationships. About how they feel about what's happening. About the scenes and sequences she's planning.

We talk about how good films are made. About keeping it real, even if real means messy. Messy can be good. There's a tension and a drama to it, whereas fakery and neatness are always dull.

We talk about letting the audience piece things together and draw their own conclusions. Don't say too much. Let your viewers enjoy moments when things are uncertain. Let them get engaged.

We talk about pacing, so the audience meets the big moments the way you think they should.

I don't want to say too much. Half the things I know I wish I didn't. I think I was probably better at TV when I knew almost nothing at all.

'It's a lot to remember', she says.

'But the thing is you don't need to. Just feel your way, be honest, and everything will fall into place.'

You see people in TV running into their own limitations all the time, all their cockiness gone, bewilderment on their faces. Not this girl. Her face just shines with the pleasure of flexing her talent. She's doing a brilliant job, which makes me proud and happy.

Then we talk about this place. I tell her how much I like it here. It makes me feel safe and calm, like there's nothing to battle and nothing to be done. Like the world has shrunk and everything is knowable, and where and how it should be. It's the feeling I had when I was a little boy in bed, and I heard my mother come home from work and run herself a bath.

She says that the feeling is the feeling of being loved.

Then the pastries are ready and it's time to leave.

December 18

Last night, I left work feeling very tired and empty and cold. I started to think of all the people I've let down for the sake of TV. The birthdays and weddings I've missed, and the little tea parties people have to introduce their friends to their newborn babies. And so many lesser occasions – casual meet-ups for a drink and a chat, wrap parties and leaving dos, and screenings of films made by friends.

Each of them felt like no big deal at the time. Maybe even, if I'm honest, like a sacrifice to the gods of television, pleading for favour and luck. Whatever I was doing instead always felt terribly important and invigorating, no matter how flawed or far-fetched. Real life just couldn't compete. And by the time a particular project had failed, something else would have taken its place. That's the nature of the job. It's a present-tense sort of occupation. You carry on, looking forward.

Looking back, these dozens of let-downs and disappointments appear utterly appalling. My life is littered with them. Which is to say, full of friends and good people I've treated like litter.

I felt soul-sick and chilled to picture so many happy faces. Trippy and out of sync, like a bad case of the flu.

I went to an old-man pub for a drink and asked the landlord to light a fire. It didn't help at all. My bones still ached when I left, and I went to bed in my clothes.

Today, as well as feeling sorry, I feel sorry for myself. For all the late nights, early mornings and lost weekends that felt like they'd make all the difference, but ultimately, of course, did not. All the films those sacrifices were made for seem a long time ago now. I can barely remember most of them.

But I've no business feeling self-pity. The truth is that there's nowhere I'd rather have been, and nothing I'd rather be doing.

Selena knows that. Knows me, and seems to like me nonetheless.

'I'm not the man you think I am', I told her once, not long after we met. She said, 'Oh yes you are.'

She's cooking in her kitchen, singing softly to herself, which she does whenever she's happy. She brought me a drink just now, and a pill for my wound, and kissed me on my forehead. She's wearing baggy pyjama bottoms and a vest, her hair loose and messy, pushed away from her face with the back of her hands as she goes about making supper. I can't imagine anyone has ever looked so lovely.

We've been doing this for years now, off and on. Sometimes with months and months between one time and the next. I knock on her door, late at night, and she stands aside and lets me in.

It's a fucked-up kind of relationship, for sure. But in its fucked-up way, it seems to work for both of us.

I can feel the chill leaving my bones.

December 19

I'm sitting opposite a guy in his early twenties in the meeting room. He wrote to me a little while ago asking for a job, as more than a dozen people do every week.

These emails are generally long and dull to read. The senders tend to fill them with reasons why employing them would be a good thing. A good thing for them. There's often not a single line about why employing them might be a good thing for me. 'I really, really want a job and I really, really want to work in TV' isn't going to get you anywhere.

Worse, you can often tell that the same email has gone to 30 other people like me. 'Dear Truman Locke'. That's a giveaway. Only slightly less bad than 'Dear Sir/Madam'.

The guy sitting opposite wrote a short, simple email that certainly seemed like it was to me and no one else. 'Dear Truman, I watched your film last year. That must have been a bitch to make. If you're looking to do more of the same, I think I can help, and I find myself looking for a job. How would you like to meet?'

No childish stuff about it being his dream to make TV programmes. Nothing annoying about his life-changing gap year. No information at all about who he is or what he's done, in fact. But I do know that he's confident, and I know that he can tell a tale. 'I find myself looking for a job' is the beginning of a story. So much more intriguing than simply wanting or needing one.

I found myself agreeing to meet him.

He doesn't look like telly people usually do. He's very big, and looks as hard as iron, except for his eyes, which are kind, and his smile, which is disarming.

I don't know why so many people want to work in television. It's better than working in a factory, I suppose, or in a shop or a call centre. Better in the sense that you'll earn more money, though not necessarily a lot more, and in the sense that the work is more interesting and varied. But lots of things are better than working in a factory from that point of view. And in many ways TV is much worse than working in a factory. I worked on a building site one summer when I was a boy, and have never felt so much part of something, or so useful, or so happy and tired at the end of the day. The value of my efforts and the part I'd played could be measured quite precisely in neat rows of bright red bricks, laid by someone else, but carried to the bricklayer by me. I was helping to build homes for families.

Most TV is pretty bad, and making it is just as punishing and difficult as making the stuff that wins Baftas and Emmys, only with no time and no support, and a creeping sense that you're wasting your time and energy; that what you're really doing is helping old people and sick people pass the time on lonely afternoons, or helping terrible people sell exorbitant loans to vulnerable people via the ads that bad TV attracts. There's nothing glamorous at all about driving 200 miles after a long day filming miserable vox pops on your own in the rain, checking into a budget hotel, and eating dinner out of a vending machine, knowing you have to get up in six hours and do it all again. Lots of people every year realize this, and leave the industry to do something more rewarding and worthwhile.

The guy sitting opposite says he knows how I operate, and thinks it's an approach that might suit him.

The thing about filming miserable vox pops on your own in the rain is that, whilst it's arguably the lowest form of making TV, it's still quite difficult. You have to know how to operate a camera, which means that you have to know how to judge lighting conditions and exposure, and be aware of things like white balance and shutter speed. You have to be able to frame things properly, so that the things you film don't look ugly. You have to be able to monitor and record sound at the same time as you're doing all of this. And also charm the people you're filming with, to get them onside and produce them into delivering a good performance. And you need a half-decent editorial brain, to know what to ask them and when you're on to something good. Finally, you need to manage your time, get yourself from A to B, take care of your kit, and download and organize your rushes. Depending on the sort of show you're helping to make, you might need to be able to edit your rushes as well. You need a lot of skills to be able to do all of this on your own. You might well be able to put those skills to better and more profitable use outside of the TV industry.

The guy sitting opposite says, 'You're a man who does what's required.'

Maybe half of the people who write to me are profoundly idealistic. They want to work in TV because they want to change the world. If that's what you want to do with your life, TV is a very bad way of going about it. People don't watch TV to be politicized or energized. They basically want to be told that the world is okay, and that people are okay. And I'm not just talking about cosy early evening programmes, and talent contests and panel shows. Reassurance is what people want from documentaries as well. Maybe even more so. We already know that life is tough. We want to know that life is beautiful and wonderful as well. Evidence of that can be hard to find in real life. What TV does for people is go out and find that evidence for them, and distil it into a form that is easy and enjoyable to consume.

The guy says, 'Eyes on the prize'. He says that's his entire philosophy.

One girl who came to see me wanted to make a programme about a UN-backed campaign to eradicate smallpox in Rwanda. I said that I wasn't in a position to commission programmes, and that I didn't think anyone who was would commission such a programme in a million years, because no one at all would watch it. She said I was ignorant and arrogant and stupid. She looked like she wanted to hit me.

The guy says, 'Rules aren't for you and me, are they? Rules just get in the way.'

Who the fuck is this guy? He's menacing but charming as well.

I think I like him. He's deeply cynical and I find that refreshing.

I did lots of things before I came to TV. I worked in a bookshop, and spent my days reading, one chapter a day, and never more than that of any single book. After six months, my head was brimming with ideas. I ran a crumbling old cinema that nobody went to, for less than the minimum wage. Man, I loved that place. I worked in the city as a headhunter, and hated every minute, but made a ton of money. I taught in a school. I worked (illegally) in a restaurant in New York.

And in the end I didn't come to TV; TV came to me. I met a sweaty, stick-thin, hollow-eyed guy in a bar, who offered to buy me a drink. I had been stood up. He'd been there all day. He was a TV producer who had alienated all of the people who worked for him, and they'd abandoned him, en masse. He needed a writer, for a film that was late and over budget. He offered me a large amount of money to do the job, at a time when I had none. He'd drunk so much I didn't think he'd remember, but he was at his desk at nine the next day, wearing the same clothes and a frightened, please-God look. I did the job well, and never looked back.

The guy sitting opposite says he did a bad thing at school and got expelled.

I liked TV because it felt like the Wild West; a place to ride out and stake your claim, where energy and ingenuity would quickly be rewarded, wherever you happened to come from in life. That's also why I'm good at it. I had no real wish to work in TV as such. I didn't expect it to be glamorous. I didn't want to educate people, or make the world a better place. I didn't expect it to make me happy. I just wanted to find a job that suited me and seemed to value the things that I'm good at.

The guy sitting opposite says he has no qualifications. But he knows how to do lots of things. 'Things they don't teach you at school', he says. 'Things that you might find useful.'

I ask him, 'Have we met?'

He says, 'No, but you know my Auntie Len. And she says you're alright.'

December 20

A friend of mine who works in TV, but in entertainment rather than factual, wanted to take on a bright and ambitious young person to bolster his team. Easily done, you might think. But good researchers are hard to find. The obviously talented ones get snapped up quickly, and companies tend to hold on to them. As for the rest, it can be hard to know whether they're talented or not. When someone's 21 or 22, you don't have much to go on. Save, perhaps, for a graduation film or a reference from a tutor. But my friend has a real dislike of film and TV courses. He thinks that most of them are taught by people too second-rate or washed-up to really know what they're talking about, and that they make young people believe they know far more than they really do, most of which needs to be untaught when they actually start work. He reckons that if you're happy to waste three years of your life and take on 40k of debt to get a job that is more about your attitude and personality than anything you may have learned, you don't deserve a break. So he placed an advert in a leading youth-focussed entertainment magazine: 'Are you passionate about TV? Do you want to work in the TV industry? Write to me at the address below.'

15,000 people replied.

Most of them, including my friend, had made an assumption that is quite odd when you think about it. The fact that you like beer or cheese doesn't make you think that you'd be good at making them, does it? Or that making them would be fun?

My friend thought he was being clever by asking anyone responding to his advert to send in three ideas for a programme. Some people sent in more than three, which gave him more than *50,000* to wade through. Almost all of them were terrible. Of course they were. Having a good idea for a programme is a very hard thing to do.

My feeling about all the people who sent in their ideas is similar to my friend's feeling about people who study TV at university; if you place so little value on your ideas (no matter how bad) that you're willing to email them to a stranger with very little hope of a response, you're too naive to work in an industry that's full of tigers and sharks.

I still don't know much about the guy who came to see me yesterday. Beyond him being Selena's nephew, I mean. He offered me no references, and Selena's phone's been off.

Maybe that's all I need to know.

That and the fact that he's clearly an operator. I can always use one of those.

I'm pleased she told him about me. Pleased to exist in the everyday parts of her life, outside of our own private bubble.

December 21

The company is having a brainstorm today, which isn't going well. This is what happens when you do away with an organically assembled gang of people, who all more or less get along, and replace them with fresh recruits on short-term contracts. Of the five people round the table, three started work here only this month, as part of the boss's masterplan. The conversation is stilted because we're basically strangers.

We've been around the table talking about shows we long to make. One of us would love to make a documentary horror film – a real-life version of *The Exorcist*, maybe. Someone else would love to make a film in space. The girl next to me said she's always wanted to make a series about teenagers in a war zone, dealing with all the damage and danger, but also the universals of teenage life. The guy opposite said he dreams of making the definitive doc on Diana, Princess of Wales, and looked deeply embarrassed, as well he might.

Now we're going round again, answering hypothetical questions: what moment in life do you wish you'd filmed? If you could spend a day with anyone, who would it be? If you had a key that could open any door, which ones would you open? If you were invisible, what would you do?

These things can be effective with a bunch of people who know each other well, as a stimulus to creativity. The idea is that they break up your usual patterns of thought. You're supposed to enjoy the process. It's supposed to make you laugh. You take the piss and think aloud, take things apart, mash things up and play. If you're lucky, you might stumble upon a good idea, or maybe the beginnings of one. And if not, at least you're having fun, deepening your bonds and investing in the future; it'll be even more playful and productive the next time you do it.

My turn to ask a question now: 'How far are you prepared to go? To get the things you want.'

With strangers, wary of each other and respectful of other people's contributions, it can be horribly awkward. A development producer who joined last week is bright red in the face and can't look anyone in the eye. It's all too personal and exposing, all way too soon. We're not deepening our relationships. We're reinforcing everyone's natural reserve and suspicion.

Ordinarily this sort of thing makes me despair. But not today, because it's revealed something interesting – that two of us don't seem to be strangers at all. There's a weird dynamic. A familiarity that feels tense and resentful. Unless I'm much mistaken, my new boss has fucked his new Head of Factual Formats, but – in the office at least – is trying to carry on like it's business as usual.

Her family is Indian, and she speaks with a clipped, precise accent that makes her sound vaguely aristocratic. Her bearing gives the same impression: upright and regal, and slightly detached. Not today, though. In place of her usual loftiness, a girlish eagerness to please. All me-and-you smiles and smitten glances she thinks only our boss can see.

He is determinedly ignoring it.

Maybe he thinks he made a mistake, and wants to go back to how it was before; him impressive and in charge, her hard-working, cool and professional. But that's one sort of genie that's hard to put back in its bottle.

Maybe my new boss is less stiff than he seems. Maybe this is a good thing. Maybe there's a future here after all.

On the other hand, maybe not.

He was something to live up to. Rigorous and stern. A grown-up version of working in TV. I can't help feeling disappointed.

December 23

I never take holidays. 'Holidays from what?' I always think. Talking shit and drinking wine and coffee is what people take holidays to do. We're lucky. We get to do that every day.

But there's no avoiding holidays at this time of year. Today the office closes for two whole weeks. If I could skip straight to January, I would.

I don't have anything against Christmas as such, though I don't much enjoy it either. I usually just buy a few books and hibernate. The thing I dislike is being forced out of the game. What gets me up every morning is the possibility that today might be the day. Generally speaking, I've always got chips on the table. Losing ones, usually. But not necessarily. Any day could be a winning day – a day when things change and life speeds up. But for the next 13 days, there's no chance at all of my number coming up. No chance at all of a new adventure.

It's a time for realizing where you belong, and being where you ought to be. People have been talking about their plans. Now they're starting to say their goodbyes.

If this was an ordinary week, with ordinary odds of new things happening, I would probably have ignored the text I just got.

People are hugging and shaking hands, and putting on their coats.

Someone asks 'What will you do?' 'Just the usual', I always say. Though in truth that's something I'd do anything to avoid.

Even drive out of London to a lonely place to meet with someone who declined to give me a name, for purposes as yet unknown.

December 24

I'm at a quiet little harbour, in a seaside town. The fishing boats are bobbing against one another, like they're trying to keep warm. There'll be no more fishing until after Christmas now.

I've been here an hour. Since that day on my doorstep I've had an ache in my belly I can't get rid of, and the cold, damp air is making it gnaw.

I haven't seen a single other person since I got here. People want to be snug on days like these.

Then there's a hard, dark figure on the other side of the harbour, stark against the whitewashed walls.

A car pulls in at the end of the pier where I'm sitting. A man in a heavy black coat gets out and stands by the bonnet, his hands behind his back, looking my way. There's no expression on his face, but the meaning is clear: you stay right there, sunshine.

Another man – my man – just as tall and wide as the first, gets out of a second car – my car – and does a peekaboo wave to the first.

Selena's nephew, Tom, on his first day of work experience.

The hard dark figure makes his way around the harbour towards me. Slowly, like he's enjoying it. I'm trying to think past the fear in my chest. Neither fight nor flight is really an option. I don't doubt that Tom can scrap, but he's mainly here for show. If this is what it looks like, I'm going to have to talk my way out.

Rankin sits down beside me.

'You're looking well', he says. 'Considering.'

I do a sort of 'humph' noise, that I hope sounds manly. I can't think of anything better to say. I'm not planning on saying anything till he's explained why we're here.

We both have a good long look out to sea.

'Fucking hurts, doesn't it?' he says. I say, 'I don't remember', but that's untrue. Being shot hurts like an absolute bastard. 'Especially there', he says, prodding my belly and making me wince. 'That little spot right there.'

'I've been thinking', he says, 'about me and you. About you mainly. And why you did what you did.'

Here it comes.

'At first I thought it's because he's got no balls', he says. 'And then I thought maybe he does. Maybe he's got some big ones.'

I'm not sure where this is going. It was always hard to tell with this guy. Now everything sounds like a prelude to being shot.

'You remind me of me', he says, eyes flicking towards Selena's nephew. 'Always pulling strings. Got yourself tangled though, eh?'

I give him a non-committal grunt this time.

'I know what you need', he says. 'An arm around your shoulder. A bit of reinforcement when you need it. A bit of guidance from someone who gets you.'

He looks at me, not blinking. 'That's me', he says. 'I'll be the boss, but we'll be like partners.'

What?

'You do what you do', he says. 'And I'll be here to help you when you need it. Bring a little bit of influence to bear, every now and then, eh? Grease the wheels. We'll need to think of a name ... '

Then I get what he's on about. He thinks we should set up a TV company.

I'm preparing to say all the reasons why this couldn't possibly work. So many reasons, I don't know where to start.

'I'll pay you both', he says. 'Till you start making proper money.'

'Both?'

He looks towards the car, and the man opens the rear door on our side. It's Mills, in a bottle-green coat, looking luminous.

Rankin stands up and gives her shoulders a squeeze and a rub as she gets to us. 'Brrrr', he says. His face is full of kindness and warmth. He directs her to the bench between us.

She looks from me to him and back again.

'You're on board with this?' She smiles and nods, perfectly happy and relaxed.

It feels odd to ask someone to clarify exactly why they shot you, but in this instance it would be useful to know. I hope that Rankin shot me for all of the bad things I did, and not just because I lied about the film. I hope he already knows that I semi-accidentally fucked his girlfriend. I suspect he knew about that before I did.

On balance, I decide to let sleeping dogs lie.

We'll need liquid assets. Developing ideas chews through cash. Rankin says he can help with that; significant funds will be coming his way in

March. I can cover our costs till then, from the money I made from selling the reel. It's probably no less tainted than the source of Rankin's 'funds'.

Now I think of it, setting up an indie is a great way to launder cash.

Start-ups can struggle for work, though. It's best to launch them with a commission. Something noisy and impactful, to prove you're a serious outfit.

Rankin pulls a box from his pocket. Inside is a key. The key from the robbery at the depository.

'Problem solved', he says.

There's a fresh surge of fear in my belly.

I ask him how he got it, and he shakes his head.

I ask him about the people who stole it, and he shakes his head again.

Mills says, 'Don't worry. We just need to figure out what the key is for.'

She says this with firmness and authority. I think she's more than just on board with all this. I'm starting to believe the whole thing is her idea. A source of money and security, to help her take care of her mother and brother.

And of course her baby. We'll come to that when Rankin's not around.

Maybe shooting me was her idea? Maybe she talked Rankin out of something worse? Just a bit of painful payback, and leave it at that?

For the moment, I'm imagining the locker at King's Cross, its secrets intact for 20 years, amidst all the breakneck change in that part of London and the millions of people passing through. But wouldn't the bad people be there at the station, waiting and watching? They've already killed three people. Three people that I know of.

I'm imagining opening the locker, cameras rolling, heart in my mouth. The perfect ending to a gripping story. A sensational discovery. A coup.

I'm imagining how Rankin might feel about working with a former copper. And how she might feel about working with him. It's hard to picture them getting along.

But we have a chance here to do the right thing. We could hand whatever we find in to the police. Most of it, anyway. We could hand it to Lockwood herself; win favours from the police in general and bring her career in law enforcement to a glorious end. She could help us tell the story, exactly as we planned.

I tell them, 'I might be able to help with the question of what the key is for.'

Mills looks up in surprise. I'm pleased to have a surprise for her on a day of surprises for me.

Rankin smiles wolfishly, showing me his teeth.

Maybe the film could begin at the end, at King's Cross, with the opening of Pandora's box, and all the demons inside set free. No one would switch over after an opening like that.

Mills says 'We have to cut Donovan in. It's part of the deal we made.'

'*Donovan*!?'

'You were in trouble there', Rankin says, chuckling like a kindly uncle.

Mills tells me how she bought him off with the promise of a once-in-a-lifetime story. Might be useful to have a journalist on our side, she thinks. He might sometimes have stories for us. She seems to have everyone wrapped around her little finger.

I'm conscious that I must be looking bewildered. She pats my knee and says, 'You're welcome.'

The other part of the Donovan deal is a collaboration on a film about Ray Monroe. An old-fashioned exposé.

'He's got a ton of stuff', Mills says. 'People who will talk. They just don't want to be the first.'

I'm thinking how useful Lockwood would be on that film also. Patiently piecing it all together.

And I'm thinking of Carole Monroe and the box of letters and photos. It would be the perfect way of putting a film in motion. Maybe she'd even take part?

'You and Donovan need to make friends', Mills says. 'I'm sure you'll be buddies in no time.'

So here I am. Running my own company, with the oddest assortment of people: a gangster in love with the glamour of TV; a string-pulling, problem-solving genius, who appears to have everyone right where she wants them, and is also the mother of my unborn child; my girlfriend's brawny nephew; a righteous copper; and a journalist who seems to hate me. A rabble of misfits, with an interesting array of talents.

This looks to be the scenario whether I like it or not. But I think I do. Sensible, orderly, business-like start-ups are ten a penny and easy to ignore. This one might be messy and real enough to work. I can't help feeling excited, in my belly, like I did starting out, almost 20 years ago. Thoroughly outmanoeuvred and outflanked, but thoroughly okay with it.

Everything depends on the key, though, and there's one problem still unsolved. How do we explain where it came from? To the police, the commissioners and everyone else?

'It's okay', Mills says. 'I've had an idea … '